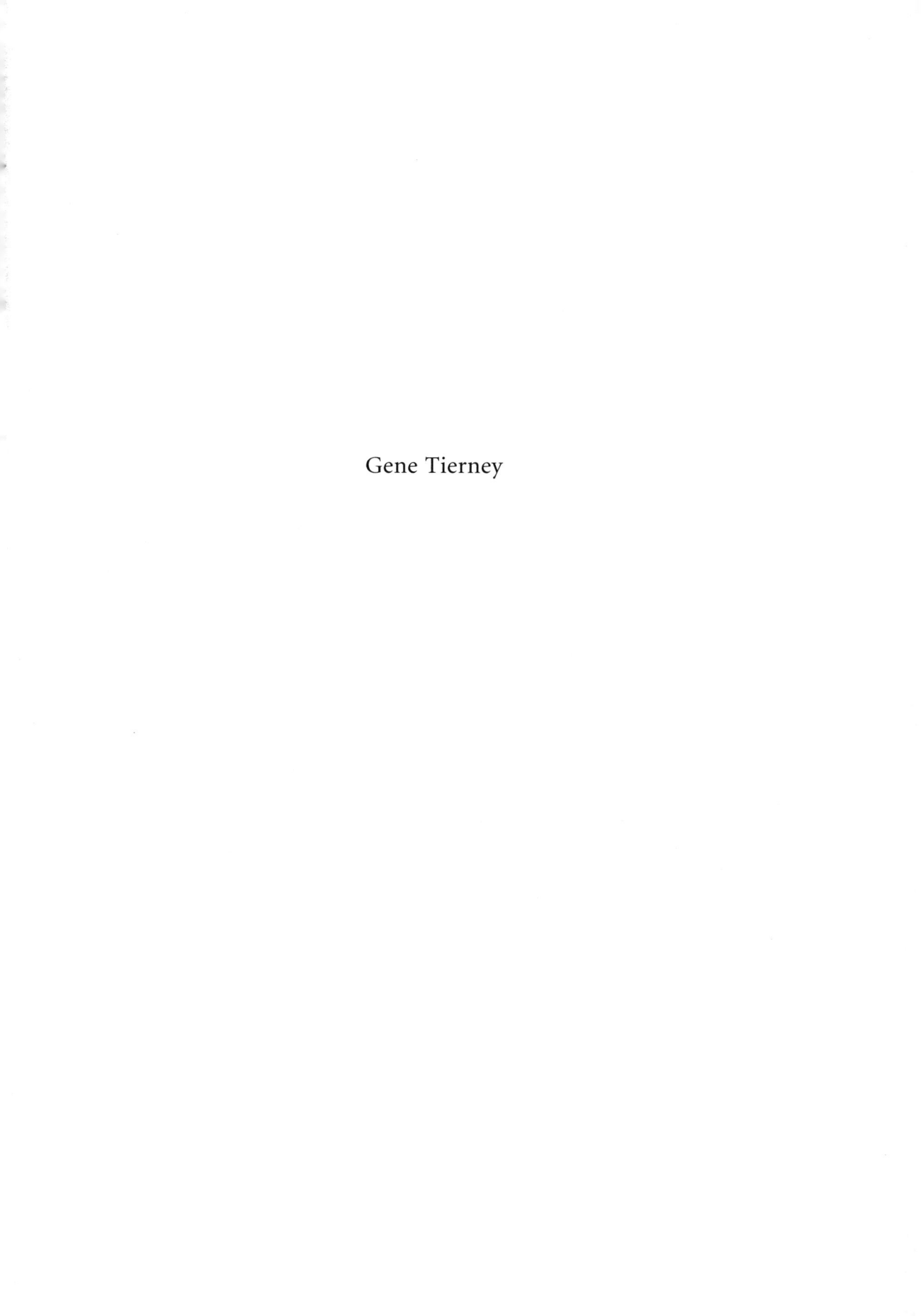

Gene Tierney

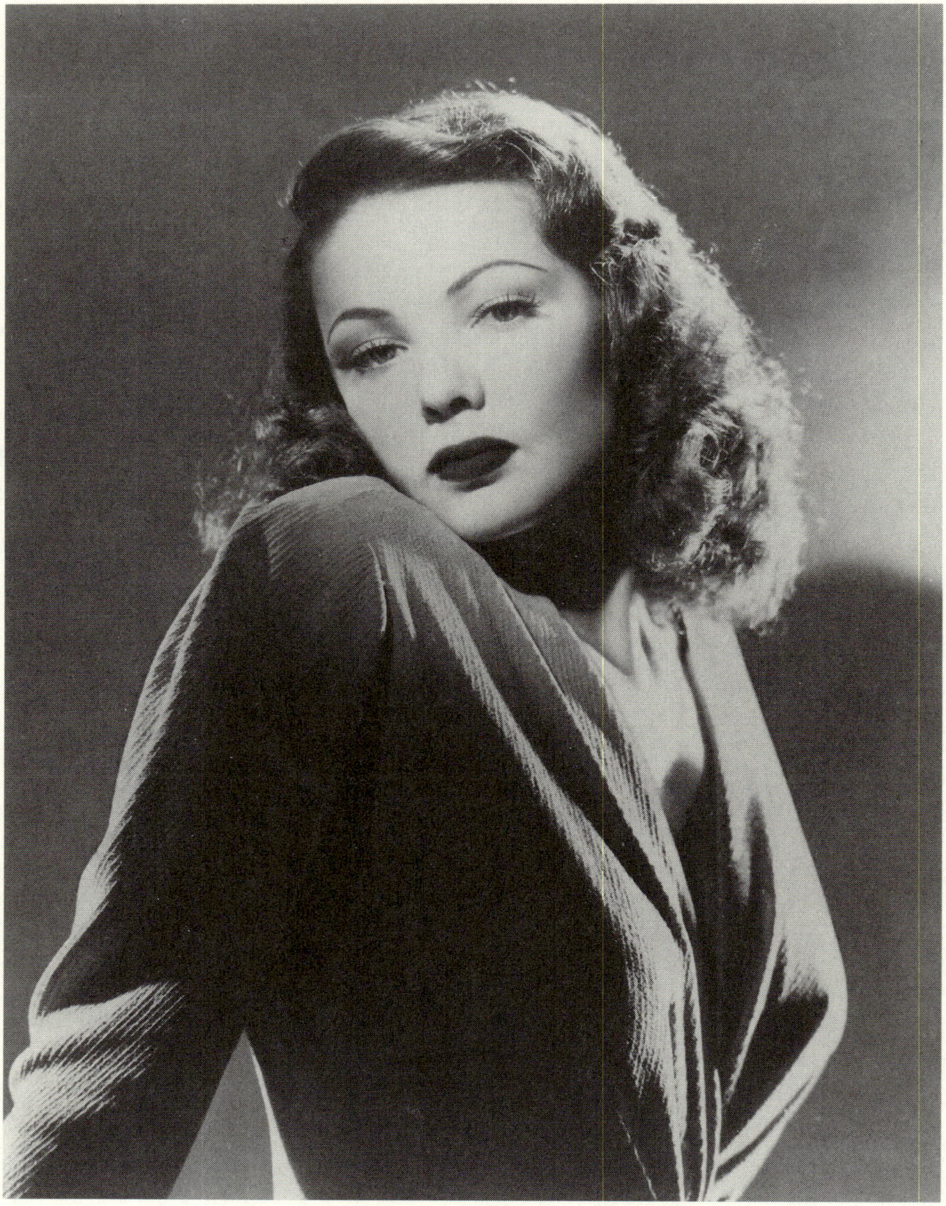

Gene Tierney

A Biography

Michelle Vogel

Foreword by
CHRISTINA CASSINI

McFarland & Company, Inc., Publishers
Jefferson, North Carolina, and London

Frontispiece: A glamour portrait of Gene Tierney in her prime (circa 1940s).

LIBRARY OF CONGRESS CATALOGUING-IN-PUBLICATION DATA

Vogel, Michelle, 1972–
Gene Tierney : a biography / Michelle Vogel ;
with a foreword by Christina Cassini.
p.   cm.
Filmography: p.
Includes bibliographical references and index.

ISBN 0-7864-2035-9 (illustrated case binding : 50# alkaline paper) ∞

1. Tierney, Gene.
2. Motion picture actors and actresses— United States— Biography.
I. Title.
PN2287.T48V64   2005   791.4302'8'092 — dc22   2004026709

British Library cataloguing data are available

©2005 Michelle Vogel. All rights reserved

*No part of this book may be reproduced or transmitted in any form
or by any means, electronic or mechanical, including photocopying
or recording, or by any information storage and retrieval system,
without permission in writing from the publisher.*

On the cover: Publicity still for *On the Riviera* (1951)

Manufactured in the United States of America

*McFarland & Company, Inc., Publishers
Box 611, Jefferson, North Carolina 28640
www.mcfarlandpub.com*

For Matt — My husband … my everything

Contents

Acknowledgments	viii
Foreword	ix
Preface	1
1. Brooklyn to Broadway	3
2. Hollywood Beckons	20
3. Hollywood — Take Two	29
4. Bride to Be	38
5. Belle Tier	49
6. Hollywood at War	62
7. It's a Girl!	77
8. *Laura*	89
9. Heaven and Heartbreak	97
10. *The Ghost and Mrs. Muir*	111
11. Cassini vs. Hughes	137
12. From Countess to Princess?	152
13. The Darkest of Days	161
14. The Ledge of Insanity	169
15. Home, Howard, Happiness…	174
16. Back to Work	181
17. The Final Curtain Call	191
Filmography	199
Bibliography	227
Index	231

Acknowledgments

In no particular order of importance, I would like to thank the following people and places for their help and support.

David Rosen for finding a scrapbook of treasures and allowing me to purchase its contents.

Hart Galleries, Sylvie Bernard, Lou and Mary Jo Mari and Pierre Nolot for their generosity in sharing items from their collections.

Wesleyan College for access to its Gene Tierney Family Archive.

Three inspirational teachers, the late Rob Mutton, Lucy Croxford and Gary Chapman. From my tender age of eight, they taught me a love of reading and the joy of writing. I love what I do because of them.

To my parents, Pam and Bob, and to my mother-in-law, Jean, for absolutely everything, everyday.

My extended family and friends (of which there are simply too many to mention) for your support in everything I do, no matter how wacky the idea!

My gorgeous husband, Matt: words could never describe how I feel about you. I love you.

My stepsons Josh and Reeve, thank you so very much for making the informed decision not to clean the toilet with my toothbrush or put frogs in my bed!

Oleg Cassini for his charming generosity and openness in sharing his memories of a life once shared with Gene Tierney. Without him, this book would be a mere shadow of what it's become.

Christina Cassini for her generosity in sharing memories of her mother along with personal family photographs.

Last but not least, I must thank Gene Tierney. Her existence, her talent, her extraordinary life, inspired me to write this book. Within her sea of tragedy, may we never forget her triumphs. With the magic of film, may we continue to enjoy her beauty and her acting for many years to come.

Foreword

Paris, February 11, 2005

It is difficult to be the daughter of a star.

As far back as I can remember, my love — the natural love that a little girl has for her mother — was always accompanied by a certain amount of admiration which was shared by those who knew her. She was a naturally refined beauty with amazing crystal green eyes. She had a quick wit, a good sense of humor, a charming laugh and a lovely warm smile. She was a woman full of genuine kindness.

Looking back, I can see now that my mother, unfortunately, did not have the necessary aggressiveness to resist all that she was confronted with in life. Most certainly, my mother had many exceptional and joyous moments that I did not witness.

Her Academy Award nomination for Best Actress in *Leave Her to Heaven* (1945), meeting the queen of England, meeting Picasso, filming *Advise & Consent* (1962) after a seven-year break, sitting next to Jack (President John F. Kennedy) at the White House after so many years had passed ... there are many such instances that meant so much to her before my birth and those that I was too young to witness first hand.

As an infant and very small child I had nannies that took care of me. My mother, being at the height of her career, did not have much free time to look after me. Later on I witnessed many difficult moments, both physical and unhappy ones.

My mother loved her grandchildren dearly. But she saw them rarely due to both her mental and physical illness. She always remembered to send them cards on their birthdays and for Christmas and Easter, and the cards were often accompanied by a thoughtful gift. My children affectionately called my mother "Bama." They enjoyed writing "Bama" thank-you notes, which she often had framed and hung in her bedroom. Like most grandmothers, she would brag about her grand-

Gene Tierney

children to her sister, brother and friends, and she always had up-to-date pictures of them that I sent from France.

I believe this book faithfully traces the life my mother led, and while reading it, I was able to relive a part of my own life. Thank you, Michelle.

Christina Cassini

Circa 1999: Gene Tierney's youngest daughter, Christina Cassini (center), pictured with her children (left to right) Jasmina, Alexander, Cedric and Delphina. As of February 2005, both girls are now married with their own children, while Alexander is in finance and Cedric is in college studying economics (photograph courtesy Christina Cassini).

Preface

She married a count, was engaged to a prince, and was romanced by a future U.S. president. She had the lifelong devotion of one of America's most eccentric billionaires, and according to Darryl F. Zanuck, founder of 20th Century–Fox, "Unquestionably, she was the most beautiful woman in movie history." She was Gene Tierney.

Gene Tierney's life, if it were not true, could easily be categorized as one of the most highly fabricated fictional stories ever written. She went from the dizzying heights of starring in many 1940s film classics, such as *Laura*, *Leave Her to Heaven* (of which she was nominated for a Best Actress Oscar) and *The Ghost and Mrs. Muir*, to the depths of personal despair when her daughter, Daria, was born severely retarded. She had lived it all, or so it seemed. Gene had experienced great triumph and even greater tragedy at a very young age, all of it before she turned 25. Yet, her biggest challenge was still to come in the form of an illness that was surely triggered by the pressures of her life, both good and bad.

By the 1950s, Gene's down-spiraling mental condition threatened her booming film career and her life to the point that she was institutionalized for full time treatment. At times, the so-called cures seemed far worse than the condition itself. Gene suffered through years of drug-warped days, radical psychological counseling, and, worst of all, dozens of electric shock therapy treatments that caused periods of her life to be erased from her memory forever. Her name and the fame it brought her in the outside world meant nothing to the doctors and nurses who bound her naked body in icy bedsheets to shock the demons from her mind. Gene Tierney was just another patient, a woman who had gone mad.

Yet, in an inspirational story of survival after nearly a decade of battling her wavering mental condition, Gene Tierney bravely returned to Hollywood after a break of seven long years. It was the biggest comeback of any Hollywood star in movie history, and the public loved her for it.

This is her story. It is the first complete biography since her death, covering

Preface

everything: her rise to fame, her romances, her mental illness and her triumphant return to Hollywood. Despite her miraculous comeback, Gene eventually walked away from a film career at a time that most actresses would consider premature. By her mid–40s, she had retired to Texas with a devoted husband, and for the very first time in her life she was truly happy. In her darkest of days, the very thought of happiness, a day without burden, had been only a dream. Gene Tierney retired content with the fact that she had made it, lost it, and made it back in an industry that so many hopefuls fail to conquer at all.

Gene Tierney's on-screen presence and her ability to transform herself into a variety of characters throughout her career were rare qualities that few stars have. She had what the industry commonly refers to as the "It" factor. Moviegoers sat up when she appeared on screen, listened to every word she had to say, and when she left the scene, anticipated her return. She had the ability to use her beauty when she needed to, but she did not rely solely on her looks for any one performance. There was depth, vulnerability, a soul behind that pretty face. In reality, it was a tortured soul, but I believe her inner demons helped her create such loved characters as Laura Hunt and Lucy Muir, and such hated characters as Ellen Berent and Isabel Bradley. Gene said it herself: "I had no trouble playing any kind of role. My problems began when I had to be myself." Gene Tierney was a movie star in every sense of the word. Sadly, she's no longer talked about like Monroe, Hepburn or Garbo, but she left her mark on Hollywood, just as they did in their own special way.

An extensive filmography with interesting anecdotes from behind the scenes, together with rare photographs spanning her life and career, makes this book a definitive reference on Gene Tierney, the actress, the person, the movie star. I hope it will ensure that her star doesn't fade to black like so many now forgotten names who gave heart and soul to Hollywood's golden age.

On a personal note, I started this book because I admired Gene Tierney the actress, but after finishing it, I now admire Gene Tierney the person. She lived a roller-coaster life of triumph and tragedy, but I know you'll enjoy reliving every moment right along with her. I know I did. Most of all, I hope her story inspires you to be a bit stronger and a bit braver when life's road gets bumpier than you'd like it to be.

1

Brooklyn to Broadway

If only there were a director in real life who could yell "Cut" when life's battles became too much to bear. Unfortunately, there wasn't a lot of inner peace to the real life role of being Gene Eliza Tierney. No movie script would come close to echoing the dramas scripted for her by destiny. Her 36 movies and many unforgettable portrayals will live on. Yet through it all, she proved that her best and most courageous performance was the one she gave on life's stage playing the role of herself. With all of its triumphs and tragedies, her story could not have been written or directed by the best of them and believed as the real life tale of one woman.

Gene Eliza Tierney was born in an elaborate brownstone house in Brooklyn, New York, on November 19, 1920. She was the second child born to Howard Sherwood Tierney, a successful insurance broker, and Belle Lavinia Taylor Tierney, an ex–gymnastics teacher. Lovingly, she was named in memory of her late uncle, her mother's brother, who died of diabetes at the age of 17. Insulin was yet to be discovered, and his death was considered a family tragedy of such despair that he was never spoken about again. Now his namesake, his niece, would eventually ensure that his name and its spelling would long be remembered.

Her elder brother Howard Jr., now three years old and otherwise known as "Butch," would welcome another sister, Patricia , three years later, but on the day of November 19 his new baby sister, Gene, was something of a treasure. Life in Brooklyn was comfortable, but Gene's father, Howard, felt that he needed to find a place where his children could run and play. After her first five years in Brooklyn it was time for a change. Howard Tierney was looking for a house that had access to some open land, a property that would present opportunities for countless adventures for his young family to experience. He found the ideal place; an old farmhouse in Green Farms, Connecticut, was for sale, and to him it was the perfect home.

The Tierney forefathers had owned land in the area generations before, back as far as George Washington, and so with the newly acquired farmhouse Howard began to reclaim the land of his relatives for himself and his family of today. Eventually, as money would allow, 35 surrounding acres were bought, most of it covered in milkweed and some parts with views of Long Island Sound.

Later in life Gene remembered the peacefulness of those early days. "You could wake up in the morning and peek out your window and see deer loping in the woods. I have never known a place more serene," she said. Howard Tierney was earning around $15,000 a year at the time, and the family had many servants, a boat, a horse and three cars. The children had a German nanny, Louise, to take care of them throughout the day. Louise was 16, and Gene delighted in listening to her sing German lullabies as she followed after her around the house. Once, Gene came running back from the brook that she had just found on her new property in Connecticut and exclaimed that she had "just met a princess, with a crown and a bright shiny dress with sparkly things all over it." Gene's mother's concern only caused her father to laugh and hug his daughter with proud amusement. "What harm can her princesses do?" he said.

Gene started her education in the area at St. Margaret's, a school that her mother had attended at her age. By the still early age of eight it was noticeable that she was not a very good student but bright and happy in personality and always telling stories, so much so that Gene's mother began to worry that she was becoming a compulsive liar. Princesses are quite the normal runaway thoughts that little girls have, but when Gene told all the children in her class that "It's my birthday and everyone is invited to my house after school for a big party," it was time for that fatherly speech about the differences between lies and harmless storytelling. It was not Gene's birthday at all; she just wanted a party. The only inkling that this lie had occurred was toward the

What a doll! A three- or four-year-old Gene poses for the camera (photograph courtesy Lou and Mary Jo Mari).

1. Brooklyn to Broadway

end of the party when Gene's mother heard the children saying "Happy birthday, Gene" as they left to go home.

As happy as the Tierney's were in the modest farmhouse, they soon decided they'd like something a little bigger. So, in 1928 Howard Tierney sold the farmhouse, and the surrounding land and decided to purchase the meadow across the street. It was literally a walk across the road, not more than 400 yards from the original farmhouse but the land was good and he felt it unnecessary to look any further. The land was swiftly purchased and a new house was built, this time to the Tierneys' own specifications. Much more elaborate than the farmhouse, this was an impressive piece of architecture

Young Gene with her mother, Belle Taylor Tierney, in their home state of Connecticut, circa 1928 (photograph courtesy of Lou and Mary Jo Mari).

in its day. It was a two story residence with two fireplaces, both downstairs. There was a bedroom for each of the children upstairs. The master bedroom was downstairs and overlooked the garden. There were also a guest room, a study and servants' quarters that were accessible only by the back stairs. Gene's father had invested wisely; he had bought stocks that were constantly climbing. Wall Street was booming at the time, and so was his bank account. The completed house ended up costing $60,000, enough money spent to feel easy about calling it a mansion. The Tierneys certainly had what you would modestly call "a comfortable life," a rich existence, one without financial troubles.

That same year Gene realized she was not going to pass her school year. Too much fantasy and not enough reality made for bad grades. Something had to be done. A girl of eight has the same budding fashion desires of a woman much older. Gene's mother knew that bribery was needed for Gene to pass this school year, and if clothes were going to do it then clothes it would be. The two of them went out walking. Hand in hand they strolled along strips of shops until they stopped outside a shop window where a gorgeous velvet coat sat, nestled warmly in a box. The coat had fur edges and a matching muff, perfect for a Connecticut winter. "You can have that coat if you pass, Gene," her mother said. Gene's green eyes glistened with excitement. There was nothing to do now but to pass this school year. She *must* have that coat and she would study as hard as could to ensure that it was hers. The bribery worked. Gene passed and got the coat. To parents who were not struggling for a dollar, buying the coat to inspire their daughter to pass the school year was not much of a sacrifice.

As fashionable as she felt in her brand new coat, nothing made Gene more miserable than looking down at her feet. She had to wear corrective shoes, square toed, heavy shoes that made her cringe. "No one will ever like me in these awful shoes," she cried. But she was wrong; everyone liked her, boys especially.

In 1930 the family prepared to sail for Europe for a six month stay abroad. This time there was concern over another coat, and again it came down to fashion. Since Gene's mother figured the family would be gone for quite some time she bought Gene and her sister Pat long, oversized coats with enough room in them for growing. In six months they would fit the girls just fine, but on the day they were purchased they were loose and long and just plain unfashionable. The coats dragged along the ground as they walked, and Gene constantly tried to convince her mother that this would not do. "Look at us. These coats are too big. Who knows who we'll meet in Europe. We look terrible. I'm not going if I have to wear this ugly coat."

Gene's pleading went unnoticed. They went to Europe, and both Gene and Pat wore their coats. Gene watched as people stared at her and her sister in these oversized monstrosities. Before sailing, Gene had said to some young friends, "It will be nice seeing our castle again. We were taken from our ancestral castle when we were mere babies. But we are going back home now, of course. I can just picture the dear old servants lined up in the great hall ready to welcome us back." She had a whole group of children gathered around now, all listening to her wonderful story.

"Is it one of those real castles, with towers and things?" a little boy asked.

"Oh, yes, and a moat" she beamed. The storytelling continued, and Gene's tales of her castle made her a very popular little girl. "Goodbye," she shouted as she walked onto the boat waving. As far as Gene was concerned the story had gone over amazingly well. She was now on a boat bound for Europe, and the children back home went away thinking she was a real princess.

1. Brooklyn to Broadway

The saying "it's a small world" rings true in this case. For one day in Paris a group of tourists ran up to Gene's father shouting, "Mr. Tierney, which way is your castle?"

"My castle!" he said in astonishment. Just as he turned around to look quizzically at Gene she slipped by him and through an open door. It was time for that speech about storytelling and lies to be given to a certain little girl — again!

After returning from Europe and back into the throes of schooling, Gene happily took up acting in various school plays. In the fifth grade she played Jo in the timeless classic *Little Women*. The acting bug hit and she said casually, "Maybe someday I'll be a real actress and go on the stage."

Of course Gene's brother, Butch, took every opportunity to tease and taunt his sister. Upon hearing Gene's statement he began to mock and taunt and laugh as brothers so often do. "You an actress!" he snorted. Butch's friend's laughed along with him while Gene did her best to ignore them. Soon enough, though, Butch's friends would leave Butch behind in the house and take Gene for long strolls around the family's property. She was a popular girl, charming, full of personality and beautiful.

At 15 Gene was not at all interested in finishing school in Connecticut. "I'm not going to another school around here," she said. "I want to go abroad. Switzerland, that's where I want to go to school." It all sounded very glamorous. Finishing school in a foreign country would take her a long way away from Butch and Pat and her parents. In a whole other country she would be all alone. The family discussed it and discussed it some more. Eventually it was decided. Gene was packed up and sent off to Switzerland. There were many tears before leaving, but this was a trip of self-discovery and adventure. As sad as she was to say goodbye to her family, she was also filled with the excitement of having some sense of independence, at last.

Her trip across to Switzerland was made much more pleasant when she ran into actor Douglas Fairbanks, Sr. They talked for hours and became great friends. His being a man of the world gave her the extra reassurance that she needed and convinced her that she was about to embark on a great adventure, two years of fun that she would always remember. He somehow made the trip exciting before she even arrived.

It was 1936; Gene stared out of her window at the exclusive Brillanmont School for girls in Lausanne. She gazed dreamily at the snow-capped mountains in the distance. She realized now that she was half a world away from Butch and Pat and her parents. Connecticut and New York seemed like a lifetime ago. She was in Switzerland, at a school for girls where only French was spoken between the students and teachers. Many girls from many countries were gathered together. All spoke their native languages back home, but the universal French vocabulary had them all understanding each other completely, even giggling in the same way the American girls would be doing back home. As much as Gene enjoyed her new friends, she was still desperately homesick. The only thing that stopped her from writing a pleading letter home and asking to be rescued was thinking of her little sister, Pat.

In Pat's eyes, Gene was a leading a fantastic and exciting life abroad, and Gene didn't want to disappoint her. She wiped away her tears and stayed strong. Gene would sit for hours writing letters home that would tell of great adventures, just knowing that Pat would be reading every word with envy. Gene's inventive storytelling ability carried her through most of her childhood, and this time it was used in a positive way to please Pat. She was mature now, and she had learned the difference between a lie and a tale. This time the tale was to please her little sister, but this time she was lying to herself.

Gene stuck things out, and one Christmas she was invited to spend Christmas in England. Gene's roommate, Sylvia Muir, was going home for the holidays. She invited Gene home for a traditional English Christmas, and Gene accepted without so much as a thought of declining the invitation. She excitedly packed; she was thrilled by this new adventure. There would be no school, and Christmas in yet another country would be exciting. That Christmas was the start of good things to come. The following Christmas was spent in Norway at yet another girlfriend's home, that of Dagney Paust.

In September 1937, Gene wrote one of her chirpy, informative letters back home. Inside she was torn apart, homesick for her parents, brother, sister and friends, but her letter is full of youthful exuberance. There is no sign of her wanting to be anywhere else but Switzerland.

In her newsy letter Gene addresses her parents as a child would; she begins with, "Dearest Mommy and Daddy." Her description of the Alps and its surroundings is worthy of being in a travel brochure. She describes herself as being "half way up to heaven," in an adorable little peasant village. She and her group are staying in a chalet that Mlle. Henri (whom Gene describes as a young teacher who is foul) had rented. They even had the foresight to hire three maids to do the dirty work for them. Clever! She excitedly tells her folks that she and her roommate, a Greek girl, have the best room in the chalet. It's a room with a view, which a young Gene breathtakingly describes as "super."

Les Marecottes consisted of roughly six chalets, a herd of 60 cows and an abundance of goat sheds. It had a post office, a church and a graveyard, in which Gene predicts she'll soon be buried in if she is forced to walk up one more mountain! Their only luxury was electricity, which was provided by nature itself. The abundance of waterfalls and raging torrents in the area provided the power needed to run the village.

1. Brooklyn to Broadway

Even so, the water was heated only three times a week, so it was a real scramble among the girls to take a bath on those days. She tells her parents (probably to their horror) that everyone is dirty most of the time, simply because the cold water is almost glacial and far too cold to wash with. When hot water day comes, the five girls, the foul teacher, Mlle. Henri, the trained nurse, Madame Hougenauts, and her two "brats" all have to take turns to bathe, in the same water! She's obviously less than pleased with the primitive bathing conditions.

At the time of this letter, Gene was lucky enough to be first in line for a bath, so the water was hot and not lukewarm with another person's stench. She excitedly tells her parents that she is clean for a change. Her excitement heightens again when in the next sentence she says she even managed to get her hair washed, a major accomplishment.

She describes her hair as getting quite long, but she's not even thinking of cutting it. She assures her mother that, although her hair is longer than she would remember it to be, she is doing her best to manage it responsibly and is keeping it neat. With the help of her new Greek roommate, she is trying out new styles too. The latest style consisted of little curls, all up the back, and she describes the style to her mother as similar to the way "Tournie" would do it. She then mentions that she received a letter from "Tournie," who was sailing for England on the Aurania. Gene tells of the hysterics she was in while reading the accounts of her adventure.

She moves back to describing her surroundings and again mentions that they're camped right in the middle of the Alps, and they are scheduled to take tons of different climbs. She describes the village as fascinating and says she's never seen anything like it in all her life. She says the peasants are very friendly to them and simple in what they expect out of life. Their lack of materialistic needs seems to be a complete fascination for Gene. She tells her mother that the women are content to knit all day, especially in winter when the weather is extremely bitter. The men cut wood in the forests so their families can build fires to keep warm by at night, and with that they survive until the warm weather comes. When that happens, so many people descend on the village that the peasants are more than happy to greet fresh faces and shout "bonjour" to everyone they see.

As friendly as the peasants are, the strangers still fascinate them. Gene says that when she takes a walk down the cow path to the village, all the peasants gather in a group and whisper and stare at her. She says it made her feel a little strange at first. She even thought her petticoat might have been showing, but after checking for that fashion nightmare, she was relieved that everything was in place. When she went back to the chalet she asked her teacher why they did this. Her teacher explained that it wasn't her in particular. They did it with all newcomers.

Her days started early, at 5 A.M., and that wasn't for a leisurely breakfast but for starting their climb on one of the steep mountains. They had to take their

Gene Tierney

climbs early, before the sun was up and it got too hot to climb. Gene says she's getting toughened by these early rises and tough workouts. Their next climb, the day after this letter was written, was to begin at the ungodly hour of 3 A.M.!

Gene tells her mother that when she gets home she can challenge her to a walk, anywhere, any length, anytime and in any weather. She was looking forward to the late afternoon climbs the most, partly because they wouldn't have to rise early to do them, but mostly because after the climb to the top they would get to sleep under the stars and rise early the next day to watch the sun rise from the peak of the mountain.

She says that halfway up on their last climb rain started to pour and they had to run to find shelter. The only thing they could find was an old shepherd's chalet, and it stank to high heaven because it was where the shepherd regularly sheltered his livestock in the storms. The girls held their breath amid the lingering stench of damp cows, doing their best to huddle together and not get any wetter than they already were. It all proved useless in the end. Gene says they waited and waited for the rain to stop, but it just seemed to get heavier, so finally they had no choice but to descend the mountain in the downpour. They were soaked and covered in mud by the time they reached the bottom. A real sight, especially since it wasn't hot water night.

She says it wasn't unusual for the weather to change so suddenly like that. It happened regularly. At the time of her writing she says the sun is shining "like mad," and it took just one day of sunbathing for her skin to turn "as black as coal." She says her parents wouldn't recognize her.

She talks of her relationships with the other girls in the group and tells her parents of a discussion they all had the other night about countries and customs. She says she learned that Greeks preferred to eat dinner at 10 at night and that in

A young, somewhat fuller faced Gene Tierney emerges as a young starlet in this rare early promotional still.

1. Brooklyn to Broadway

England, most people believe in phantoms and ghosts. After that conversation she says she was beginning to think that America was the only normal country in the whole world.

She speaks of "the Greek" who is very creative and is helping her with a rust colored sweater that she is knitting. She says she is halfway done with it, and when she's completely finished, "the Greek" is going to teach her how to embroider her initials on it in brown, a nice contrast to the rust wool. She excitedly tells her parents that she's been invited by "the Greek" to visit her in Greece next year when she, Hunna and Uncle De go traveling around.

She then sympathizes with the girl because her previously beautiful skin changed dramatically and the poor girl broke out with "hickies" everywhere. She went to a skin specialist in Lausaunne, and luckily for her the prognosis was good. The doctor told her that it was nothing to worry about, and as soon as she set foot back in "good ol' Greece" her skin would be as good as new. It was the drastic change in weather that had played havoc with her usually blemish free complexion.

Gene talks of one girl who is getting over her love for women on her own advice that it is "foul and awful" and nice people just don't love their own sex. She says that except for that she's really a very nice girl who's had something of a sad life. Despite coming from a rich family, she'd always been left to governesses,

A fresh faced teenager, Gene poses by the pool, innocent to the future pain that would cause a lifetime of struggles for her. This rare studio snapshot shows a young girl determined to make it as an actress.

Gene Tierney

never her own parents. Her mother is Lady Levita and her father is a high ranking member of Parliament. She says the girl admits that her parents were strangers to her, and how can she possibly love strangers? Her riches meant nothing to her because she lacked love and proper parenting. Gene says the whole family is "disgustingly rich" with lavish homes in London and Scotland, and one by the sea.

Perhaps the only inkling of Gene's acute homesickness lies within her next paragraph. Gene tells her parents of how much she loves getting letters from home and that just knowing that people miss her makes her feel special. She sarcastically says that she thinks only *half* of them *really* miss her!

She goes on to say that she received a sweet letter from Mrs. Jones, Meredith Manning, who was another American girl, Betty Swan, Peggy Esseray, who was an English girl, and another American girl named Betty Ann Shields. These were all girls who had previously stayed with Gene and who had left and gone back to their respective countries. Gene had obviously made a good impression, because she seemed to mention getting many letters from people all over the world.

She encourages her parents, and anyone else for that matter, to continue to write her and send clippings from America because she wants to keep up with what's going on back home. It is about there that she ends her 17 page handwritten letter with "heaps of love to you all, Gene."

This was one of the many informative letters that Gene wrote home, not only to her parents, but also to her sister, Pat, and her brother, Butch, not to mention her long list of friends. It seems that most of her spare time was spent knitting and writing letters back home. Maybe, in hindsight, the length of her letters home and the frequency in sending them was the only clue of how much she was missing Connecticut.

The best surprise of all came at the end of 1937. It was the sight of Butch roaring up the road toward Gene's school. There he was, driving his old American jalopy, packed to the brim with a bunch of college friends. All of them were ready to take on Europe, and Butch was willing to take his sister along for the ride. "You be ready tomorrow when we come to pick you up," Butch said. Gene nodded and ran inside to pack. The very next day she was ready. Ready with 16 suitcases of clothes to pack into a car already crowded with college guys. "Have I brought too much?" she asked. Most boys would of course toss one bag into the car and leave the other 15 behind, but Gene's way of asking had all of those boys hooking up a trailer and taking every bag and a very happy Gene along for a new adventure.

Between June and December of 1937, Butch, Gene and several of Butch's friends toured Europe. They visited eight countries together. It was the perfect end to the two years spent at Brillanmont. It was a time in her life that she would always remember, just as Douglas Fairbanks had told her on the sail over two years before.

By now it was 1938 and nearing the end of Gene's time in Europe. After two

1. Brooklyn to Broadway

years in finishing school a 17-year-old Gene was about to return home. She had done well in her schooling, making the honor roll each year since the eighth grade. Her two years abroad were full of mixed emotions. She missed her family terribly, but she made great friends, one of whom was Maria Seiber, the daughter of Marlene Dietrich. She could now speak fluent French, excelled in horseback riding and enjoyed the relaxation of reading, painting and writing poetry. The poetry writing subsequently became one of her lifelong passions. Although she was thrilled to go home and be with her family, she was now sadly breaking ties with her new family in Europe.

Upon Gene's arrival home, a now 14-year-old Pat greeted her first. Gene could hardly believe the way her little sister had grown. With no more puppy fat, she was a pretty young girl who was quick to tell Gene that she had put on quite a bit of weight while being away. Gene had gotten up to 145 pounds; her five-foot-seven-inch frame wasn't built to carry that bulk, and she did look pudgy. She looked at herself in a full-length mirror, agreed with Pat, and set about at getting her thin frame back.

A 19-year-old Gene strikes a fashionable pose in one of her first modeling photographs after making her elaborate Connecticut debut (photograph courtesy Lou and Mary Jo Mari).

She had one more try at a local school. This time it was Miss Porter's School in Farmington, Connecticut. The school worked Gene to the bone, and without much effort and without even realizing it she was back to her ideal weight in no time, a svelte 122 pounds.

Summer vacation was approaching, and the Tierneys decided to pick up and go to California. Howard Tierney stayed behind to run the family business. A relative had a connection at Warner's studio in Hollywood, so when the family reached the studio they were given a backstage tour. Bette Davis was shooting a scene for her new picture, *The Private Lives of Elizabeth and Essex*, on the lot and came over to speak with Gene and Pat during a break. Gene was starstruck; she was totally captivated by the performance that she'd just witnessed.

"Miss Davis," Gene said tentatively, "I'm about to make my debut and I was wondering if you'd mind if I had a copy of your dress made from the movie *Jezebel* for my debut dress." Bette Davis smiled and said she'd be flattered. Just as Gene was about to continue her backstage tour, director Anatole Litvak turned to her and said the famous line, "Young woman, you ought to be in pictures!"

Gene was stunned. Butch laughed uncontrollably at the very familiar line he was hearing. He found it especially amusing now that it was being pitched to his sister. His laughter soon ceased when he began to realize that Litvak was serious. A screen test was swiftly set up for the very next day. The test was simple enough. It was to be the standard personality test. Gene was to be alone onstage in front of a camera, reading the lines from a Dorothy Parker monologue titled *A Telephone Call*. Gene was so excited. She seemed to breeze through it and the test felt as though it was over with in no time.

The rest of that day Gene, her mother, Butch and Pat saw more sites around the studio as they waited for the verdict on Gene's screen test. That evening Gene's mother took the phone call that they'd all been waiting for. It was a Warner's executive who casually told her that her daughter photographed well. They'd like to offer her a standard studio contract of $150 a week.

Gene called home immediately to ask for her father's permission to accept the deal. He was not impressed. He reminded her that she was still a child, had not yet made her debut and was to come home to be introduced to Connecticut society, as any other girl of her age would do. As disappointed as she was, she knew never to question her father. The screen test was a surprise, and getting the contract offer was even more surprising. She put this experience down as being a wonderful story to tell her friends when she got back home

It was now September and almost time for Gene's debut. The year was 1938, and as much as Gene liked the glamour of getting dressed up in her copied dress from *Jezebel*, the socializing, the mingling and the smiling with those "society types" just did not impress her enough to make it her life's work. She was not content to look pretty and smile and wait for a man to choose her as his wife. She had spirit and a need to be heard. She wanted to accomplish something for herself. Being a debutante, having high tea and mingling in a society circle was not what she envisioned for her future.

On the night of September 24, 1938, Gene Eliza Tierney was presented to society at the Fairfield Country Club in Connecticut. Her name was published on the

1. Brooklyn to Broadway

Gene and her brother, Howard, lovingly known as "Butch," scan the paper for a suitable apartment for Gene to rent in New York City, 1939 (photograph courtesy Lou and Mary Jo Mari).

society page of the *New York Times*. Gene read and reread her name in the paper and secretly hoped that one day her name would be published more frequently in newspapers, only this time as "Gene Tierney — Actress." The night went well, and Gene had done exactly what her parents wanted her to do. She'd now made her debut and was formally a member of Connecticut society. With all of that done it was now time to put a proposal to her father. It was time to turn on that Tierney charm,

Right: A beautiful full length shot of Bette Davis in the Civil War love story *Jezebel* (1938). Gene was so taken with Davis' dress in the film that she asked her if she could get a copy made to wear to her debut. Davis was flattered, and Gene was beaming with excitement. This was her first real dream dress.

Below: A closer, more detailed shot of Bette Davis in *Jezebel* (1938) pictured here in "that dress." Gene had an exact copy of this dress made to wear to her debut. Take a closer look at the lace bodice and the fullness and detail of the tulle skirt. Original or replica, this dress would not have come cheap.

1. Brooklyn to Broadway

and if she did it right she would get exactly what she wanted. She decided not to waste a second and put the proposal to her father on the very same night as her debut, before going to bed. "Daddy, I want to go on the stage," she blurted out. "I want to at least try it. I know I can do it, I want to do it. Please let me try."

Howard Tierney knew that once his daughter made her mind up about something it was much easier to go along with it than fight it. "All right, he said, "But there are to be conditions." Gene only heard the words "all right." He had agreed to let her at least try, and that was all she needed. That was all she wanted.

He went on, "I will not have any daughter of mine walking the streets by herself. I can spare a little time once a week, on Wednesdays. You will meet me in the city on Wednesdays and we will make the rounds together — agreed?" "Oh, agreed, Daddy" she shrieked. "Agreed!"

And so it began. Gene would get dressed up in her best clothes, perfect hair, perfect makeup and set off into town to meet her father for the pounding of the pavement. The first morning Gene put on her gray fox fur coat, one that her father had bought for her, a bright red hat with a purple bow and red lipstick to match the hat. The moment her father saw her he laughed out loud. She was ready to show Broadway that they were missing something and she was it! Her father saw that she meant business.

The 8:15 A.M. train ride into the city was a pleasant one, but the most dissatisfying part was the walking of the streets, the enthusiastic speeches about how she wanted to become an actress and then the knock backs. It became an all too familiar circle. The train ride to the City in the morning was full of hope and chatter. The train ride home was full of silence, tired feet, and one 17 year old's very bruised ego. Howard Tierney would go home and wink at his wife over Gene's shoulder, "No luck today either," he would say, using the most despondent voice he could muster. He was convinced that Gene would believe he was sounding sympathetic. He figured Gene would soon get tired of this merry-go-round of disappointments and eventually come back to his way of thinking. In Gene's eyes he would still appear to be the supportive father for helping her at least try to realize her dream of becoming an actress.

Unfortunately for Howard but fortunately for Gene, one Wednesday was very different from the previous three that she'd experienced. George Abbott wanted to see her. His success was already proven. It was not unusual for him to have two or three hit shows on Broadway at one time, and he wanted to see Gene Tierney!

Gene was shaking on the inside but smiling on the outside. As she entered his office, her father waited patiently in the waiting room. It seemed like hours. When she reemerged, all of ten minutes later, he anxiously asked, "How was he?"

"Well, he was very sweet," she said. Nothing more was thought about this meeting until Gene was ready to go on a ski trip to Vermont with some of her friends a week later. The morning before she was to leave she opened an envelope addressed to her. She read the letter to herself and suddenly said, "I can't go. I *have* to go back into town."

Gene's friends were horrified. "What do you mean you have to go into town? This trip has been planned for ages. Who is this Mr. Abbott anyway? Tell him to wait until you get back." Her friends were relentless. Gene was part of the clan, and her not going was just not going to be accepted. Little did they know that the letter read, "Mr. Abbott would like you to read for a part." That was enough for Gene to drop everything. This was her chance. She wanted this more than anything, and nothing, let alone a ski trip, was going to get in the way of it.

Gene went to the meeting and met George Abbott for a second time. He asked her if she could read in an Irish brogue. "Sure," she said, and proceeded to pick up a newspaper and read an article aloud in a thick Irish accent. The part that he wanted her to play required a thick Irish accent. Her short demonstration must have impressed him. She did her part well, but the moment she finished she dropped the newspaper at her feet and ran off stage.

"She hasn't had a scrap of experience," she heard one man say. "Experience comes with opportunity," said another. "Let's give this one a chance." Suddenly, Gene Tierney had scored her first big acting part. Her graduation from Miss Porter's school was in June, and by December she was realizing her dream as an actress. Not just anywhere, but on Broadway. This was her first *real* paying job. She remembered how excited she was when she received a $30 payment for a modeling session for a prospective cigarette layout, even though the shots were never used. This time she would be acting, every night, and getting paid to do it.

Gene had to move to New York to be close to the stage, so with her father's approval of the intended accommodations she would lodge at the American Women's Club. Howard Tierney felt that it was safe because men were not allowed past the first floor. Gene was determined to make this work. She was living off her own money now, and she needed to be fairly frugal in order for it to spin out and make ends meet. She would ride the subway when necessary. She ate cheaply in drugstores and bought all of her clothes at bargain stores. One of her favorites was Klein's on 14th Street. Gene had an eye for fashion and could make any cheaper outfit look as if it belonged on a store mannequin in Bloomigdale's.

The play was called *Mrs. O'Brien Entertains*, and Gene's part was that of Molly O'Day. Her paycheck was decided upon at $75 a week, but Gene went through the first five days of rehearsals terrified of being fired at any moment. At that time an actor could be replaced without notice or compensation, if found to be unsuitable. No real reason had to be given for the dismissal. If they didn't like you, you were out. On day five George Abbott reassuringly tapped Gene on the shoulder as if to say, "You made it, kid." He knew she was sweating over being replaced "Today you

1. Brooklyn to Broadway

can stop worrying, Gene. Today you're an actress." She had made the grade, and there was no way she could be replaced now. The deadline had passed, and she was now a permanent member of the cast.

Opening night was in Baltimore. As Gene waited for her time to go on, she felt a strange sense of calm. There were no nerves at all. Maybe it was numbness, because when it was time to go on stage a terrible sense of panic washed over her. Her voice dropped and she went limp. She had stage fright! At the end of the first act she looked across at Abbott, waiting for him to look at her disapprovingly. She felt she had let him down terribly. He had given her this first big chance, and now she had let him down. Abbott grinned at her and whispered, "Pick it up, Gene." She went back onstage and never succumbed to stage fright again.

Mrs. O'Brien Entertains was technically Gene's first speaking role on Broadway. She'd previously appeared very briefly in a play titled *What a Life*. Her role was simply to carry a bucket of water across the stage. Usually such a minor part would go unnoticed but her presence impressed the reviewer of *Variety* so much that he wrote, "Miss Tierney is certainly the most beautiful water-carrier I've ever seen!" Without uttering a word she managed to make her mark on this reviewer. It was the sign of things to come.

The critics always viewed Gene's Broadway performances favorably. Just as she had hoped on the day she was a debutante, her name appeared in print yet again, this time in the *New York Times*. Brooks Atkinson, the most important critic of that time wrote, "As an Irish maiden fresh from the old country, Gene Tierney in her first stage performance is very pretty and refreshingly modest." Others wrote that it was almost worth going just to see this new young actress perform in her first role.

As kind as the critics were to Gene in her first speaking role, in an overall perspective, *Mrs. O'Brien Entertains* was one of George Abbott's few failures. By the time it got to Broadway it had run 37 performances, lasting all of four weeks.

Although Gene's stage career began and ended within one month, it was enough for her to be spotted by a Hollywood talent scout. A contract was presented to her. She was now 18 years old, and all of a sudden she was being offered $350 a week and a chance in the movies! Gene was elated. She thought back to Bette Davis giving that brilliant performance at Warner's in *The Private Lives of Elizabeth and Essex*. Now it was her turn. She was going to be an actress, just like her.

"You're not going anywhere!" Gene's father yelled. "The stage has credibility. Hollywood is another story. You're too young, and the things you hear that go on out there!" Gene was heartbroken. She spent many nights quarreling with her parents, but eventually, as usual, Gene won out. Her parents agreed to let her go, and before too long, she and her mother set out for Hollywood. Columbia pictures was their destination. Gene was on her way to becoming an actress after all.

2

Hollywood Beckons

While back home, Howard Tierney arranged to set up a company to manage his daughter's soon to be growing bank account. The company would be known as Belle Tier, and it would manage and invest all of Gene's income. Her father would distribute all ingoing and outgoing funds as he saw fit.

A month after arriving in Hollywood, Gene was exasperated. "Pictures!" she would say. She was yet to see the inside of a set. There was excuse after excuse. "You're too young. We're not ready for you yet. We're paying you aren't we?" Paying her they were. She was getting exactly what her contract promised, but Gene wanted to act. She didn't want to sit around and wait, wait, wait. Waiting was not one of Gene's strong suits, and so she wrote all of her frustrations down in a letter to George Abbott.

The only fun that Gene had at Columbia was socially. Through her agent, Leland Howard, Gene met the billionaire owner of RKO Studios, Howard Hughes. Leland Howard was at the time married to actress Margaret Sullavan. He had made his fortune working as a Hollywood agent and later became a successful producer. Howard Hughes was a powerful man in 1939. In 1933 he had set out to build the most progressive airplane the world had ever seen. He set up a secret hangar just outside Los Angeles and hired Glen Oderkirk and Dick Palmer, two expert engineers in the field of aviation, to help in the project that he would call H-1, aka Hughes—1. After working day and night for two years, Hughes believed he had created the fastest plane in the world. It was the first to incorporate retractable landing gear as well as other aeronautic breakthroughs such as countersunk screws and flat rivets to lessen wind resistance

By September 1935 the H-1 was announced as *the* plane that would break all current air speed records. Not only that, if Hughes succeeded he would make himself known as a worldwide figure. Hughes' eccentricities were legendary. He insisted that he be the one to pilot the plane and that the test for speed would be carried out only on the very first flight. With this plane being a completely new design,

2. Hollywood Beckons

there was no way of knowing whether it would fly at all, let alone break any speed records. The current record was that of 314.32 miles per hour, set by a French aviator, Raymond Delmotte. Hughes was convinced that he could break the record, and right he was. He reached a speed of 352.39 miles per hour. He not only broke the record — he broke it easily!

Hughes put his name into the record books overnight. He had flown faster than any other man in a plane of his own design, and America loved him for it. He made the front pages of every newspaper of his day, and he was honored with a traditional American ticker tape parade down the streets of New York City.

A classic pose of eccentric billionaire Howard Hughes. Gene had a brief romance and a lifelong association with him.

Hughes loved airplanes, movies and women, and the major Hollywood agents of the time were only too happy to appease Mr. Hughes' appetite with an introduction to a new starlet that might be of interest to him. Leland Howard had Gene Tierney on his books and decided fairly quickly that Hughes would most definitely be interested in meeting her. Most other men of the time used their cars as a pick-up tool to attract women. Hughes went a step beyond that. He used his plane!

At 19 it was easy for Gene to fall for an older man of wealth and power, and Hughes did his best to seduce her. On one occasion he flew both Gene and her mother to Tijuana, Mexico, where he booked an entire restaurant and a band. He had her hotel room filled with gardenias, all before their first date. Another time, Gene had mentioned in passing that she had not seen a friend from boarding school for two years. She lived in Santa Barbara, and the distance made it impossible for them to keep in contact. Before Gene could blink, they were in his car and heading for the airport. As they arrived, his plane was warming up on the runway, and he flew Gene to Santa Barbara to visit her friend for an hour.

Whenever he left town he would call up any restaurant that Gene and her mother were likely to attend and say that all orders by them were to be billed directly to him. That summer Gene complained that she had terrible stomach pains. It was so bad at times she would be rocking back and forth on the floor in pain, sweat rolling from her forehead. Hughes insisted that he send his personal doctor, Dr. Vernon Mason, to evaluate Gene's symptoms. A surgeon was brought in, and after further examination they both concluded that her appendix should be removed immediately. Gene had the operation, but two weeks later the pain returned. Now without her appendix, it was a mystery as to what was causing the problem. After further tests she was told she was suffering from a chronic condition called "nervous stomach," a problem that she would have to endure for many more years.

Gene remembered Hughes as a sweet, quiet man, never implying that anything physical should be expected of her in return for his kind deeds. His kindness drew people to him without his pushing for it, and it wasn't long before Gene fell for the charm of Howard Hughes.

A studio pose of Gene, this time in "country gear." The studio liked to give young starlets that innocent, pretty, yet ready for anything look.

As much as he tried to involve himself in Gene's life, their romance was short lived. Gene knew of his reputation and soon realized that she wasn't the only girl he was seeing. His attention span was short when it came to relationships, and Gene was not willing to be one of many. Hughes settled on being a very good friend, and in future years he drifted in and out of her life. He became someone she could rely on when needed, and need him she did when personal tragedy struck years later.

Gene spent her time at Columbia watching others work while she was waiting patiently for something to happen for her. In a desperate need to publicize her, Columbia suggested that she change her name. Something a little more flashy, they suggested. Something people would remember.

Rita Hayworth, although only a couple of years older than Gene, had been

2. Hollywood Beckons

Would you care for some tea? Gene pours herself a cup from her elegant silver teapot. This was a promotional photograph to play up Gene's debutante status for the public (photograph courtesy Lou and Mary Jo Mari).

molded by the studio into a sex bomb. She was born Marguerita Carmen Cansino. She never got beyond the first year of high school, but when it came to making her mark in Hollywood, no one trained harder than she did. She dyed her hair, lost weight, took lessons in voice training and drama, splurged $500 on a dress and reserved a table in a nightclub in full view of Harry Cohn.

Her manipulation was brilliant, and after 14 "B" pictures, Marguerita Carmen Cansino was reborn as "Rita Hayworth, leading lady/sex goddess." She did whatever she could to make her mark on Hollywood, and changing her name was the first of many changes for her.

Gene didn't want to hear about any of these Hollywood publicity stunts. She liked her name, she was proud of her name, and she wanted to keep it. "But Gene is a boy's name" they would say. "How about we spell it Jean instead?" Although the pronunciation would be the same, it was not the name she was born with and she wanted to keep *her* name. That Tierney stubborn streak had kicked in again, and the studio knew that any name change suggestion, as slight as it was, would be followed by an emphatic "No!" from Gene.

They eventually agreed that if she had what it took to make it, the name "Gene Tierney" would be remembered easily enough. And they were right. She managed to get more than enough publicity with her own name; she certainly didn't need any fabricated studio hype to help her.

Gene Eliza Tierney was eventually known as the Hollywood "GET" girl. The first initials of Gene's name spell "GET"—she eventually "gets" what she wants. It was a long and very bumpy road, but, eventually, personally and professionally, she did get what she wanted.

Another suggestion came from a cameraman who told her that her slightly chubby, cherub face would photograph better if she lost a few pounds. She took this advice seriously. Anything to improve herself and her appearance would give her a better chance of getting a part.

She quickly mailed a dollar off to *Harper's Bazaar* magazine for its "lose a pound a day diet." It was a dollar well spent. Gene lived on salads and lean meats and eliminated starches from her diet for the next 20 years. She followed the diet religiously, and in doing so she kept her weight steady at 117 pounds for two decades. She said later in life that she was hungry for most of those 20 years, but her dedication to her art and her desire to succeed at it was well worth the sacrifice of a good meal.

On a professional level, Gene was tired of waiting for Columbia to find something for her to do, and George Abbott beckoned her back to the stage. "Come back to Broadway, Gene. We'll find you something here," he pleaded. She trusted George. He knew best. As soon as her six-month option with Columbia was up, she went back home. Columbia did its best to persuade Gene to take up another six-month

2. Hollywood Beckons

In a rare, somewhat cheeky pose, a young Gene has her hands on hips while giving the lens an "I'll show you" look. It was that same Tierney stubborn streak that convinced her father to go ahead and let her try to realize her dream of becoming an actress.

Gene Tierney

option at the same salary, but as usual, she had made up her mind and no one could change it. She was going home.

Back on Broadway, George Abbott kept his word and cast Gene in a play titled *Ring Two* at $100 a week. After two months of rehearsal the play opened in November. It lasted two nights and Gene was heartbroken. "The only flops you've ever had have had me in them. I'm a jinx. Do you think I'm a jinx?" she cried. George convinced her that all good actors suffer this same hardship, and his plays being failures had nothing to do with her at all. Coincidences, that was all.

Gene was starting to develop a crush on George Abbott. He was 53, tall, suave and had a brilliant mind that fascinated her. He was equally infatuated with her. Eventually he got up enough courage to ask her out, and as much as Gene wanted to accept, she wasn't quite sure that she should. She asked an assistant director for advice. "That's up to you," he said. A politician's answer if ever she had heard one.

Gene decided to accept. On their first date George was very nervous. He brought her a bag of hard candy, and they went out to dinner. The usual easy talking between them had suddenly ceased. Both of them soon realized that any connection between them was purely that of a father/daughter relationship, nothing more.

George let Gene down as easily as he could by telling her that he could never marry her. "There will be days when you'll want to dance and I simply won't feel like dancing," he said. Their 34-year age difference proved too much of an obstacle for any romantic relationship to blossom, but they enjoyed a lifelong friendship. Gene recalled later in life bumping into George at a nightclub in Palm Beach, Florida. "He was 90 and still played tennis every day. Even then I still found him to be an attractive man."

After the letdown of *Ring Two* there was not much chance to sit and ponder what went wrong. Gene pounded the pavement again. She had heard that the actress signed to play the young ingénue in *The Male Animal* was pregnant. She couldn't continue, so Gene went after her role with great enthusiasm. Howard Shumlin wrote and directed the play and hired Gene as the replacement for Mary Lou Davies. Ironically, a year before Shumlin had ejected Gene from his office, and now he was hiring her for his play. He remembered no such incident, maybe because Gene was in his office for all of three minutes.

Gene would play the younger sister of the female lead. This time she was noticed. She made the theater pages in all of the papers. Suddenly people knew who Gene Tierney was, and she liked it. Her photo appeared in *Harper's Bazaar* and *Collier's*. All reviews of her performances so far, even in unsuccessful plays, had been favorable. The press liked her, and that was half the battle in making it. Richard Watt's of *The Herald Tribune* said, "I don't see why Miss Tierney shouldn't have an interesting career if the cinema doesn't kidnap her."

Night after night Gene went onstage. She felt at home in the theater and was

2. Hollywood Beckons

enjoying her success in her longest running play so far. The play had been running only two weeks when all of a sudden it happened again. Twentieth Century–Fox approached her and offered her a screen test. Darryl F. Zanuck, the head of Fox, had seen Gene himself. He had gone to a performance of *The Male Animal*, and before she even opened her mouth he nudged his executive next to him and said, "Sign that girl."

That same night Zanuck and the same executive went to the Stork Club for a quiet drink. Casually looking around the dance floor, Zanuck spotted a beautiful girl dancing with a very smitten college boy. Again Zanuck nudged his executive and said, "Forget about that girl in the play. Sign this one instead. Go and find out her name." The executive went over and asked the girl her name. "Gene Tierney," she said. He went back to Zanuck and told him what she had said. With the name sounding familiar Zanuck flicked through the program for *The Male Animal*, and in amazement he saw that she was the same girl. "I've tried to sign the same girl twice in a matter of hours and without even realizing it," Zanuck said. "Whatever it takes, I want her under contract." He wasn't willing to hear the word "no" from her, so he was willing to go her way and give her what she wanted. He just wanted her at Fox.

Gene remembered back to Columbia and how her hopes for the movies were soon dashed with countless excuses of why they couldn't use her just yet. She liked the stage. It was her base and she wanted to stay there. She refused Fox's initial offer, but Fox refused to give in. Zanuck wanted Gene to sign, and he would do just about anything to change her mind. "I told you," he shouted. "Give her what she wants. Tell her this deal will be on *her* terms."

Yet again Zanuck's studio executive set out to convince Gene that this would be much different from her time at Columbia. "You do not have to come out here. We'll test you in New York. Just recite something, that's all." It sounded harmless enough. She wouldn't have to pick up and leave Broadway just yet. She could do this test between her Broadway performances. She wouldn't miss a beat. She finally agreed to the test and recited a heartbreaking speech from *Our Town*.

When she had finished she looked around and stared in surprise at what she was seeing. The cameramen were crying. One was mopping his running nose. "You know something, Miss Tierney?" said one cameraman. "You had every one of us in tears. Look at us. We were all sobbing like babies."

And so a second chance at Hollywood and the movies suddenly presented itself. Gene's father helped negotiate the contract, her terms were set out, and they were all agreed upon. She would have work within 30 days of signing her contract or the contract would be void. She would not be made to pose for cheesecake shots in bathing suits. (This was a clause she would later ignore. She posed for many bathing suit photos throughout her career. She had the figure to do it, so why not?)

Gene Tierney

She would not be made to dye her reddish brown hair. (This was another clause that she ignored for her platinum blonde role in *A Bell for Adano*.) Her slight overbite would not be cosmetically altered, and her nose was to stay the way it was meant to be — absolutely no plastic surgery! Finally, she wanted the option of spending six months of the year in pictures and six months on stage.

Zanuck agreed to all terms, so Gene couldn't say no anymore. These were her terms, and just maybe this time it would all work out. With her father as her agent Gene negotiated a lucrative $750 a week contract with Fox. With no formal training she was again ready to make her mark on Hollywood.

The family company that Gene's father had set up to manage her income was put to use again. Belle Tier would hold all money earned by Gene. Her father would look after all ingoing and outgoing money. It was Gene's job to earn it and his job to manage it. It seemed to be a good idea at the time, but it soon became the center of a family dispute that would lead to financial and emotional heartache for Gene for the rest of her life.

3

Hollywood — Take Two

Four months after her opening night in *The Male Animal* it was time for Gene's second attempt at Hollywood. This time she hoped things would be different from her time with Columbia. She was tentative about leaving a successful Broadway play, but she was ready to take on Hollywood for a second time. It was a famous story around town that George Jean Nathan had bet Gene that she'd return to Broadway within one year. He lost the bet. As much as she loved the stage, the only time she ever returned to the theater was as an audience member.

A month or so after being in California, frustrated, she told a friend, "I had them all in tears over my dramatic performance of *Our Town*, and I've been playing sexy roles ever since." As frustrated as she was, Gene found her current situation amusing. She was getting paid and she was at least working. She wasn't hearing excuses like those at Columbia. She was making movies. She was now officially an actress.

The studio stuck to the agreement and she was put to work within two weeks of signing her contract. Her first role of 1940 was *The Return of Frank James*, alongside Henry Fonda. She was to play Eleanor Stone, a female reporter who ends up being the love interest of Frank James, played by the legendary Fonda. Not a bad role for a beginner, but she was suddenly acting with the intimidating male lead in Fonda. More often than not he would memorize his lines perfectly. He was known as "one take" Fonda, and Gene was so impressed with his dedication to his art that she vowed to be known one day as "one take" Tierney.

The Return of Frank James was a success at the box office, but Gene dropped her head in embarrassment when she heard herself on screen. "I sound like an angry Minnie Mouse," she said, horrified. In a drastic attempt to lower her voice she took up smoking cigarettes, and it worked.

Gene's performance in *The Return of Frank James* won her an award. An award is usually something to boast about, but not when it's being voted "The Worst Female Discovery" of 1940 by *Harvard Lampoon*. It wasn't exactly a flattering title

Gene Tierney

to have attached to her name, but Gene took it in stride and moved on to her next picture, *Hudson's Bay*.

Paul Muni was to be her leading man, already the winner of one Academy Award. She was facing yet another tough task up against an experienced actor. Nigel Bruce played a minor character. He was known as Dr. Watson of *Sherlock Holmes* fame. He was a gentle old man who sensed Gene's frustration one day when a scene that she was filming repeatedly went wrong. "Come here, my little darling, and let me press you to me," he cooed. As seductive as that sounded, all Gene got was an affectionate hug of reassurance. It was exactly what she needed before facing her first romantic scene with John Sutton. This was to be her first screen kiss, and she was as nervous as any young actress would be. The scene was shot three times, but Gene had no memory of its being anything but routine when asked about it years later. It must have been equally forgetful for Sutton; he walked right past Gene without recognizing her when she was filming her next film, *Tobacco Road*.

Again, this film was no masterpiece, but once again Gene was working, she was acting, and that's what she wanted to do. That's what she was there to do. John Ford directed the film, and what better way for her to learn the craft of acting than to be directed by the master himself? *The Hollywood Reporter* described the film as "the most daring movie of all time." A seduction scene between Gene and Ward Bond no doubt fueled that statement.

Gene was cast as a seductress halfwit hillbilly, Ellie May Lester. The scene required Gene to seduce Bond. The script called for them to roll around in the dirt as they groped and pawed at each other. This type of raw animalistic sex scene embarrassed Gene, and she asked John Ford to clear the set. He agreed. Gene was happy, and he got what he required of her without having a tense actress worried about who was watching her in such a display of passion.

The role of Ellie May was anything but glamorous. Each morning Gene was sprayed with a coating of olive oil. Her

A pretty portrait shot of Gene in her first "released" film role, playing Eleanor Stone in the Western *The Return of Frank James* (1940).

3. Hollywood—Take Two

arms, legs and face were covered with oil, and then she was wiped over with dirt. Her hair was caked with mud and oil to give it a stringy, unwashed appearance. She wore a stained calico dress that was nothing more then a rag. That was the extent of her makeup and wardrobe for the entire film. The crew nicknamed her "Dirty Gertie."

Gene would spend over an hour each night scrubbing the dirt from her body and untangling her hair. Her scalp itched constantly from the mud and oil that was applied daily, but instead of complaining, she felt that she was finally making it as an actress. She was creating a character that was a world away from her regular way of life, and she loved it. This *was* acting!

Even through the dirty face and the torn and tattered clothes of her character, there was something about Gene Tierney that shone brightly. She had now completed

Around the release of *Tobacco Road* in 1941, in order to promote the film (which has nothing to do with bowling) Gene attended a charity tenpin bowling day at Sunset Center in England.

three films in 12 months. None of them would come close to earning an Academy Award, but all were good enough for the studio executives to know they needed to keep her signed. Although she was technically acting, the studio was placing her in these roles only to keep her working. Her contract required that, and the studio delivered. Fox had no idea what to do with this exotic looking woman. The studio knew they wanted her, they knew they had to keep her, but until they worked out what to do with her, they just kept her working. In anything!

Gene knew she was being nurtured along, and she soon grew dissatisfied with her second attempt at making movies. At least it was more fun this time, and socially she was having a ball. She became engaged to actor Robert Sterling. Her parents disapproved strongly of this union. Her mother made the trip out to see her daughter, and the engagement was broken very swiftly.

Gene still longed to go back to Broadway for a spell. She knew she had the six months in Hollywood and six months on Broadway option agreed to in her con-

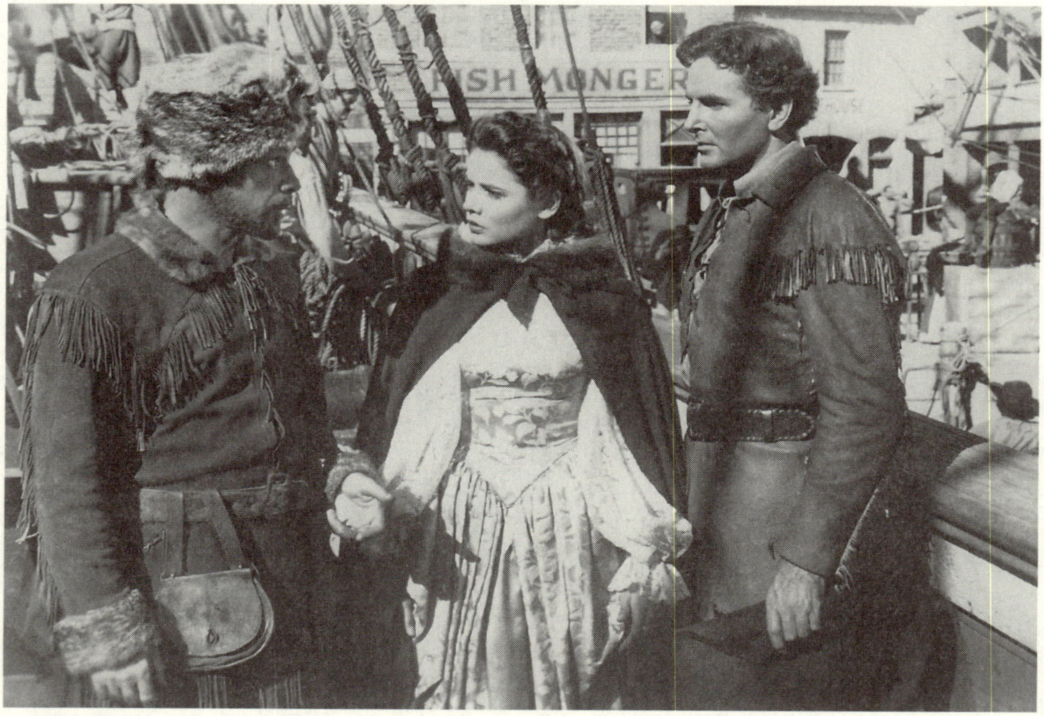
ISH MONGER

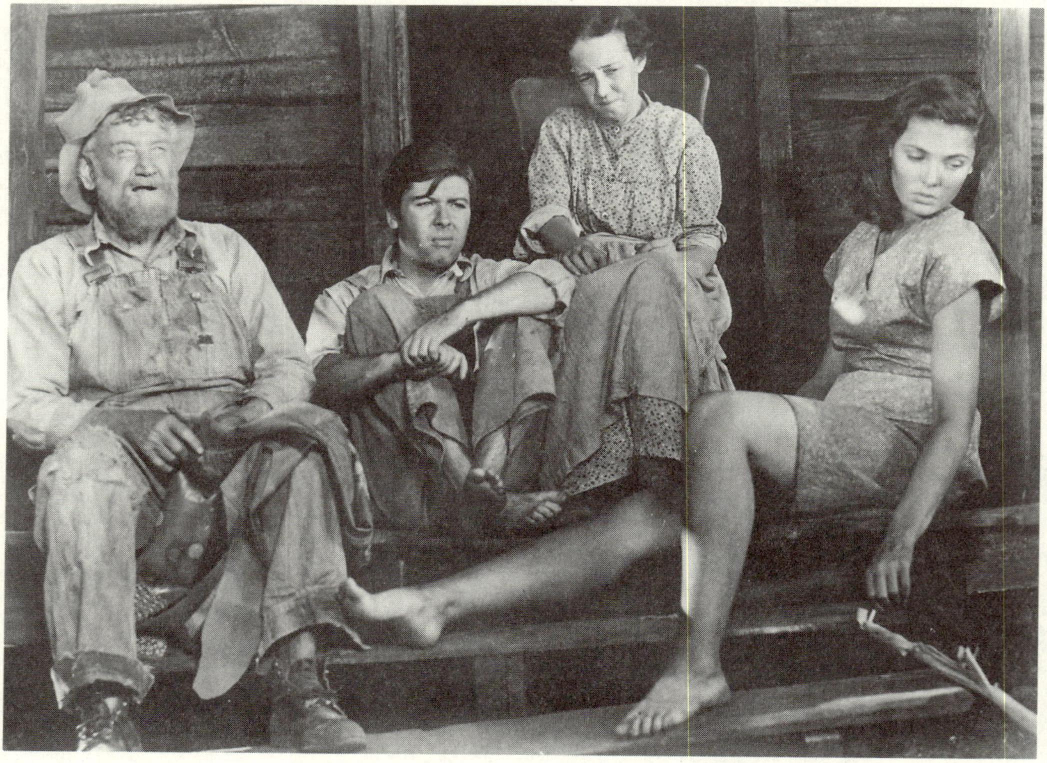

3. Hollywood—Take Two

tract, so understandably she was over the moon when she was asked to read for a play by John Golden. The play was *Claudia*, and when Gene read for the part, Golden and the author, Rose Franken, agreed that Gene was perfect for the lead. Gene was thrilled. She now needed only the approval of her studio to close the deal, and before long she would be back in the theater. But it wasn't long before Gene's bubble was burst. She hadn't realized that her still being a minor prevented her making decisions about her Broadway/Hollywood career. Gene's father, still in control of her finances, also made her decisions, even contractual ones. He had already advised Fox without her knowledge that she would waive her option to go back to Broadway for that year.

There was nothing Gene could do but turn down the part. This disappointment was the first of many that

An early pinup pose of Gene (photograph courtesy Lou and Mary Jo Mari).

would be brought to her by her father's decision making. Dorothy McGuire ended up being second choice for the role in *Claudia*, and the play was a smash hit. As much as it hurt, Gene found some comfort in the fact that she was the replacement girl in *The Male Animal*. She owed her contract with Fox to that part, and her

---

Opposite, top: A 21-year-old Gene as Barbara in **Hudson's Bay** (1941). *Opposite, bottom:* The hillbilly Lester family in the controversial *Tobacco Road* (1941). Gene plays Ellie May Lester. The crew nicknamed her "Dirty Gertie" because of the layers of mud and dirt packed on her for each scene. Who said film work was glamorous?

career was taking off in Hollywood. There was no reason to feel disappointed for long.

Gene was dating many men, none of them seriously. She didn't have time to dedicate herself to a serious relationship. Eddie Albert took her sailing. Desi Arnaz took her out to dinner one night and talked the entire time about how much he loved Lucille Ball. Gene politely listened, and sure enough, Lucy and Desi married soon after. She casually dated actor Robert Morley, who introduced Gene to the finer points of eating certain high class delicacies. Caviar was a favorite, and Morley delighted in spoiling her by ordering Gene as much as she desired.

The studio set up publicity dates for Gene. They wanted her to be seen with nice, wholesome types. In 1940 there was no one fitting that image more than Mickey Rooney. Gene said, "Mickey could make me laugh simply by ordering a meal." She enjoyed his company and looked upon their "set up dating" as being out with a great companion.

Gene is approximately 19 years old in this early Twentieth Century–Fox promotional shot (photograph courtesy Lou and Mary Jo Mari).

Other dates set up by the studio were not so pleasant. Fox arranged for Gene to be seen out with singer Rudy Vallee. Nothing thrilled Gene's mother more than this union, but to Gene this man was much older than she, and she wasn't the slightest bit interested in going as far as across the street with him. Gene's mother adored him as a singer, so Gene allowed her mother to come along on their dates. "Besides," she said, "someone had to show an interest in him."

It was nearing the end of 1940, and Gene's social life was busy. Her studio-arranged dates and her dates of choice saw her out and about almost every night. She felt in control of her life, and she was happy with her decision to date several

3. Hollywood—Take Two

men instead of looking for one steady boyfriend. As with most things in life, just when you think you have everything under control, something unexpected moves in and changes everything. That unexpected something for Gene was fashion designer Oleg Cassini.

Gene attended a party at the home of actress Constance Moore and Johnny Maschio. She came to the party alone, as did Oleg. She was invited because Johnny was her agent. Oleg was invited because he had designed Constance's clothes in *I Wanted Wings.* They were soon attracted to each other and talked for hours about everything, in English and in French. Although there seemed to be some chemistry between them, Gene was still hesitant to give out her telephone number. A persistent Oleg refused to leave the party without it. What's a girl to do? She jotted it down and handed it to him.

Oleg was employed at Paramount studios as a $200 a week fashion designer. He was 28, once married, now available and according to Gene, "the most dangerous looking character I had ever seen." He was considered something of a playboy, but Gene wasn't looking for a serious relationship. His playboy ways would in no way bother her if she was not serious about him as an exclusive beau. She intended to keep him at a safe distance.

A few days after the party Gene received a phone call from Oleg. He wanted Gene to go out with him on New Year's Eve. "I'm so sorry," Gene said, "but I'm just *so* busy." She had no desire to go out on a date with him. She already had a date, but Oleg charmed her into breaking it after convincing her that she would have a much better time with him. He kept her on the phone for two hours, refusing to hang up until she agreed to go out with him. She gave in and called to break her original date with the excuse that she was ill and just couldn't think of going out anywhere.

Nothing more was thought about her little lie until Gene and Oleg ran into her date, Raymond Hakim, on their night out together. Raymond was surprised to find her up and about so quickly. "Feeling better, I see," he said as he shot a look Oleg's way. An embarrassed Gene excused herself. She and Oleg laughed about it later.

That New Year's Eve was the start of a new year and a new relationship for both of them. They started their date at Ciro's and moved on to club after club, talking, laughing and dancing till dawn. On reflection Gene said later, "I hadn't been with Oleg for half an hour before I decided I liked him."

There has to be an added pressure when a girl accepts a date with a fashion designer. One wants to look her best and make a good impression, especially on a first date. Certain professions could easily make a girl feel uneasy about her appearance. Dating a plastic surgeon would be a good example. Is he looking at you because he can't take his eyes off you, or is he looking at the wrinkle he could easily iron out with some quick scalpel handiwork? When he tells you your nose is cute, does he mean it, or is he really saying he could make it even cuter? Anyway, my point being there really *are* certain professions that carry added pressures into a relationship. Dating a fashion designer has to be one of them.

With that in mind, Gene thought she'd put together the perfect outfit. It was one she'd designed herself, and she waited nervously for Oleg to pick her up. When the doorbell rang and Gene opened the door, Oleg stood in disbelief. "For heaven's sake," he said with a frown, "take that pink stuff off. You look like a cream puff." Gene was wearing a navy and pink print dress and a navy hat with pink roses and masses of pink tulle surrounding the brim. A navy cape with pink satin lining covered her shoulders. Her pink gloves and bag were, in her eyes, the perfect accessories. As taken aback as she was by his reaction, she swallowed her pride and took his advice. After all, he was the expert. She went to her room and changed into something simple. When she reappeared Oleg admired the new outfit with as much enthusiasm as he showed in disliking her first choice. His compliments gave her some satisfaction. This new outfit was another one of her own designs.

In future years, when Gene wanted to go shopping, Oleg would refuse to go with her. Shopping for clothes gave him the fidgets. Gene would go out, pick what she liked and then come home and model her purchases for him. Anything he found to be unflattering to her figure or simply too "cream puffish" would be returned. Their arrangement worked, and under his expert guidance, she consistently remained one of Hollywood's best-dressed women.

Oleg intrigued Gene. He was born Count Oleg Loiewski Cassini de Capizucchi in Paris on April 11, 1913. He was the son of a Russian Count, Count Alexander Loiewski. Forced to leave revolutionary Russia, he spent the better part of his European life in Italy. When his mother opened a dress shop, its success was partly due to Oleg's ingenious designs. He started sketching for his mother's store, and when many customers liked the designs he was coming up with, his mother decided to send him to Paris to improve his talents by studying with the famous French designer Patou. By the time Oleg had reached his early twenties, it was decided he should try his luck in America.

In 1936, at the age of 23, he bought a ticket on the Italian liner *Saturnia* and sailed with a dream to the land of opportunity, America. The Italian government had imposed a currency restriction at the time. Only $100 was allowed to be taken from Italy. With his $100 limit in his pocket, a few names and addresses of friends of his mother's to contact upon arrival, a tennis racket and a dinner jacket, Count Oleg Cassini sailed from Italy to America.

By the time the boat docked his $100 had diminished to $25. He had bought all of his new friends drinks on the trip across. With the site of the Statue of Liberty approaching, the thought of having so little money left did nothing to dampen

3. Hollywood—Take Two

his spirits. He had reached America and was bursting with excitement. Later he would renounce his title of Count Cassini and become an American citizen.

Now four years after his arrival in New York, Oleg was employed at Paramount Studios. Socially he was recognized as an up and coming designer, just as Gene was considered an up and coming actress. They were equals in every way, and they were in love. As fascinated as Gene was with Oleg, he was equally fascinated with her. "She was stunning," he said as he remembered their first meeting years after it had occurred. "It is difficult to describe just how breathtaking she was. Photos never really did her justice."

He paused as if to remember how best to describe her features. "She had soft golden skin. It seemed to glow. And her eyes, very light, green/blue, magical. The effect on me was magnetic. She was wearing a simple black dress with a string of pearls. She had shoulder length brown hair that curled at the ends. There was not an angle in her face that was not perfect, although her teeth were slightly bucked—which only added to her allure, as far as I was concerned. Without that slight imperfection she would have seemed unreal, so completely beautiful as to seem synthetic, and therefore uninteresting. She was about five foot seven, with broad shoulders, an elegant body, and long limbs. Spectacular." This description was given by Oleg years after their first chance meeting. Gene certainly made an impression.

Many dates followed that first meeting, and soon enough, within one week, they both realized they were ideal for each other. This was the exclusive man that Gene had said she had no time for, and suddenly she was talking about marriage!

In all their hours of conversation, Gene always talked of her family with great enthusiasm. Oleg knew that if he were in her father's position and *his* daughter came home telling him that she was going to marry a count, he would not allow it to happen. Putting himself in Howard Tierney's shoes made Oleg realize that if he didn't marry this girl now, her family would ensure that it would never happen at all. He couldn't lose her, so he devised a plan.

"Gene, go home, change your clothes, give some excuse to your mother, and we'll go to the airport," he said. Gene nodded and agreed. She loved this man, and as much as she loved her family, somehow she knew that if they got wind of this romance, it would be over.

Oleg dropped Gene off at her house around 10:30 A.M. He picked her up an hour later, down the block away from any prying eyes. Oleg had planned everything. He had chartered a plane through his friend Bill Josephy, whom he had awakened from a deep sleep. "Wake up. You're about to be the best man at a great marriage," he shouted into the phone. When Oleg told Josephy whom he was marrying, Josephy almost fainted. "Jesus," he said, "you work fast!"

4

Bride to Be

Rain was falling heavily by the time they arrived at the airport, and waiting for it to ease only made Gene anxious and full of doubt over what she was about to do. "Don't you think we should at least talk to Mother?" she said. "Absolutely not," Oleg replied in a stern tone.

Suddenly their hasty marriage plans weren't solely up to them. All of a sudden it seemed Mother Nature had reason to put a stop to their wedding too. The pilot told them it was too dangerous for their plane to take off with the rainstorm coming in. They had no choice but to return home, their romantic plan foiled by bad weather.

Oleg drove Gene home in silence. He sensed a feeling of dread. He felt their chance of getting married without any hassles had presented itself, and now there was no hope without a family battle. Once home, Gene tried to convince him that it would all work out, just not as they first planned. "It need not end this way. Let me talk it over with my family. They'll love you when they get to know you."

"No," he said, "I'll not go through anything like this. I refuse to have to explain myself to them, about my divorce and everything else. I will not go through it. So if you want to see me again, if you believe in your feelings and instincts, call me. I will not call you." Oleg was frustrated and later regretted putting that to Gene, but he stuck to his word and did not call her. He did, however, sit by the phone waiting for her to call him. Gene eventually called after a few very long days and told him that the marriage had to be cleared by her family. She would just not feel right about sneaking off without involving them.

Oleg eventually backed down and agreed to meet Gene's mother. It was an agreement that he later regretted. "Some say the mother is prettier than the daughter," Belle Tierney said with a laugh as she met him. This was not a comment that would impress anyone at any time, and it did nothing to impress Oleg on that first contact. He did not like Belle Tierney and she did not like him. She did all that she could to turn Gene against him, even to the point of insulting him to Gene's face.

4. Bride to Be

"Good looking men fall for you left and right. Why are you so insistent on *him?*" she yelled.

These were the exact battles that Oleg wanted to avoid by that planned elopement. Everything that he predicted had come true. He was fighting for Gene and Gene's family were fighting for Gene. She was in the middle and torn between the two, and Oleg knew that he was anything but a sure bet to win the fight. The stress proved too much for the young lovers to endure. They parted company, and over the next few months they drifted in and out of each other's lives. Both dated other people, yet the flame for each other was far too strong to die out completely.

Gene soon came to the realization that her own parents' marriage was coming to an end. Knowing that the father she worshipped was leaving her mother for her mother's best friend was heartbreaking for Gene. The one constant in her life was the family base that she thought was always there for her to fall back on, and now that was crumbling around her. Her parents' divorce hit her hard. It was an emotional blow that would leave a lifelong scar.

Gene's memories of her father standing before her, Pat and Butch and lecturing them about the importance of honesty and morality and doing what was right in life suddenly turned into a "do as I say and not as I do" speech. Gene had believed in her father and in his words. All of a sudden he was not the man she thought him to be, and that realization did emotional damage that would never heal. The solidity of her family unit was the one thing in the world that she trusted and relied on, and now it was gone.

Personally, life was dealing Gene a bad hand, and professionally she soon came to realize that Hollywood was not an easy place to be either. Her roles were limited and initially not what she thought she was suited for. She knew that professionally she had to hang on and hope beyond hope that Fox would eventually find the exact niche to fit her look.

In May of 1941, Gene called Oleg from New York. He was always glad to hear from her and noticed that she sounded different. He soon learned of her father's infidelity and realized that her world had been shaken by it. "I love you. I *must* see you," she pleaded over the phone. Oleg was thrilled. He hadn't realized that she still cared for him that much. As thrilled as he was, he tried to remain in control of the situation and agreed to see her, but with the intent of laying a few ground rules this time.

They arranged a meeting of sorts, and Oleg was happy to see Gene again, this time under circumstances that he knew would eventually have them back as a couple again, as long as she agreed to his terms. "Can't we just go back to the way things were," she pleaded. "Hmmphhh," he sighed. "I do not want to be toyed with again. If time is required, it will be because I wish to take *my* time. If we are to resume, you must agree to certain things. You must not date anyone else, not even studio publicity dates. You must respect my wishes. If I wish to meet your parents, it will be done when *I* am ready to do so." On and on he went as Gene listened to this list of terms. Oleg always spoke with dramatics. His words were almost comedic, full of theatrics that should have seen him become an actor instead of a designer. Gene eventually agreed to Oleg's terms, and they became a couple again, this time for keeps.

That spring, Gene was cast in her fourth movie alongside Randolph Scott and Dana Andrews in a Western entitled *Belle Starr*. It was a part originally given to Barbara Stanwyck, who at the last minute pulled out. Gene was under great pressure at the time. Her split up/make up with Oleg, the realization that her parents' marriage was beyond repair, the pressures of being a 19-year-old starlet, all took their toll. She had always looked and appeared much calmer than she was. Her life's pressures manifested themselves in other ways. Physical ailments would constantly plague her. Her stomach problems still came and went without warning. Whatever pill the doctor prescribed to help her she would take, but when the pain became too much, no pill would work. She would have to double over on the floor and wait for the cramping to ease before continuing her work.

Her new role was something of a step up from previous ones. She was promised her first star billing, but just as filming on *Belle Starr* began, Gene began to suffer terrible eye problems. Her eyes would swell up for no apparent reason, becoming red, puffy slits that would hamper her vision and her looks to the point that she would have no choice but to stop work until she recovered.

The itching was unbearable, the pain reducing her to tears. A string of allergists were called in to look at her. One gave her a shot of Adrenalin; it almost stopped her heart from beating. None of them really knew the cause of the condition, so no one knew what to give her to cure it. Another allergist told Darryl F. Zanuck that it would be a condition that she would face for the rest of her life. This news had Zanuck thinking seriously of replacing her. She was in danger of losing this role, but with the knowledge that her condition would be lifelong, she knew that Zanuck would also consider letting her go completely.

Just like her stomach problems, her eye condition would come and go without warning. When her eyes returned to normal, she would work. When they flared up again, she stayed home and waited for the phone to ring, telling her that she was no longer needed on *Belle Starr* and subsequently no longer needed at Fox.

As cold as it sounds, the studios were running a business. Every day lost in filming is money down the drain, and no amount of sympathy for any star's illness would stop them from cutting her loose. Gene knew she was on borrowed time with Fox. She was letting them down, and the more she worried the worse her eye condition became. Oleg became Gene's rock through the stresses and strains of the allergy, constantly telling her that she always looked beautiful to him. Their

4. Bride to Be

Gene in a scene from *Belle Starr* (1941) with Randolph Scott. Dana Andrews (Union uniform) is in the background. One could argue that it was Scott who single-handedly saved Gene's career. When a severe eye condition forced her to stop work and shut down production on *Belle Starr*, Scott assured the studio that he wanted no extra pay for the time it took Gene to get well, just as long as they didn't fire her. "You'll find me on the golf course," he said. And there he stayed until Gene was well enough to return to work.

relationship became stronger, and once again, between Gene's days of torment with her eyes, they spoke of marriage.

Fox was a long way behind the shooting schedule on *Belle Starr*, and Gene was the reason for it. If it weren't for the patience and understanding of Randolph Scott, we may never have seen or heard of Gene Tierney/Actress again.

Scott was on loan to Fox for a limited number of weeks. His contract entitled him to additional salary for every day over the predicted shooting schedule. With the number of days they were behind because of Gene's inability to work, Scott was facing a dilemma. He knew that by holding Fox to his contract would mean that they would either have to pay him the additional money or replace Gene with another actress. Even if they paid him the money and kept Gene in the role, he knew that the resentment from Fox would be enough to make it a very rough road ahead for Gene and her career.

"We need Gene in this picture," he told Zanuck. "I waive my rights to any additional payment for every day over schedule. I'm here to say you don't owe me a cent more. Until Gene is well and ready to work again, you'll find me on the golf course." With that he walked out of Zanuck's office and did indeed head straight to the golf course. Without a doubt, his unselfishness gave Gene the slack that she needed at Fox to finish *Belle Starr* and keep her contract with the studio. He may have saved her career.

Eventually a doctor pinpointed Gene's problem as a stress disorder, an allergy of sorts to the pressures of everyday life. The condition was called angioneurotic edema, a malady that Gene would suffer spasmodically her entire working life. Not long after her first eye problem she decided that upon her death she would donate her corneal tissue to the New York Eye Bank for Sight Restoration to be used for corneal graft operations. She knew the despair of a temporary eye problem. She took comfort in her pledge that, upon her death, she would help someone who had a permanent eye condition.

Gene's relationship with Oleg grew stronger through her difficult period of shooting *Belle Starr*. He doted on her when she was housebound by her eye allergies and reassured her that everything would work out when she believed that it wouldn't. One thing for sure, Oleg's prediction of trouble over their relationship proved to be accurate. Gene already had more than enough stress in her life, and the nightly shouting matches with her mother over Oleg did nothing to ease her torment. Her father wrote her a stream of hurtful letters. One of them stated that he would have her declared legally insane if she married Oleg.

That was the final straw for Gene. She knew she loved Oleg, and no amount of convincing would make her parents see that she was serious about marrying this man. They were unwilling to give him a chance and saw him only as a foreigner who was ready to mooch off the money their daughter was making in pictures. There is nothing more challenging to a child than parents saying they won't allow something to happen. In Gene's case the forbidden relationship with Oleg only made him seem even more attractive. There was nothing more to talk about. They planned to elope for a second time, and this time nothing was going to get in their way!

Just before their planned elopement, Oleg came to pick Gene up at the studio after a day's filming. She was very strict about eating the right foods, and at this time she was on a new diet, a sweet-free diet. Oleg walked into Gene's dressing room, kissed her, and presented her with a huge box of candy. Frustrated by his tempting her with such a gift, she frowned. "You know I can't eat candy. Please, take it away!" she squealed.

4. Bride to Be

"Open it!" Oleg demanded. He looked stern and serious, so Gene gave in and sighed as she began to open the lid of the box. She blushed with embarrassment as she stared at the sparkling diamond nestled among the chocolates. It was an exquisite marquise diamond ring, her engagement ring.

A few days later they bought tickets for the midnight flight to Las Vegas. To avoid being found out they both thought it best to use aliases. Gene used her character name Belle Starr and Oleg used Oleg Loiewski. Gene left her house dressed casually in a blouse and skirt, telling her mother she was going on a picnic. She met Oleg at the airport and saw that he had attempted to dress like an American businessman. He was wearing a long polo coat and a felt hat. He topped off the outfit by carrying a briefcase. They sat several rows apart on the plane. Gene took out her compact from time to time and gave him a reassuring wink in the mirror. Little did Gene know that he had become terribly airsick. He tried to hide it from Gene but later confessed, "I was so sick, I must have looked like a lemon."

On arrival in Las Vegas a chauffeur and limousine met them. "Where to, Miss Tierney? My name happens to be the same as yours, so I keep tabs on you," he said excitedly. Finding that statement a little off-putting, to say the least, Oleg directed him to Judge Brown's house. He was the local justice of the peace who had agreed to perform the ceremony.

Back at home, both studios were searching frantically for the couple. Paramount had sent a wire to Oleg's house, and Fox was even more frantic over Gene. If Gene was married she would no longer be considered a minor. Belle Tier, the company her father had set up between him and the studio, was still in place because she was under 21 and not yet legally considered an adult. Upon her marriage that contract would be null and void, and a new contract would have to be negotiated. Howard Tierney knew that Gene would soon arrange a new contract that would terminate the need for Belle Tier to exist. He had contacted many people about the elopement and somehow found out exactly where they were to be married.

The phone rang through the entire wedding ceremony, and Gene pleaded with Judge Brown not to answer it until the ceremony was over. It made for a nerve-wracking wedding, but they ignored the phone and got to the end of the ceremony. Oleg and Gene finally became husband and wife on the afternoon of June 1, 1941.

In their hasty escape Oleg had forgotten to buy Gene a wedding ring. He stared blankly at Gene when Judge Brown said, "With this ring, I thee wed." He had bought Gene a beautiful diamond engagement ring, but the buying of the wedding ring had been overlooked. Luckily, Gene was wearing gold hoop earrings. She slipped one of them off and handed it to Oleg to use as a substitute wedding band. They eventually got around to buying the real thing when they arrived home. Gene chose not to wear those earrings again. She saved that one earring for years after. It was much more than just an earring now.

Gene Tierney

As Oleg kissed his bride, Gene felt safe in the fact that they were now legally husband and wife. She gave Judge Brown the nod to answer the ringing phone. What a surprise! It was for Gene. It was Harry Brand, the director of publicity at Twentieth Century–Fox. "Gene, you can't do this!" he yelled into the phone.

"Harry," she cooed, "I've already done it."

"Well, in that case," he said, "don't move. I'll fly right out and we'll have champagne and wedding cake at the Apache Hotel." At last someone was willing to celebrate their union. Sure enough, Harry Brand arrived, but he wasn't alone. A stream of reporters and photographers came with him. This elopement was milked for all its worth.

For a few months, at least until Oleg's citizenship papers were processed, Gene was officially a countess. She thought her new title funny, and since it wouldn't last it was something of a novelty to laugh about. Oleg had come to America as Mr. Oleg Cassini. He did not flash his title around town. He had applied for American citizenship long before he'd met Gene, and it wasn't long before the official papers would be final.

Within the first few hours after the ceremony Gene and Oleg called their parents. When Gene told her mother that she had a new son-in-law, she said, "Well, you can keep him," and hung up the phone in Gene's ear. Gene later heard that Belle Tierney fell to the floor and wept uncontrollably for the entire evening.

Gene's father was next on the list to call. Surprisingly, his reaction was calmer than expected. With all things considered, his smoothness was more fearful than if he had yelled into the phone as Belle had done. He wanted to speak with Oleg.

"Well, you must be quite a man," he said. "I'm sure that anyone my daughter loves will be just fine with me. I'm looking forward to meeting you.... Oh, and by the way, I'll be sending you some papers to sign. Nothing crucial, just some agreements making you part of the Belle Tier Corporation. It's for Gene's protection and her future — and yours, too, now that you're part of the family. But more importantly, you have my blessing. I hope you will be very happy together."

His words appeared to be sincere, but both Gene and Oleg feared that something was brewing. The very next day they found out what it was, and it wasn't pleasant. They decided to get the next flight back to Los Angeles. Gene wanted to try and patch things up with her mother, but upon arrival they were met with newspaper headlines that shocked both of them. The front page of the *New York Journal American* had a statement from Gene's father: "I think Gene has gone Hollywood.... It's unfortunate that she married a man of this fellow's notoriety." Another cutting statement to the press voluntarily given by Gene's mother was, "Gene is just a misguided child. She has been carried away by this suave man of the world."

This was the first of many onslaughts from family and friends. The phone rang

4. Bride to Be

continually. People whom Gene hadn't seen in years were telling her "it's not too late to get out," and "we can get you an annulment in no time." Only a handful of friends sent wedding presents. Many that they both thought to be friends didn't even write or call to congratulate them.

Their marriage seemed to sort out their true friends from those who had only seemed to be friends. It was the start of a professional and social boycott. Gene desperately tried to make contact with her parents, but both rejected her. "When you leave him we will talk," they said jointly. After her many failed attempts to talk with her parents face to face, she decided to communicate with them through the press, just as they did with her. With maturity far beyond her 20 years, she retaliated in a most dignified fashion. In March of 1942, on behalf of Oleg and herself, Gene released a statement to the press. It read as follows: "We are your product. We are living examples of yourselves. You should have faith in us and be proud of us, if you are proud of what you have taught us. I didn't do anything wrong — I just knew whom I wanted to marry."

The cracks had begun to show between Gene and her father long before Oleg was even a factor. This treatment of her and her new husband was the end to the father/daughter relationship that she had once treasured. Gene's mother was another story. As controlling as she was, Gene loved her. Her mother would often regale friends with stories of how she and Gene's father had eloped when she was young. She of all people should understand her daughter's situation.

To top it all off, the Paramount telegram that was sent to Oleg's house was not one of good news. He had been fired, and no doubt this was another stem of the conspiracy between studios and parents to make it as hard as possible for the young couple to survive.

Gene and Oleg did their best to ignore the outside strains, and Gene moved into Oleg's quaint cottage on Cherokee Lane. He rented it for $50 a week, and they called it their Honeymoon Cottage. Gene was the perfect young wife, puttering around, hanging curtains, fluffing pillows, painting walls and making what was once a bachelor pad into the home of a young married couple. Oleg delighted in watching her flutter around fixing this and fussing over that. She enjoyed her newest role of wife to the man she loved.

Oleg's mother, now living in Washington, came out to meet her son's new wife. She was very impressed with Gene's skills as a homemaker, and she and Gene got on famously. That afternoon was going along smoothly when, unexpectedly, Belle Tierney turned up at the front door. She was polite but stiff and formal and came only to tell Gene that her father wanted to talk to her about her insistence on being married. The only suspicious thing about this new contact was that he wanted to meet Gene in, of all places, Chicago.

Both Gene and Oleg knew a plan was in the works, an annulment kidnapping

Gene Tierney

Newlyweds Gene and Oleg play a game of cards in bed (photograph courtesy Lou and Mary Jo Mari).

of sorts. Gene had no time to consider going anyway. She was due back to work on *Belle Starr* to finish up the final scenes, and then she was off to Arizona to begin a movie with George Sanders and Bruce Cabot called *Sundown*. Belle Tierney left after her proposal had been declined, and that was the start of a bumpy road ahead for Gene and her mother's relationship. Gene was never close to her father again, and Oleg had very little to do with either one of them.

Gene's parents' marriage was now over, not officially, but her father had moved on and was now living with "the other woman." The once very affluent Tierneys had come down to earth with quite a thud. A news story dated November 7, 1941, from Westport, Connecticut, stated that a $5,000 mortgage was foreclosed on the Tierney family home on Clapboard Road.

Gene's statement to the press in March of 1942 broke down the barriers between her and her mother. They reconciled later that month, and as a gift to her mother, Gene bought back the family home.

By November of 1942, Belle Taylor Tierney and Howard S. Tierney were divorced. The once close Tierney family had perished. No matter what Gene now felt for her father, she was heartbroken, for herself but mostly for her mother. Belle Tierney was a proud woman who had believed that her marriage was forever.

4. Bride to Be

Gene and husband Oleg Cassini on a night out at the popular Stork Club nightclub.

As if that weren't enough of a burden to take into a new marriage, things got worse. Socially the couple was cut off. Invitations to parties, tennis matches, film premieres, basically anything involving other people were all of a sudden dried up. This was a couple who before marriage would be out on the town every night. You would think their social calendars combined would have them turning down invitations left and right. For more than six months after their wedding, Gene, Oleg and Butch, Gene's police dog, would sit together and be content in their own company. Gene would often get invitations addressed only to her. Oleg was shunned completely. Socially, they were simply not recognized as a couple.

Oleg did all he could to prove that his love for Gene was genuine, even signing a document relinquishing any rights to their community property if they were to divorce. Still the eyes of suspicion turned on them from every direction. Looking back, it was a miracle their marriage lasted those first few weeks.

Newly married with an unemployed husband, Gene would take Oleg's costume

Gene Tierney

sketches to Darryl F. Zanuck, hoping that with her influence at the studio he would give him a job. Every time, the sketches were returned to Gene without comment. Oleg explains: "It is a cliché that Hollywood was a small town in those days, but it is true. Zanuck was in touch with my old friend Ginsburg at Paramount, and with Jack Warner, Louis B. Mayer and Harry Cohn as well. Working hand in glove, they gave me a very tough year. But I survived, and so did the marriage."

Later in life, Zanuck and Oleg became good friends. One night over dinner, Oleg couldn't help but ask why Zanuck refused to employ him. "Oleg," he said, "it was nothing personal. Gene was a very important property. We could have given you work, but that would have made your life easier. We decided to boycott you in the hope that if we made the marriage more difficult, Gene would lose interest in you."

Oleg had suspected the boycott when it occurred, but hearing all those years later that he was right, and directly from Zanuck himself, it was a hard fact to swallow. When other studios got wind that Gene's studio had no interest in her husband, they too shut the door on any Cassini designs that were submitted to them. It ended up being a turbulent year for the couple. Gene was still arranging to work on her next movie, *Sundown*, while Oleg did all he could to find work and battle a conspiracy against him at the same time. The studios eventually backed down, and as soon as they realized that the marriage had survived that very rocky year, they lifted the boycott, and Cassini designs were given consideration once again.

5

Belle Tier

As one pressure was lifted for the couple another battle was looming, again coming from Gene's family. The relationship between Gene and her father had broken down to the point where the only communication between them was through their respective lawyers. It was starting to get very messy. Howard Tierney went as far as taking Gene to court over her contract with the family company, Belle Tier. Gene's newly married status allowed her to override the legality of still being a minor. It also allowed her to be responsible for her own career and her own earnings, all things that Howard Tierney was dead set against.

A new contract was agreed upon between Gene and the studio. Belle Tier would no longer automatically receive a 25 per cent cut of her salary. Howard Tierney sued his daughter for $50,000, claiming that Belle Tier should still be recognized as her agent. For the entire time that Gene was under contract she didn't control a single cent of her own money. Anything she purchased would be run through the family corporation, right down to a dress or even a new lipstick. Unfortunately, Gene's trust in her father was such that she didn't consider asking for a company statement to view the funds for herself. On one occasion when she asked for a breakdown of funds in the company account, Howard Tierney said, "Don't you worry your pretty little head over it Gene. I have it all under control." Gene left it at that and didn't ask again.

The court battle that Howard Tierney initiated only ended up showing him up as the fraud that he was. As the court case progressed, Gene's business manager began to get company figures through his office. One day he called Gene in. "Guess how much your share of this company is worth, Gene." Gene shrugged. "How much?" she asked. "How does zero, zero, zero sound? There isn't a cent left."

Gene was shocked. It seemed that her father was letting her down more and more, and now he had actually stolen from her too. She slowly found out the truth behind his deception. Her father's insurance business had failed after a long bat-

Left: An alluring shot of Gene from *Sundown* (1941). She poses in the same outfit and is seen on the cover of *Life* magazine to promote the film in 1941. *Above:* Gene in a romantic embrace with her leading man to promote *Sundown.*

tle with his partner. He drained the money from Belle Tier in the hope that he would come out on top and keep his business. The more he took from Belle Tier, the more he used someplace else, and to no avail.

It was calculated that he stole about $30,000 over the course of two years from the Belle Tier fund. Gene stated later in life that she would have given her father that much and more if only he'd come to her and asked for it. She wanted the truth, and only now she came to realize that for so many years his words only masked his devious actions. Gene's mother confessed to Gene that in his desperation to rid himself of his debt he considered ridding himself of his own life. He carried a gun for many years, reminding himself that if he did get that desperate, he could pull the trigger and his life insurance policy would rid him of the debt that he'd incurred.

Howard Tierney's divorce from Gene's mother was the easier option. His new wife paid off all his debts. She never attempted to repay Gene a penny of her lost funds from her early years of work that were put solely into Belle Tier. Belle Tierney refused to ask for any alimony or settlement of any kind in their divorce. The

5. Belle Tier

Gene as "Poppy" in *The Shanghai Gesture* (1941), in a scene with Mother Gin-Sling, played by Ona Munson. Just look at that hairstyle! As forgettable as the film is, it's entertainment in itself just watching Munson cope with that horrible wig!

papers were served on her, but she refused to read them. She signed them and in doing so signed away all of her rights to claim a cent from her soon to be ex-husband. She later said that she refused to look upon their marriage as a business deal. She did not want to sue the "other woman" for alienation of affection (an old law in divorce proceedings) and instead went back to work and supported herself. She worked as a bridal consultant in Washington, D.C., and maintained until the day she died in the spring of 1978 that Howard Tierney loved her and her only. "He wouldn't have left me for anything else in the world, but he needed the money," she would say. That strange justification kept her sane. She never remarried.

Gene often considered another possibility. If her father had come to her and asked for the money that he needed instead of stealing it from her, she might have been able to help her parents stay together. He might not have fallen into the arms of another woman, for money or for whatever other reason. Gene was starting to lay blame on herself for her parents' divorce. She thought she could have prevented it. That may or may not have been true. If only she had known there was something to prevent in the first place.

In November of 1942 Gene and Oleg moved into a new house in the Franklin Canyon district of Beverly Hills. Howard Tierney decided to drop in for a visit. He had yet to meet Oleg and looked upon this as an opportunity to meet his new son-in-law. Gene remembered the meeting as "strange and tense." She politely showed him through her new house but stayed reserved, as if she were showing a prospective buyer what he would get if he decided to purchase the place. Oleg was surprised at his father-in-law's outwardly pleasant demeanor but had also experienced that part of him on his wedding day over the phone. Oleg was polite but guarded, just like Gene. Howard

Gene with Tyrone Power in *Son of Fury* (1942). They even have matching bathing costumes.

left after an hour, and Gene would not see him again for 16 years. The only other time she attempted contact it was too late. He died in 1963, just a few days before her phone call.

Howard Tierney paid a high price for his deception. He lost not only his business but also a daughter and a son. Howard Tierney, Jr. (Butch), later went on to become a successful businessman. Any secretary he employed would know the line to deliver if his father made an attempt to contact him. "I'm sorry, Sir, but Mr. Tierney doesn't have a father." Gene thought the line harsh, but Howard had caused his own pain by destroying a family that truly loved him.

It was a time of mixed emotions for Gene. The estrangement of her once close family, the news that she would be suffering from a permanent eye condition that would flare up without warning, and her two-week-old marriage to Oleg Cassini made something of a whirlwind time for a woman of just 21.

Within the first two weeks of her marriage she worked to finish *Belle Starr* before heading off to New Mexico alone to start work on *Sundown*. There was no time for a honeymoon, and now Gene's work commitments would mean the new-

5. Belle Tier

lyweds would be separated. There was no solid reason for them to be apart, but the movie's producer, Walter Wanger, asked that Oleg stay behind in Los Angeles for the duration of the shoot. Gene suspected that another last ditch effort to split up her marriage was in the works. Wanger had served with Gene's father in World War I. She was sure a favor was being asked of Wanger, and this time it was coming directly from Howard Tierney.

Gene was cast as Zia, the daughter of an Arab trader. The location crew had miraculously created the look of East Africa in an area called Ship Rock Hill, New Mexico. The heat was stifling. Gene hated the stench of the camels. She hated them even more after one of them attempted to take a bite out of her behind as she walked past it. There was no way to get to the set but to walk. She would have to climb to the top of the steep slope to the set twice daily to shoot her scenes. They even used donkeys to haul equipment up and down the hill. It certainly made for an authentic feel,

In a live radio broadcast Gene tells America why she decided to will her famous eyes to the New York Eye Bank for sight restoration. After suffering a rare eye condition early in her career, Gene realized how reliant we are on healthy vision. After a full recovery and with perfect eyesight herself, she decided to will her eyes in the hope that she might be able to help someone else.

but there wasn't a hint of glamour on that set. The harsh conditions combined with her desperately missing her husband made for a miserable time.

Gene was costumed in what best would be described as a harem girl outfit. She wore a low slung skirt with her navel exposed, a daring piece of the anatomy to expose at the time. She wore a black and gold threaded bra with a skimpy over vest that covered the top part of her. Assorted veils draped her head and shoulders. Her hair flowed down her back, long and wavy, almost to her waist. Her harem girl portrayal made the cover of *Life* magazine in the summer of 1941. Because of that exotic image of Gene, that issue of *Life* is still one of the most desired magazines for collectors to obtain.

Gene Tierney

Daddy's little girl. The stately portrait shot of Howard Tierney, Sr., on Gene's night table shows an undeniable devotion to her father. Sadly, his eventual betrayal would change those feelings forever (photograph courtesy Lou and Mary Jo Mari).

The location work lasted three weeks. Gene would spend any free moment she could find writing letters back home to Oleg, most of the time telling him how miserable she was without him. When she wasn't writing to him she was reading letters from him. The only moments that got her from one point to the next were the telephone calls between the letters. Bruce Cabot, whom she was starring with in the picture, would drive once, maybe twice a week, into the closest town. Gene would take the opportunity to ride along with him, and there she would make her calls home to Oleg.

When Gene returned home she asked Oleg what was wrong with his hand. The knuckles on his right hand were raw. "It was just so frustrating here without you," he said. She later found out he had hurt his hand himself by pounding his fist on a wall when he missed her.

Gene's next picture held a lot of excitement for her. On paper it looked like a success, even without a single scene yet shot. If the quality of the ingredients make the cake, then certainly the quality of people involved in *The Shanghai Gesture* would ensure that it would be brilliant. Unfortunately this recipe (and theory) failed somewhere along the line.

The German director Josef von Sternberg, who was best known for launching the career of Marlene Dietrich years earlier in *The Blue Angel*, was making his comeback on this film. He hadn't worked in years, and the expectation of this man creating again had many people excited, no one more so than Gene. The best news of all was that Oleg was hired to design all of the costumes, Gene's included. Gene was on loan to United Artists for this picture. The term "on loan" makes it seem that the studios happily swapped stars back and forth without something being in it for them. Once again, the studios were running a business. Any star "on loan"

5. Belle Tier

from another studio was being rented to the studio and making the picture for a higher price than the star's studio was paying them under contract.

It was profitable to lend stars out to make pictures elsewhere. It was like a rental agreement, and the studios made good money in doing it. Another factor in favor of this film's being a surefire hit was the longevity of the play on Broadway. *The Shanghai Gesture* was a runaway success on stage. Florence Reed and Mary Duncan starred, but neither of them was considered for the roles in the movie version. Gene was to play Mary Duncan's role of Poppy Charteris. She was the illegitimate daughter of Mother Gin-Sling, played by Ona Munson, who is best remembered as the lovable Belle Watling in *Gone with the Wind*, a film she made three years earlier.

Walter Huston played Gene's father, and Victor Mature played Omar the Arab. Everything on paper pointed to this film's being a roaring success, yet it could not have been received more badly. The critics attacked it from every angle. Gene was given the first bad reviews of her career, and Oleg's costume designs went unnoticed.

Toward the end of the picture there is a scene where the main characters are having dinner. A small carved figurine depicting each of the characters is placed in front of their plates. Once the scene was shot Gene asked von Sternberg if she could have the figurines as a memento of the film. He of course agreed and Gene took them home and displayed them proudly on her mantelpiece. On the night of the first bad reviews Gene came home from work only to find her figurines gone from where she had put them. She thought Oleg might have moved them someplace else, but she looked and she looked and found them to be no where in the house. Upon asking Oleg where they were he yelled, "Ahhh, so you want to see them do you?!" He stormed off down toward the back of the house. Gene followed. "Come let me show you," he shouted. "I have blown them to bits."

Although he sounded very convincing Gene thought he was joking. Soon enough Gene realized he wasn't joking after all. There on the ground were the shattered pieces of the figurines from *The Shanghai Gesture*. Gene leaned down to pick up a few small pieces. She was stunned. "How could you do this?!" she screamed. "You knew I wanted to keep them!"

"Those characters deserved to die," he said smugly. "I have executed them. At least now we won't have to be reminded of that dreadful movie." Execute them he did. Literally moments after reading the first bad review of the picture, he grabbed the figures from the mantel, lined them up along the back fence and decapitated them one by one with his hunting rifle. By destroying those figures, Oleg ensured that there was no daily reminder of that picture in their home. It gave him a sense of closure to be the executor of each character from the film. Shot by shot, he had the last word.

Gene Tierney

With the horrors of *The Shanghai Gesture* behind them, Gene went about making her next picture, *Son of Fury*. You were always only as good as your last picture, and as much as Gene wanted to forget the panning of her last film, she needed the public to forget it as well.

Tyrone Power was cast to play her leading man. He was to play the nephew of George Sanders' character, Sir Arthur Blake. As usual Sanders was portraying the aristocratic character with a hidden agenda. Gene was cast as Eve, the love interest of Power. The film wasn't a bomb, but it wasn't what you would consider a success either. It held its own, with overall performances and a story line good enough to erase the memories of *The Shanghai Gesture* from people's minds. It served its purpose. There was always something about Gene's performance and onscreen presence that somehow managed to advance her career, even after a so-so picture.

The early days of Hollywood were punishing for actors and actresses. The schedules required of them were grueling, to say the least. It was not unusual for Gene to finish one picture in the morning and report to the set for her next picture that same afternoon. A normal day would have her up at 4 A.M. She and Oleg would get dressed, grab a quick cup of coffee with the intent of heading out the door no later than 5 A.M. Oleg would make the drive through the darkness of Beverly Hills to Fox Studios, where he would drop Gene off for her day of filming.

Gene's dressing room was large and elaborate. She had a team of professional hair and makeup people who would work on her from her time of arrival, usually at around 6:30 A.M. They would have her ready to report to the set by 9 A.M. and be on call constantly, always ready to touch up their living masterpiece throughout the day when needed. Oleg would spend most of his days at the West Side Tennis Club, mingling with other people who needed to fill in their days with something to stop them from going insane when without employment.

Although the ban seemed to have been lifted, the studios still doubted a Cassini design. There was no studio in Hollywood ready to embrace him for fear of being shunned themselves. It was far easier for any new studio that he approached to turn him away just like the studio before them and the one before them. When one studio took a stand and had the courage to employ him, only then would the others sit up and take notice. In time it would happen, but until then Oleg felt useless. Gene did her best to support him, but Oleg was a man of pride. He wanted to work and at least feel that he was making some type of contribution to their marriage.

Through an orchard of fruit trees 100 yards above the guest house, Oleg would watch day after day as the renovation on their house took shape. He started to realize there was no reason why he couldn't lend a hand himself. There was work in his very own backyard, literally. Instead of watching the work get done, Oleg approached the Mexican construction crew and convinced them he would be as

5. Belle Tier

A candid shot of Gene welcoming home her husband, fashion designer Oleg Cassini. It seems their faithful dog, Butch, is even happier than Gene to see him.

hardworking a contributor as the rest of them. After all, it was his house, and no one cared more about the quality of the finished product more than him, and of course Gene. This was his work, to be done with his own hands, for both of them. Out of desperation he took a $5 a day job hauling stones up the hill to the main house that was being renovated on their property. Gene and Oleg were living in the guest house until work on the main residence was complete.

Incredibly, they bought the property with the main house and the guest house included for a mere $6,000. They put down a $2,000 deposit, leaving a $4,000 mortgage to be paid off at the rate of $100 a month. Four years later they would sell the renovated house, the guest house and the property in its entirety for an impressive $125,000. Once the main house was complete they intended to move in and use it as their main residence, with the intention of renting out the guest house to help subsidize their renovations.

For eight hours every day Oleg worked and sweated with the rest of the laborers. Gene would come home from the studio around 8 P.M. Exhausted, she would go straight to the hot tub with her script. Oleg, also exhausted from his day, would read with her. Intent on getting her lines memorized for the next day of shooting, she could not relax and enjoy her bath without insisting on reading her script at the same time. In the kitchen she would sit eating dinner, fork in one hand as she ate and script in the other as she read. Finally she would end up in bed, using those last moments of the evening to memorize her lines. Oleg would sit in a chair next to her and act as her leading man or whatever other role she required him to be at the time. Finally, they would call it a night, turn out the light and get ready to start the routine all over again in no more than six hours time.

On the very few days off, they enjoyed going for long walks around their new neighborhood. One afternoon on a walk along Wilshire Boulevard, Oleg spotted a mangy mongrel puppy in a pet store window. He was $2, and Oleg, a sucker for a dog needing a new home, went into the store and came out with this new addition to the family. On the way home they named him Salami. Unfortunately, Salami wasn't very appreciative of the rescue effort. He began to tear up and eat the furniture, and when he was done there he demolished the garden. They had no choice but to give him away. The Cassinis were destined to be a one-dog family. Butch, of German Shepherd ancestry, was a loyal companion for many years. Unlike Salami, Butch had no interest in redesigning their garden or making a meal of their furniture.

On the money side of things, both of them had made an early decision not to employ a business manager to look after their finances. The experience with Gene's father had left a sour taste in both their mouths. If your own father robs you without conscience then it would be just as easy, if not easier, for a stranger to do the same. Together they worked out a budget and, like any young married couple, followed it, and did very well at shuffling their finances around.

5. Belle Tier

With both of them now working around the clock, they decided to employ Madeline, a French housekeeper, to help keep the guest house in order. As small as it was, there wasn't a lot to do to keep it clean, and so most of her time she would spend in the kitchen cooking. Since both Gene and Oleg were no experts in food preparation, Madeline was looked upon as a godsend. She would prepare many old French recipes for them to enjoy after a hard day at work.

One day when Madeline was away for the day, Gene happened to come down with a cold. Intent on being the doting husband, Oleg raced to the kitchen to make her something soothing to help her. Not long after, he came back with a bowl of soup. Gene took her first mouthful and screamed, "You're trying to poison me!" Oleg stood before her and convinced her that his was an old Russian remedy for fixing

A sultry Gene poses in character to promote her new film, *The Shanghai Gesture* (1941).

colds rapidly. "Drink it down," he ordered sternly. Gene, frowning and wanting to feel better, swallowed every mouthful until she got to the bottom of the bowl. As she handed the empty bowl back to him he laughed uncontrollably, finally confessing that he had made the recipe up in the kitchen as he went along. The list of ingredients were horrendous. The Cassini soup consisted of two cups of boiling water, one raw egg, one beef bouillon cube, a dash of Worcestershire sauce and the juice of one lemon. No wonder Gene cringed after taking her first mouthful.

Gene soon recovered from her cold and started her next picture, as usual within quick succession of finishing the one before. It seemed as though she was churning out as many performances as she could in the shortest time possible. Maybe there was an inner voice telling her that she would turn her back on Hollywood far earlier than most. She seemed driven to keep working without rest, without so much as a few days between going from one set to another. This time she was working with Henry Fonda again. She had a lot more experience since her days on *The Return of Frank James*, and her dedication to her work almost gave her the unofficial title of "one take Tierney." Gene and Henry were the perfect twosome. They knew their lines inside out. Rarely would there be a retake because of a forgotten or misread line. Both were a director's dream. The film was called *Rings on Her Fingers*. It was another test for Gene, this time having to utilize her comedic skills.

Despite the fact that Gene and Henry Fonda had worked together previously and liked each other, it just wasn't easy for Oleg to take to his new wife's leading man. "Henry Fonda made it difficult for me to like him," Oleg explained. "When he and Gene were working together on *Rings on Her Fingers*, he struck me as rather arrogant. He had that wonderful voice and easy manner, and he seemed to exude a confidence that he could seduce Gene anytime he wanted. He made it very clear that he considered me just a hair in the soup, a distasteful encumbrance on the set. There was a real tension between us, but never a confrontation, a lot of double entendre barbs flying back and forth. Later on in life we became quite friendly."

On Sunday, December 7, near year's end of 1941, they were filming *Rings on Her Fingers* on Catalina Island. Just as they were about to roll camera an assistant came running down the beach screaming that war had just broken out. "The Japanese have bombed Pearl Harbor," he frantically yelled. "We must pack everything up and clear for the mainland — NOW!"

The worst place to be at this time was on an island. They had no choice but to get back to the mainland, but there was still much uncertainty about what had just happened. There were rumors of Japanese submarines patrolling the California coast. The waters they were about to sail through might well have been sabotaged with active mines. There was no way of

In a scene with Henry Fonda, Gene listens intently to all he has to say in *Rings on Her Fingers* (1942).

5. Belle Tier

knowing. Everyone piled into a boat: Gene, Oleg, Henry Fonda and all of the crew that were on the island. Stunned with the news of America at war, there was little conversation on that boat ride back to the mainland. Their silence is no surprise. What could possibly be said anyway?

6

Hollywood at War

The timing of the war coincided with Oleg's citizenship papers being processed. He would soon be considered an American citizen, therefore giving him the right not only to live freely in his new country but to fight for that freedom for every one of us. With Oleg's citizenship papers not being processed until July 22, 1942, it was not possible for him to contribute physically until that time. He volunteered for military intelligence. His language skills put him in a great position to give useful service in that department. The ability to speak fluent English and French made it the perfect role for him. Unfortunately, he did not receive a reply to his letter until a year and a half after it was written. In time, he would be needed, his letter would be answered, but without knowing what the future held, he thought carefully about whom to approach next.

In a desperate effort to do something, anything, he and Victor Mature decided to join the Coast Guard. Oleg received his citizenship papers on Tuesday. He enlisted in the Coast Guard on Saturday, and he was swiftly inducted on Monday. After the Pearl Harbor attack the U.S. sent private yachts out to patrol the coast, looking for Japanese submarines. Both men were accepted, with Mature volunteering his own 64-footer, *The Bar Bill*, as the patrolling yacht to be used.

Oleg was given the title fireman first class, but he was thrown straight into the kitchen as a cook because of his Italian name! Oleg explained, "I spent all my time preparing the most elegant continental cuisine. The men were very appreciative, except for Victor Mature, who was constantly hungry. He would invade the galley between meals, focusing on, of all things, the mayonnaise, which he ate *au naturel* from the jar with a tablespoon."

Besides being hungry, it seemed he was always thinking of a way to kill two birds with one stone. Oleg continues, "So that he would look presentable when accompanying Rita Hayworth to film premieres on his night off, Victor cleverly volunteered to be our lookout. This enabled him to spend all day everyday working on his tan, while looking out for the enemy at the same time." Perhaps the best

6. Hollywood at War

A scene from *China Girl* (1942).

part of this service, aside from sitting on the deck with a good cigar after dinner, was the amount of time I got to spend at home."

Gene and Oleg had been separated enough during their marriage, so the Coast Guard duty proved to be a bearable existence for both of them. The men would go out, eight aboard the yacht, for a 48-hour patrol and then come back to port for 48 hours' leave. The two days back home enabled Gene and Oleg to be together before he would head out to the unknown waters of the California coastline to patrol again. While Oleg was on duty Gene was cast in *Thunder Birds* and *China Girl*. The film *Rings on Her Fingers* was eventually finished, not long after the announcement that war had begun.

Gene pushed Oleg to become an officer. She considered his role in the Coast Guard to be less distinguished than that of the others who were serving around him. The only problem was that in order to be an officer in the Coast Guard or Navy, you had to be a native-born American. Oleg's mother researched the possibilities of his becoming an exception. With her being in Washington, she was close to the people who made these decisions, and she did her very best to get them to bend the rules for her son. Her attempts failed, but she did manage to get Oleg transferred to the U.S. Army Cavalry, an area where foreign-born officers were recognized. Basic training was given at Fort Riley in Kansas. Based on his performance there, if good enough, he would be chosen to attend Officer Candidate School.

The road ahead was no easy one for Oleg; he washed dishes in the mess hall, did drill training with the rest of the recruits and took more than his fair share of teasing for being who he was. The former Count Cassini, aspiring fashion designer and husband to a movie star, was not exactly the easiest person to be among these men. He was often involved in fistfights when their comments became too much to ignore. He eventually proved his worth and became "another one of the boys," but at times the initiation process seemed harder than the formal training. Oleg graduated from Officer's School and officially became Lieutenant Oleg Cassini of the U.S. Army Cavalry. It was a new title to be proud of.

The '40s were a time of banding together. On every level of life, someone was doing something to help the war effort. Actors and actresses would make appearances at the Hollywood Canteen, a place where soldiers would go when on leave to try to forget the troubles of a world at war. Others would tour the country selling war bonds, and still Hollywood churned out the pictures for people who flocked to theaters for a moment's peace. Somehow, within that hour and a half in a darkened movie theater, they could forget the bleakness of reality around them. Many

A classic wartime shot of Gene in front of a plane to promote her latest film, *Thunder Birds* (1942).

6. Hollywood at War

In honor of her recent film ***Thunder Birds*** (1942), Gene personally signs the name "Thunderbird" on the side of this World War II aircraft. Circa 1942 (photograph courtesy Lou and Mary Jo Mari).

A proud day indeed. It's smiles all around as Oleg signs his citizenship papers. Despite losing his title of "Count," he's now officially a citizen of the United States of America (photograph courtesy Lou and Mary Jo Mari).

movie stars enlisted to fight in the war. There was no preferential treatment for being an actor, and most volunteered their services without being called.

James Stewart was most enthusiastic. After hearing of the outbreak of war in Europe in 1939, he began to acquire as many flying hours as he could to qualify himself as a military pilot if needed. Needed he was. He enlisted in the U.S. Army Air Corps as a private, and upon graduation from basic training he was given the rank of corporal. By December 1941, after nine months of flying experience in a four-engine bomber, he was promoted to lieutenant. His calm demeanor and apparent ease at flying put him straight into the position of pilot instructor.

England was his next calling. He was sent overseas in November 1943, and

6. Hollywood at War

Gene Tierney and fellow actor and friend Victor Mature out for an innocent night on the town. Gene's husband, Oleg Cassini, voluntarily joined the coast guard with Mature. Both men patrolled the U.S. coastline on Mature's own 64-foot yacht, *The Bar Bill*. It was their primary duty to look for Japanese submarines in the nervous post–Pearl Harbor days of World War II.

soon after he was promoted to captain. The rank of major soon followed, and this gave him the distinction of becoming group operations officer for the 453rd Bombardment Group. Fifty bombers were assigned to him. By April 1945 he was released from active duty. Now at the rank of colonel and chief of staff of the 2nd Combat Wing, 8th Air Force, James Stewart, the lovable character who entertained all of us on film for most of his life, had clocked up a massive 18,000 hours of flying time and had been involved in several successful bombing raids over Germany for the United States.

Stewart was awarded the Distinguished Flying Cross for his leadership on one of those raids, on February 20, 1944, over Brunswick, Germany. The Croix de

Wartime friends. Gene chats it up with Judy Garland, circa 1942. The stern general appears less than interested in what the girls have to say (photograph courtesy Lou and Mary Jo Mari).

Guerre was another air medal awarded to him for his service. James Stewart went back to Hollywood after the war and went on to become one of the most loved actors of the silver screen. He remained in the reserves until 1968. His rank upon retirement was that of brigadier general.

Clark Gable was a gunner, and his service was a time of great personal sadness. His gunner position had him flying in situations that could at any moment get him killed. To him at the time, getting killed was the best thing that could have happened to him. He would then be reunited with his wife of two years and ten months, actress Carole Lombard. They were married in Kingman, Arizona, on March 29, 1939, on a day off that Gable had from *Gone with the Wind*. With Gable

6. Hollywood at War

being the chairman of the Hollywood Victory Committee, he had arranged for his wife to go on a war bond selling tour. Many actresses took on the job of selling war bonds, and Carole was eager to help out.

On January 16, 1942, after a long rally ending in her home state of Indiana, Carole, her mother, Elizabeth Knight Peters, and MGM press agent Otto Winkler boarded TWA flight three, bound for Los Angeles. Four passengers departed the aircraft in Albuquerque, New Mexico, in order to make room for 15 Army officers, also headed for L.A. The flight continued and landed in Las Vegas, Nevada, to refuel around 7 P.M. After refueling was complete about 7:07 P.M., the aircraft took off on its final leg to Los Angeles. The pilot, Wayne Williams, and his copilot, Morgan Gillette, flew the twin engine plane 15 degrees off course. Tragedy struck when the miscalculation caused the aircraft to crash into Table Rock Mountain. All 20 people on board perished. Lombard and several others were decapitated. The impact was so great it caused the tail of the aircraft to compress right through to the front of the plane. The plane exploded into a fireball, causing all aboard to be burned beyond recognition. Gable went to Las Vegas immediately. He had to be restrained from attempting to climb to the crash site to reach his wife himself.

Carole Lombard sold a record breaking $2,107,153 in war bonds. At the time of her death she was just 33 years old. Gable spent the remaining 18 years of his life blaming himself for arranging for her to go to the war bond rally in the first place. Friends described Gable as "lost, a man that never really returned" after her death. He never recovered, and for that very reason he was more than willing to lose his life for his country during the war. In his eyes, without Carole, his life was already lost.

He survived his almost suicidal missions of the war years and, like Stewart, went back to Hollywood. He too was awarded the Distinguished Flying Cross and Air Medal for his many bombing missions over Germany. By war's end he had achieved the rank of major. Adolf Hitler held Gable in such high esteem as an actor he offered a sizeable reward to anyone who could capture and bring "The King of Hollywood" to him unscathed. Thankfully, Gable managed to avoid any such capture.

Tyrone Power, Eddie Albert, Ronald Reagan, Art Carney, Glenn Ford, Lee Marvin and many other actors served during World War II. The troubles of war were strong enough to penetrate the lives of these people whom, until war began, the public considered to be somewhat untouchable. The personal tragedies that war brought to Gable and Lombard was heart wrenching. Equally tragic were the life-changing circumstances of war that would soon destroy the mind of Gene Tierney.

While the horrors of war still erupted, Gene was doing her part back home. Between selling war bonds and entertaining troops she was still making pictures.

Gene Tierney

In January 1943 she was offered the role of Martha in *Heaven Can Wait*. Signed to direct was the greatly respected Ernst Lubitsch, the same man responsible for casting Greta Garbo in the classic *Ninotchka*.

Heaven Can Wait was Gene's only picture for 1943, but not because she wasn't offered anything else. This time it was by choice. During the making of the picture she found out she was expecting a baby. Luckily, movie making in the '40s was a hasty business. Most movies were churned out in four to six weeks.

Filming wrapped on April 10, 1943, and Gene managed to get through the picture without showing signs of pregnancy. She kept the news a secret for fear of being replaced. Her salary would also have been automatically suspended if it were known that she was in the family way. It was Gene and Oleg's own little secret, and they were thrilled.

In the picture Gene plays a girl trying her hardest to get out of Kansas. In reality she was wishing the picture would end so she could get to Kansas to be with her husband. Oleg was stationed at Fort Riley, Kansas, and Gene thought it a wonderful idea to go out there to be with him for a while. A week before leaving, in March, Gene thought she should put in another appearance at the Hollywood Canteen to entertain the on-leave GIs. Hundreds upon hundreds of people mingled at the Hollywood Canteen. A constant stream of people would come and go. Most of them were there to dance and have fun and, of course, meet the movie stars.

That night, Gene shook hands, signed autographs and did the normal morale boosting routine that all of

Oleg Cassini, in uniform and ready to report to duty. Gene is beaming with wifely pride (photograph courtesy Oleg Cassini).

6. Hollywood at War

A group shot of the cast of *Heaven Can Wait* (1943). ***Left to right, standing:*** Father Strabel (Eugene Pallette), Cousin Albert (Allyn Joslyn), Martha (Gene Tierney), Henry Van Cleve (Don Ameche), Father Van Cleve (Louis Calhern). ***Left to right, seated:*** Mother Strabel (Marjorie Main), Grandfather Van Cleve (Charles Coburn) and Mother Van Cleve (Spring Byington).

the stars of the day did. By the middle of that week, no more than a couple of days after her appearance there, Gene woke up with red spots covering her face and arms. She called the doctor immediately and was diagnosed with German measles or rubella. At the time there was no solid connection between contracting German measles in early pregnancy and having a retarded child. Likewise, there was no immunization to prevent pregnant women from contracting it. Staying away from crowded places within the first four months of pregnancy was the best prevention a woman could hope for. Gene's Hollywood Canteen appearance was anything but quiet. That simple act of kindness would subsequently have life changing consequences for her, Oleg and their unborn child.

Gene Tierney

Not showing a lot of concern for Gene or her unborn child's well being, her doctor told her to rest, and in no more than a week it would all disappear. Gene took his advice and rested, and just as he had said, the spots were gone within a week. The measles prevented her from meeting Oleg in Kansas as planned. Now that she was well she couldn't wait to pack her bags and begin life as an Army wife and expectant mother.

The small town of Fort Riley swelled dramatically with Army wives scouting around for a place to set up house while their husbands were in town. Junction City was about a mile and a half from the officers' camp, so most of the available housing was within that area. Junction City was a small town, and at the time it was too small for the number of people needing to live in it. The main street consisted of only a few stores, and with all of the housing looking very much alike, coming home drunk was not an option in Junction City unless you could still read the number on your mailbox. The only way of making the houses individuals was to decorate them differently on the inside.

Competition was fierce when it came to looking for a place to stay, but Gene ended up finding a small bungalow for rent. It was nothing flashy, but with housing being so scarce there was no time to be vain about the extravagances of real estate. It was an acting job in itself just getting that tiny, four bedroom, clapboard cottage. But Gene had an idea and it worked. After becoming increasingly frustrated at not being able to find any housing Gene used her movie star status, so to speak, on a starstruck landlord that she had heard about from the other women. She decided to turn on that Tierney charm and dedicated her entire day to visiting him. He was starstruck all right.

Gene spent the entire day talking to him, answering all of his Hollywood questions, and just in case that didn't work, she went with the bribe approach. She had bought him a cigarette case on the way to see him and had it engraved, "From your friend, Gene Tierney." She presented it to him just before leaving, and magically within hours, and at $50 rent per month, Gene and Oleg had a new home in Junction City, Kansas! Oleg laughed when she told him about her day. He thought she was marvelous.

With the new house in California still having to be paid for and Gene being out of work for what was now four months, the only money they were living off was Oleg's Army pay. Having to be frugal only made it more fun for Gene. She took delight in buying secondhand furniture and repainting it. She was particularly proud of a set of barrels that she purchased cheaply with the vision of turning them into bar stools. She painted them white with a contrasting red band around the top, middle and bottom. She padded the seats and covered them in chintz. With matching chintz curtains to tie in with the seats, the somewhat tired old bungalow became a little piece of heaven. Their dressing table was a set of old

6. Hollywood at War

crates pushed together to make one solid wooden trestle. Gene tacked a white dimity skirt to it, to match the curtains, and she cleverly took a red rose from an old evening dress and pinned it to the middle of the gathered fabric. She found a secondhand icebox for $7, and they rented a stove for $3 a month. Gene bought a variety of scatter rugs for each room at $5 apiece and various other bits and pieces to make the place seem more like a home. It was a given they'd be there for less than a year, but Gene had the opinion that if you called it home for any length of time, it at least had to look like one.

Gene worked nonstop for two solid weeks. She hunted everything down, took it back to the house and sewed it, polished it, painted it or mended it and then put it in its place. Her final decorating bill for the entire house was a very impressive $100. Once again Oleg laughed. He was amazed at her initiative and desire to make what little they had feel special.

Gene tends to her "victory garden," the common term for vegetable patches during the war years. Here she is happily playing the role of "army wife" in Fort Riley, Kansas, in 1943. Behind her is the house that she so lovingly decorated while on leave from Twentieth Century–Fox and pregnant with Daria (photograph courtesy Lou and Mary Jo Mari).

Socially, Junction City was a far cry from Beverly Hills. The only things to do there were go to the movies or entertain friends. They did both, with Gene particularly fond of inviting groups of 20 to 25 people over for a dinner party at least weekly. She would always plan the meals in keeping with the wartime ration rules and requirements, the five rules being: (1) Is it nourishing? (2) Is it inexpensive? (3) Is it tasty? (4) Is it enough? (5) Is it low on ration points? Gene's usual meal consisted of spaghetti Bolognese, a dish that she was particularly proud of making. Her secret was to add loads of garlic and use a slow cooking process. She would

73

A newly deceased Henry Van Cleve (Don Ameche) looks on without his wife Martha's (Gene) knowledge when he's sent back to earth by the devil to assess whether or not he's been a good husband and father in *Heaven Can Wait* (1945).

serve it with hot rolls, two vegetables, a mixed green salad and dessert and coffee to finish.

    She would spend one morning a week just bicycling around Junction City, doing her grocery shopping. Most of her food she would buy at the Post Exchange. It was the cheapest place in town, with a loaf of bread costing a mere penny. She would ride her bike to one farmer to buy the fresh eggs and then ride on to another farmer to buy the chickens. Everything was piled into her basket and taken home. Sometimes she would have to make several trips back and forth in order to carry everything. But she didn't care. There was no movie star treatment in Kansas, and it was exactly the way Gene preferred it to be.

    As her pregnancy progressed she started to acquire a collection of recipe books. She studied them with as much seriousness as cramming for a law degree. She was slowly learning how to cook, even swapping recipes with other Army wives. Gene was reveling in domestic life. This was the longest stretch that she'd had away from

6. Hollywood at War

the bright lights and sound stages of Hollywood since she began her career, but she had never felt more content. With the baby soon due, Gene and Oleg decided ahead of time that if for some reason Oleg was called away before the baby was to arrive, then Gene should go to Washington for the delivery. Both Gene's mother and Oleg's mother now resided there, and so it made sense for her to be near family if Oleg was unable to be with her.

Sure enough, Oleg was approached by military intelligence. A long time had passed between his letter and these orders, and now with Gene's pregnancy, the timing could not have been worse. Gene and Oleg agreed that it was his duty to serve. They made swift arrangements for Gene to return to Washington for the birth, while Oleg reported to Newport News, Virginia, for assignment overseas.

Gene and Oleg out on the town, this time with him wearing his uniform in public (photograph courtesy Oleg Cassini).

Before Gene was scheduled to leave for Washington she decided to spread the word around town that all of her furniture from the house would be auctioned. With Oleg packing up to leave around the same time as Gene it was silly to just lock up the house and leave it all there. She made a date and a time for the auction, and she herself was the auctioneer. Oleg was stunned as he watched the crowd roll up on auction night. There she was, Gene Tierney, very pregnant, now playing the role of auctioneer and doing brilliantly at it.

At the end of the evening after everyone had left the house, Gene sat on the floor (everything had sold, even the chairs) and counted the money she'd made. She counted $200. She had made herself a $100 profit! Oleg scratched his head, a little confused as to what was right in this situation. "Is it right," he said, "to sell these things and make money when we could just give everything away?"

Gene told him that although she had paid $100 for the furniture to begin with, she herself had put in $100 more of labor in creating it. They had only appeared to make a profit. "Besides," she said, "they wanted to buy our things, so with my very own fingers I've earned enough money to pay for my train fare to Washington." She smiled as she fanned herself with the money. How could Oleg argue with that?

Gene Tierney

A few days later Gene waved goodbye to Junction City and Oleg, and set out to Washington, D.C., to have her baby.

As Gene's train traveled toward the nations capital, Oleg was told more about his new position for military intelligence. It was predicted to be a dangerous assignment, and he was given a personal code number with intelligence gear, as well as a pistol and a knife. He was then quarantined, meaning he could not send or receive messages from anyone, Gene included. Not being able to communicate with his pregnant wife while on this mission was beyond cruel. If he had known that all communication would cease, especially at such a personally crucial time, he would have declined the mission without hesitation. However, there was nothing he could do now to change things.

7

It's a Girl!

Picking up the newspaper on the morning of October 15, 1943, Oleg read an article that chilled him to the bone. It read, "Gene Tierney, actress, gives birth to a premature baby after an emergency operation at Columbia Hospital, Washington. The baby was a girl, weighing two and a half pounds." Without a second thought Oleg ran to the post commander, throwing the newspaper down in front of him and telling him to read what he himself had just read.

Oleg begged him to pull the right strings to let him get to Gene and his daughter. As much as he would have liked to have given Oleg the okay to just go right out the door at that moment, he still had to clear it with military intelligence. That clearance took several hours to complete. Oleg sat biting his fingernails. He dashed to the airport, heading straight for Washington as soon as permission was granted.

After a couple of hours of flying and wondering about the condition of his wife and child, he arrived at the hospital to find Gene sedated. He was told by a sleepy Gene that although she'd gone through a difficult birth, both she and the baby, whom they named Daria, were both going to be just fine. Her official birth name was "Antoinette Daria Cassini." She would become known as "Daria," named after Oleg's Russian great-grandmother.

Oleg was delighted. He sat holding Gene's hand and kissing her, both elated and relieved that his wife and daughter would pull through. Enjoying their moment together, they were interrupted by Gene's doctor. He signaled to Oleg to follow him into the hallway. From there he asked him to go down to his office. He wanted to talk. Now increasingly concerned at the look on the doctor's face, Oleg started asking questions. Upon reaching the doctor's office they both took a seat. Now frantic, Oleg repeatedly asked the doctor what was wrong. "Mr. Cassini," the Doctor said, "Your wife has had a very difficult delivery, but I assure you she will be fine," he paused, about to continue, and with that sentence over and done with Oleg knew he was about to start the next sentence with the word *But*.

He did use that exact word. "But your daughter is not in good shape." He bowed his head and continued, "First, she's premature ... and then ... I don't think she'll ever see, I think she's blind. There are cataracts in both eyes." He found it hard to find the words. There was no easy way to tell any new parents that they had a disabled child. The doctor asked Oleg if he would like to tell Gene the news instead of him. There was no easy way of taking it from anyone, but Oleg agreed it should come from him.

He walked back to Gene's room, numb, not knowing how to tell her what he himself had just been told. He started, stuttering at first, "Gene, there's a problem and you have to be strong." Gene tried to sit up; seeing the look on Oleg's face had already told her that something was terribly wrong. "My heart is broken. Gene, there's something wrong with the eyesight of the baby." He had gotten it out; as slow as it came, he had gotten it out, and Gene's reaction was anything but composed. She fell apart, hysterically screaming, tears streaming down her face. She lost everything that mattered at that very moment. Oleg could not comfort her. He too was heartbroken. There were no words to say to ease her pain, or his.

Military intelligence had to be notified that his mission could not go ahead. He was not leaving Gene now, for anything. It was a fight to get out of it, but eventually he was reassigned to Fort Riley. With that out of the way he went back to the hospital to sit with Gene.

By this time both Oleg's mother and Gene's mother were there. They went to the nursery to see the baby together. Belle Tierney was again in fine form, commenting, "We've never had trouble like this in *our* family," even saying, "You never can tell what can be passed on through these European families." Oleg was too numb and lifeless to even fight back. Instead,

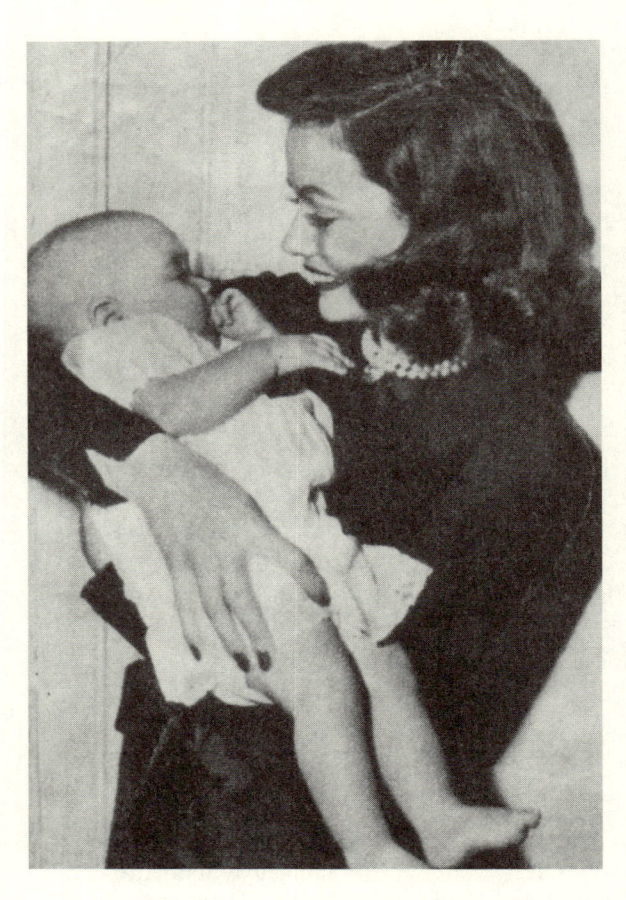

Gene beaming with motherly pride as she cradles her daughter Daria (photograph courtesy Lou and Mary Jo Mari).

7. It's a Girl!

he left. He left both women standing at the nursery window, and he ran and ran and ran, not being able to stop. Just hoping to somehow run out the pain.

Days later, back at the hospital, the doctor called him aside once more. He seemed to tell Oleg everything first, then leaving it to him to pass it on to Gene when he felt it right. This time he gave some explanation as to how Daria had ended up this way. He told of how recent studies in Australia confirmed that contracting German measles within the first trimester of pregnancy did in fact cause damage to the central nervous system of the baby being carried. The doctor had been going over Gene's records and saw that within those first few months, just before visiting Oleg in Fort Riley and just after her appearance that night at the Hollywood Canteen, she did indeed contract German measles.

No explanation of how this had happened eased the pain of what they were facing, and now the diagnosis was worse. Not only was Daria blind, but in time she would not mentally develop like other children. She would also be mentally retarded.

Once again Oleg walked back to Gene's room with more bad news about Daria. This time there were no tears, no hysterics. Oleg told her exactly what the doctor had told him, word for word, and she just stared. She stared into the distance. There was no reaction, nothing. Gene had shut down completely. Her silent reaction scared Oleg far more than her earlier tears. Oleg explained

At the height of Gene's career, a set of paper dolls was released onto the American market. Now every little girl could dress her. The paper doll set came complete with a die cut doll in Gene's likeness, eight costumes, three pairs of shoes, one pair of glasses and three hats.

A beautiful shot of Gene on the floor with her dress encircling her. A proud husband, fashion designer Oleg Cassini, admires the dress and his wife, who models the creation to perfection (photograph courtesy Oleg Cassini).

later, "Gene was almost catatonic. Certainly I could not reach her. I would see that same vacant expression again and again over the following years. I would see it every time there was bad news about Daria ... and the news was always bad."

What made matters worse, almost to the point of disbelieving the doctor's words, was that Daria appeared normal. Gene's sister, Patricia, gave her 11 blood transfusions until she eventually became strong enough to bring home. With a heart full of hope, Gene and Oleg took Daria home, hoping that maybe this time, just once, the doctor's diagnosis was wrong.

As Daria entered her first year she began to suffer hearing loss. Gene thought it had gotten worse because of Daria's having her first cold, when in fact it had just

7. It's a Girl!

gotten worse because that was the path her hearing was destined to take. She lacked fluid in her inner ear, a condition that Gene convinced herself would be surgically remedied later. The cataract seemed to be noticeable only in the corner of her left eye, a place where it could not be surgically removed. At age one her vision seemed blurred. She would hold her hands to her face as she squinted and strained to see them.

Gene refused to give up on Daria; she believed that something could be done for her. That something she hoped would come from the reappearance of Howard Hughes. He had heard about Daria's birth and offered to bring in his own doctor to examine her. His doctor in turn flew in one of the country's top doctors in the field of infant diseases.

No expense was spared. In fact, Gene secretly found out without Hughes knowing that the specialist's visit for that one day had set him back a staggering $15,000. He paid the bill without a word.

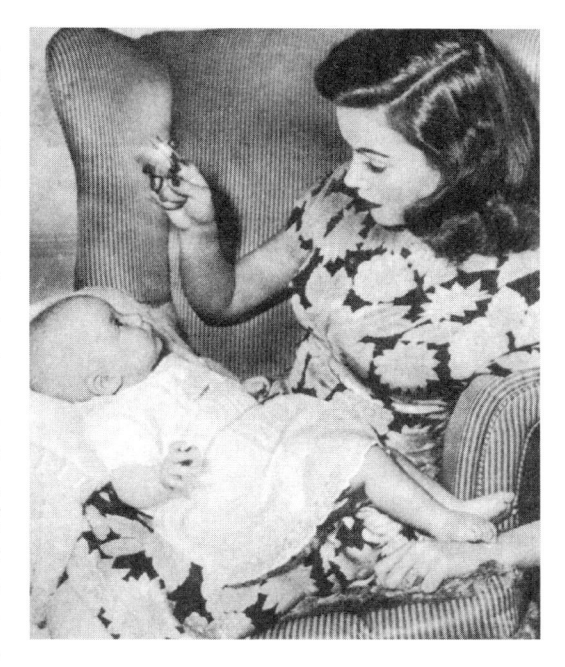

Daria appears to be alert and looking directly at the rattle in this picture. Sadly, it was these few moments of hope that would build Gene up for a future of heartache (photograph courtesy Lou and Mary Jo Mari).

Gene was hoping a miracle cure would be found and suddenly make Daria well. Unfortunately, she did not have a condition that could be fixed with a treatment or a dose of medicine. Her condition was permanent, and it was a hard fact to accept, especially for a mother who was feeling guilt over how she came to be born that way in the first place.

Oleg did his best to make things as normal as possible. As terrible as he was at remembering birthdays, even Gene's, he would never miss their wedding anniversary. With their wedding ceremony having turned into such a circus, it would have been hard to forget the date. The one thing he felt terrible guilt over missing was Gene's first Mother's Day. In Europe, where he grew up, there is no such event. He made up for it other ways and learned to make note of "Mother's Day" on his calendar for the following year. He made up for his forgetfulness with surprise gifts. Gene came home one afternoon raving about a dress she had seen in a store window but found too extravagant to buy. The next week it arrived at the front door. A gift for his "Potato" (her nickname) from Oleg. As much as they tried to

A behind-the-scenes shot of Gene going over her lines as a studio hairdresser does some final touchups. Determined to be known as "one take Tierney," Gene would study and rehearse her lines constantly.

7. It's a Girl!

maintain some sort of normalcy, caring for Daria was becoming tiring and time consuming.

In a letter dated Monday, October 30, 1944, Gene wrote to her mother about Daria's apparent "improving condition." Gene's enthusiasm in describing Daria's development within this letter is heartbreaking. She was not yet resigned to the fact that her daughter would have to be institutionalized for life.

Gene wrote of the baby doing beautifully and how thankful she was at how well she was improving with each passing day. Considering the bleakness that she and Oleg were confronted with when Daria was first born, she was understandably bursting with enthusiasm at Daria's seemingly miraculous progress. At the time of her letter, Daria was a year old and had light brown curly hair, with pretty gold highlights. She weighed 20 pounds, had chubby thighs and was 29 inches tall. According to Gene she was the average height and weight of any year old infant.

She was insistent and firm in "telling her" (probably someone back home) that their negative thoughts were not helping Daria in any way, and they should all hope and pray that Daria continued to improve, year after year. Along with Oleg's acceptance of Daria's condition, other family members seemed to be equally resigned to the fact that Daria would never be "okay." It was a mother's denial and a mother's love that prevented Gene from accepting that there was anything seriously wrong with her little girl. The doctors were wrong. They had to be.

She wrote of Daria playing on her lap, jumping up and down and playing like any happy little girl of her age. Playing horsy on her knee was their new favorite thing to do together. She wrote of her giggling and laughing all the time, and of how cute she looked when her little nose seemingly disappeared and her eyes wrinkled up as she gurgled and laughed at everything around her. She told her mother that Daria did something new and surprising every day and she was thrilled and amazed with things they thought she'd never do. She was insistent that Daria was just taking a little extra time to do these things, that's all.

She mentioned the spot in her eye and told her mother that it was now hardly visible at all. She underlined *hardly visible* and insisted that it was the truth! She said her eyes were now both the same color but she tended to cross them sometimes. She insisted that it was nothing serious, just her way of trying to look around the dot that was obstructing her view of the world. Gene was convinced that no one could detect the spot in her eye, and even the relief nurse that had been tending to Daria for months had no idea of the flaw.

Maybe the nurse was just too polite to say anything. It's obvious that with Daria being a year and two weeks old at the time of the letter being written, Gene was still hopeful and confident of her continued progress.

At the same time, Oleg was being torn apart by the awful truth of the situation. He was losing his wife, and his daughter was severely retarded. He explained how desperate he once became. "I thought very seriously about killing the baby. I would take her to the ocean. We would drown together. I would die with her because I could not live with the thought of what I had done or the shame of having to hide it. But I couldn't kill myself. My sense of self-preservation was too strong, and so I couldn't kill Daria."

While Howard Hughes was still playing the role of the white knight, doing everything he could to help Gene and Daria, it wasn't long before he would be needing some help of his own. He was about to suffer his own cycle of tragedy that would see his life change forever. While funding and producing the movie *Hell's Angels*, Hughes grew angry with the stuntman who refused to perform a life threatening maneuver that called for the pilot of the plane to nose dive toward the ground. Frustrated and angry, Hughes ripped the helmet from the stuntman's hands and climbed into the cockpit himself. He performed the stunt and crashed headfirst into the ground. Amazingly, he walked away from the crash.

In 1946 while piloting another plane, this time for personal reasons, he crashed into a house in Beverly Hills. He survived the crash, but his injuries were horrific. With broken bones too many to count, head and back trauma and severe facial injuries, he was lucky to have survived. Then again, maybe "lucky" isn't the right word to explain his survival.

Soon after the crash, Hughes began to spiral into a world of unexplainable madness. He was taken care of by a team of doctors for many, many months. The doctor who reconstructed his face was handed a blank check after the cosmetic surgery. Hughes couldn't bring himself to write an amount on the check. To him, there was no amount of money that could be paid for the work the doctor had done for him. Although he was still terribly scarred, and would remain that way for life, the doctors rebuilt his face completely, and for that he was thankful. He grew a moustache to hide what scars he could, but his once boyish features were now gone. He had lost his looks forever. Unfortunately, his mind would soon follow the same path.

With Hughes already being something of an eccentric before the plane crash, whatever injuries occurred at the time of that crash caused him to regress and become more and more paranoid. He surrounded himself with aides, a group of seven Mormon men, who Hughes somehow believed to be the trustworthiest people of all. No communication would be done by phone. He would instead prefer to sit for hours writing letters and memos to business colleagues and friends. Anything that was to be handed to him would be covered with a tissue to avoid the risk of spreading germs.

He became addicted to painkillers, but eventually no drug helped the constant pain caused by his injuries. He would constantly self-inject morphine into his system to numb what pain he could. He would sit for hours into the night

7. It's a Girl!

watching old movies with the sound turned up to full volume. His hearing was damaged during the crash, and to his ear the volume was of normal level. There is no wonder Howard Hughes was known as the "Elusive Mr. Hughes." He was most definitely one of a kind, a character not of this world.

The hope that Gene put into seeing the specialist that Hughes had arranged was soon dashed when he told her there was no hope. He advised Gene to put Daria in an institution. Gene would hear nothing of it. She didn't believe him. She knew he must be wrong. Soon both Gene and Oleg came to the realization that every doctor *cannot* be wrong. Dozens of doctors saw to Daria, all giving the same opinion. *There was no hope.*

Around this same time, when Daria was a little over a year old, Gene attended a Sunday afternoon tennis party. As she was enjoying the California sunshine a young woman approached her and asked if Gene had any memory of meeting her. Gene shook her head, telling her no. She had no idea who she was. Feeling embarrassed that maybe she should, she asked, "Should I know you?" The woman went on to say that she was in the women's branch of the Marines and had met her at the Hollywood Canteen.

The next sentence that came out of her mouth was a line that Gene would never forget for the rest of her life. "Did you happen to catch German measles after that night?" Gene stared blankly at this woman.

What cruel twist of fate would bring this very woman back to her? The woman went on talking, not realizing what she was saying. "You know, I probably shouldn't tell you this, but almost the whole camp was down with German measles. I broke quarantine to come to the Canteen to meet you. Everyone told me I shouldn't, but you are my favorite and I just had to go."

The woman stood in front of Gene and smiled, waiting for Gene's reaction. Gene was dumbstruck. This woman, the woman she was standing before right at that very moment, was the sole cause of Daria's disabilities. After a long pause, Gene politely smiled, turned and walked away. Tears welled in her eyes, tears for Daria, tears for herself, tears for Oleg and tears for a woman who had no idea the amount of pain she had caused by breaking the rules on that fateful night at the Hollywood Canteen.

Years after that chance meeting, Oleg met the same woman. She relayed the same story to him, and he had the same dumbstruck reaction as Gene did. She did not tell Oleg of her meeting with the woman at the time that it happened, so Oleg thought he was the first to know of how Daria's disabilities had occurred. At the time of his finding out, when Daria was around ten years of age, he thought about telling Gene. At that time in her life the state of her mental health was fragile enough without learning such details. He kept it to himself, thinking he was sparing Gene the pain. Only later did he find out by Gene's own admission that she

Renowned portrait artist Kanarck admires his newest work, a painting of Gene and Daria that he has just unveiled for the first time. Gene looks pleased with the final results. Circa 1946 (photograph courtesy Lou and Mary Jo Mari).

had met that same woman when Daria was still a baby. She kept the news from Oleg, wanting to spare him the same undue pain.

Now they both knew the very cause of Daria's problems. It came to them in the form of a woman Marine. The chances of both Oleg and Gene even meeting the same woman, ten years apart with the same confession, a confession that would give the answer to their daughter's problems, was a twist of fate that neither one of them could completely comprehend. What were the odds of these random meetings ever occurring? It seemed that destiny had not only cruelly sent this woman to Gene on that night at the Hollywood Canteen, but had sent her back twice more to confess her sin.

The older Daria got, the harder she was to look after. She needed 24-hour care, professional care. It was something even her parents, as much as they loved her, were not physically able to give her. Several doctors told them she would reach the average height of a normal woman but her mind would not develop past the age

7. It's a Girl!

of a 19-month-old child. She was and would remain partially blind, partially deaf and speechless. Looking at the fair skinned, pretty blonde little girl on her knee, Gene just couldn't comprehend that they were talking about *her* daughter.

By the time Daria was four both Oleg and Gene were exhausted from the round the clock care that she needed. They had tried as hard as they could to seek help and maybe find a miracle cure for her. They had tried as hard as they could to take care of Daria and tend to her needs, as any parents would do for their child. The problem was that Daria's needs were much broader and more complex than the unconditional love they gave her. It simply wasn't enough.

They had also tried hard to keep their marriage together. As hard as they tried, it was a marriage beyond repair. The end of their relationship was staring both of them in the face and it was no shock to either of them. Not only did circumstances force them to give up on their daughter, but the stresses and strains of all that had happened proved so strong that they also gave up on each other.

Gene and Oleg decided mutually to end their marriage. They began with selling their house in California. Before their divorce proceedings began they agreed that of prime importance was to look for a suitable home for Daria. After weeks of searching, Gene ended up having good feelings about the accommodation at the Langhorn School in Pennsylvania. The hardest thing Gene ever did in life was to admit defeat and let Daria go. She described her feelings of driving Daria up to the school on that first day of enrollment. "The emptiness inside me was like a cave," she said.

Gene went to visit Daria often. As she got older Gene looked for signs of improvement, but just as the doctors had warned her, there was none. Gene said that Daria would know when she visited her. "She sniffs at my neck and hugs me," she would say. That was the best display of affection that she could ever have hoped for. Since Gene's catatonic acceptance of Daria's disability the day Oleg told her of it, she had rarely cried for her daughter or for herself.

Gene's developing mental illness in the years to come made up for the lack of tears in the early years of Daria's life. She would cry and cry and cry, sometimes for herself, sometimes for Daria, and sometimes for no reason at all. She would constantly remember back to the day when she took Daria into the foyer of the Langhorn School. Daria was dressed in a pretty dress with her initials imprinted on it. Her blonde curls tumbled across her forehead. She looked just like any other pretty little four-year-old girl. The Doctor took Daria's hand and Gene began to tug her back. The doctor gently took Gene aside and said, "Mrs. Cassini, you can't keep this child. You may have another. Why don't you think about doing that? There is no chance this child will get well."

These were words Gene had heard before, and she knew that he was right. This was her last attempt at hanging on, and she did her best right to the very end.

Gene Tierney

"Couldn't I keep her around and just love her?" Gene pleaded. "No," he said firmly, "that would be unhealthy for you and hopeless for her." He then took Daria's hand and walked away. And that was it. That was the moment that Gene lost her daughter to the disabilities that plagued her.

Looking back, it seems the horrors of war spread a lot farther than the battlefields they were fought on. The people who stayed behind endured their own battles. Most of them were in some way linked to the biggest battle of all, World War II. After many years of reflection Gene would smile and say, "Daria was my war effort."

Although both Gene and Oleg kept silent when confronted by that female Marine, the woman's conscience would not be spared for long. Eventually, the story of how Gene contracted German measles was told to the media. Just as Oleg innocently picked up the newspaper that morning and read of Daria's premature birth, this woman would also innocently pick up a newspaper one morning and learn that she was the direct cause of the tragedy. Her identity has never been revealed.

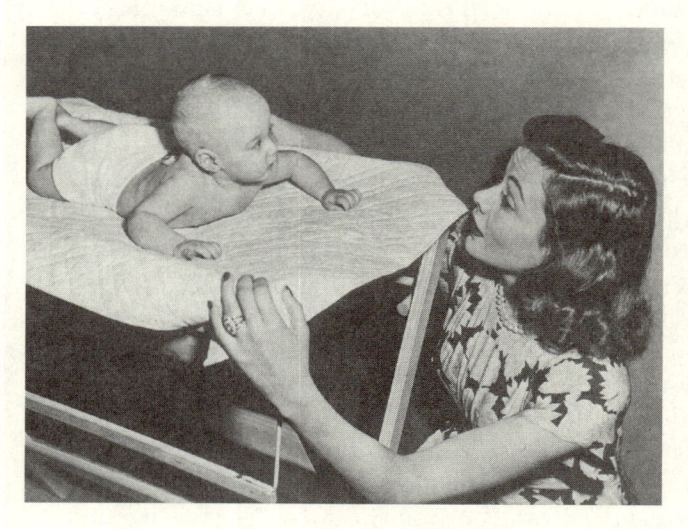

November 1944: Daria appears to be doing all the things that a happy, healthy one year old would do. Sadly, a little over two years after this photograph was taken, Gene reluctantly surrendered Daria to an institution for children with severe disabilities (photograph courtesy Lou and Mary Jo Mari).

Daria's story inspired famed author Agatha Christie to write the best selling mystery *The Mirror Crack'd from Side to Side*. It tells of a famous actress contracting German measles during her pregnancy. The baby is born retarded, and the actress sets out to kill the woman who infected her. Elizabeth Taylor would star in the 1980 movie version, with a shorter title, *The Mirror Crack'd*. Life's revenges carry the consequences that movies do not. Satisfaction is rarely obtained by those who have been wronged along real life's sometimes cruel road.

8

Laura

Between the year Daria was born and the year she was put into Langhorn, Gene made four of the best films of her career and received an Academy Award nomination for *Leave Her to Heaven*. It was not a coincidence. Oleg explained, "It was as if the birth of Daria had emptied her, and she was now filling herself up with these roles."

During the time that Gene and Oleg were at Fort Riley (while she was pregnant with Daria), a script came in the mail. Although she was taking the rest of that year off while pregnant, she took the time to read it. The movie was *Laura*.

Most of the story revolved around a painting of *Laura*. Gene would appear very briefly on screen. After reading the script Gene failed to see the magical allure that Otto Preminger intended to weave on screen. However, she trusted his vision and accepted the role a little over six months after Daria's birth. It would be *Laura* that she was most remembered for.

This was to be Gene's comeback picture. She had taken a year off with her pregnancy and wanted to be sure this very strange role would be right for her. Darryl F. Zanuck did his best to convince her, telling Gene, "You'll see. This one will help your career." Gene had second thoughts about Zanuck's words because Jennifer Jones had turned the role down before her. Why all of a sudden was it now *the* role for her? After all, she was second choice. If it was to be her perfect comeback role then she thought she should have at least been first choice to begin with. Eventually, after a lot of convincing, she listened to Zanuck and agreed to take the part. In hindsight, Jennifer Jones' instincts proved to be wrong, like those of many actors and actresses before her. Without realizing it, she had turned down the role of a lifetime. Who could blame her? On paper *Laura* seemed to be a very minor part woven into a confusing tale of suspense and mystery.

The script didn't do the completed picture justice at all. Even Gene failed to see the magic when it was written down on paper. Her decision to do the film was not based on loving the role but on believing in Zanuck's advice and knowing that

Gene Tierney

Preminger would never attach his name to a picture that he didn't believe in. *Laura* began shooting on April 27, 1944. Otto Preminger would produce and direct a cast of actors that would forever be remembered as one of the best "film noir" ensembles of their time.

Two months before filming began, Bonnie Cashin and her team of designers started on the costumes for the film. Preminger spared no expense. With a $15,000 budget the designers had a field day in creating the most luxurious costuming in a long time. Even Gene's underwear was meticulously designed with black lace panels threaded with baby blue ribbon. Her pink pajamas were embroidered with sequins. She stood for hours, passing the time by chewing jellybeans as the designers pinned and poked and tucked the many outfits into position. Preminger insisted on real diamonds and pearls being rented for the duration of the shooting. His *Laura* would not be wearing fake jewelry.

Again, Preminger would fight Fox to get such an extravagant costume budget approved. He convinced the studio they had to spend money to make money. The onscreen quality would show, the movie would be a hit, and they would make a massive profit. That word "profit" was music to the studio's ears. After all, it was really all they cared about. Since Gene's garments were made-to-measure, she had first choice on what to buy for her personal wardrobe. Anything she discarded would go back to wardrobe and be worn by bit players in future productions.

In the film, Gene is the mysterious Laura. Clifton Webb plays a writer, Waldo Lydecker. He narrates the first half of the picture and is secretly in love with her. Eventually he attempts to kill her when things don't quite go his way. *Laura* was Clifton Webb's first movie role in years. He had appeared in several films in the early 1920s and his last screen appearance before *Laura* was in the 1930 production of *The Still Alarm*.

A shot of Gene reading a scene from *Laura* (1944) in a live radio broadcast for CBS to promote the film.

The most prized prop painting ever used on film. The famous painting of Gene as *Laura* (1944) was used extensively throughout the film. This "painting" wasn't a painting at all but a photograph that was enlarged and painted over, giving the screen illusion of being a work of art.

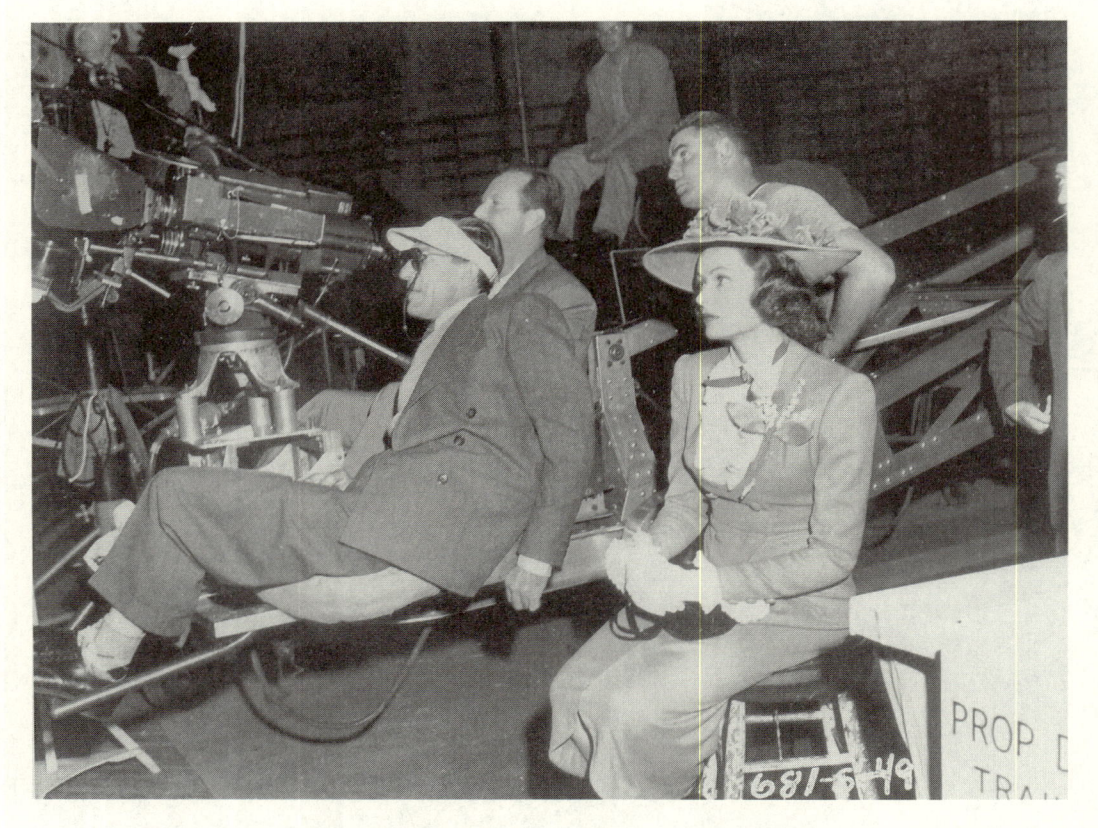

Another long day on the set for Gene. It was not unusual for her to leave home in the dark and return home in the dark. The demanding shooting schedules deprived her of sunlight until Sunday, her day off.

Although Webb was an established stage actor at the time, *Laura* was a first for him. It was his first role in a sound picture.

As casting for *Laura* began, Webb was appearing in the highly successful Broadway play *Blithe Spirit*. Otto Preminger thought him to be the ideal acid-tongued writer, Waldo Lydecker, and set out to lure him to the role. Zanuck was reluctant to have Preminger cast Webb because of his known homosexuality. He thought Webb too effeminate for the role. Preminger would not back down and was known to have many open battles with Zanuck about his reasons for casting Webb as Lydecker. History tells us he won the argument, and Clifton Webb in turn won a Best Actor nomination for his performance.

The story begins with a woman's body found outside the flat of Laura Hunt (Gene). The woman has been murdered by a horrific shotgun blast to the face. It is assumed the body is that of Laura. Dana Andrews plays Detective Mark McPher-

8. Laura

son. While investigating her supposed death, he begins to fall in love with Laura through her portrait.

The second half of the picture is told from the detective's viewpoint. Vincent Price plays Laura's slimy fiancé, Shelby Carpenter. A very clever plot has Laura, in the first half of the picture, believed to be the victim of foul play. When she eventually turns up toward the second half of the picture the roles are reversed. Laura now becomes a suspect.

The film had its ups and downs during production. Originally Preminger was to produce and co-direct with Rouben Mamoulian. Conflict erupted and Preminger fired Mamoulian and took over as both producer and director himself. No one will ever know whether Preminger's conflict with Mamoulian had to do with Preminger's being dissatisfied with the original painting of Laura. Mamoulian's wife, Azadia, was a successful Hollywood artist. She was commissioned by the studio to paint the portrait of Gene as Laura. Preminger hated the portrait, saying it lacked the mysterious feel that the painting needed to capture the audience.

With this painting being Gene's representation for a good half-hour of this picture, he wanted it to be perfect; it had to have allure and power. The painting was flat and boring. To replace it, Preminger sent Gene to studio photographer, Frank Polony. Several portrait shots were taken, and the best shot was enlarged to the size of a painting. After it was framed it was lightly airbrushed with paint, giving the appearance of brush strokes. The result was a movie prop that even today would be up near the price of the ruby slippers from *The Wizard of Oz* if it were ever to be auctioned.

The melody of the movie's theme song was by David Raksin, the lyrics were by Johnny Mercer, and what lyrics they were. No words were more fitting to describe the mysterious Laura. Mercer refused to watch the film before writing the lyrics to Raksin's music. He believed if Raksin had properly captured the mood with his melody, his lyrics would surely echo that feeling. The lyrics portray the ethereal existence of a woman who seems unreal, mysterious, alluring. He was able to capture her spirit with a minimum of words. It took just 62 words from Mercer to complete Raksin's 72-note theme, and the result was nothing short of brilliant.

Raksin praised Mercer: "I thought Johnny's achievement was amazing, that he should get that feeling into the lyric. And I know that Johnny worked hard, sweated blood sometimes, but you would never have known it. He would show up without a hair out of place — with this thing he had written on the tip of his finger." Perhaps the biggest praise of Mercer's achievement in writing *Laura* came from a fellow lyricist, the legendary Cole Porter. Mercer received a telegram from Porter saying, "*Laura* is my favorite song — among those I didn't write."

David Raksin is best remembered for writing the haunting melody for *Laura*,

Gene Tierney

A classic *Laura* (1944) pose with the main cast pictured. In the foreground is Clifton Webb and Gene Tierney (center), with Dana Andrews (right) playing the cool but infatuated detective Mark McPherson, asking all the right questions. Vincent Price and Judith Anderson round out the main cast of characters in the right middle ground.

but he had a career many years before it and many years after it. At 23 he composed the score for Charlie Chaplin's *Modern Times*. The year was 1936. Through a recommendation from George Gershwin he had already been composing musical numbers for Broadway before gradually easing his way into film. With a résumé listing more than 100 film themes to his name, David Raksin really is the man behind the music.

"People used to think if you noticed the music, it was a mistake," he said, "but there are times when you have to hear it because the music has to carry the burden. With *Laura*, you are dealing with what is ostensibly a dead girl, and a detective who is a hard-boiled pragmatic man. You have to convince people in that one scene that he is falling in love with her." His idea of using music to speak and insinuate a moment worked perfectly. "When I wrote *Laura*," he said, "I thought I really had something, which it turned out, in that case, I really did."

Right down to the music, Preminger had the perfect team creating the per-

8. Laura

fect picture. His dedication to detail would border on the obsessive, with the people around him putting in 18-hour days just to keep up. It was not unusual for him to take three hours to set up a camera angle and then decide it wasn't the exact look that he wanted after all. Gene's days started before the sun rose and ended long after it had set. She literally went for days without seeing a hint of natural daylight. Every moment was spent on one sound stage or another. Oleg, frustrated with seeing his wife fall in the front door exhausted, stormed onto the set one day and took Gene by the arm. "Come on," he shouted, "it's not worth it, nothing is worth it, we're going home." He meant business. They really did go home. The next day Gene got up at her usual predawn time and went back to work to complete the picture.

The relentless schedule had everyone exhausted, both mentally and physically, but Preminger never tired. He was driven with an internal obsession to make *Laura* a unique piece of film making. His obsession paid off. The movie was initially released in New York on October, 11, 1944. The rest of the country followed in November, and *Laura* proved to be a smash hit with the public. The Academy of Motion Picture Arts and Sciences agreed. The film was nominated for five Academy Awards. Otto Preminger was nominated as Best Director. The film was nominated for Best Art Direction and Best Screenplay. The cameraman, Joe LaShelle, was nominated and won the Academy Award for Best Photography. He was the only nominee who took home an Oscar.

Clifton Webb's first movie role since the silent era got him an Oscar nomination for Best Supporting Actor of 1945. It also got him a lot more. The stresses and strains of movie making must have taken their toll on the 54-year-old actor. Upon completion of *Laura*, Webb had a nervous breakdown and checked himself

With the radio being the only real in-home promotional source for potential movie patrons, many top stars promoted their coming films with live radio readings of scenes from their latest films. Here, Gene is photographed in the middle of a reading for Laura *(1944) on CBS radio, circa 1944.*

A portrait of Gene's favorite director and lifelong friend, Otto Preminger. His obsession with detail made him known in the industry as a control freak. However, the final product of an Otto Preminger directed film can only be called a masterpiece. *Laura* (1944) is a classic example of his brilliance.

into a sanitarium for a much-needed rest. His constant stream of high-strung characters on screen was very close to his real life personality. He was a homosexual who was inseparable from his mother, Maybelle, whom he lived with until her death. Playwright Noel Coward said at the time, "It must be tough to be orphaned at seventy-one."

Clifton Webb died of a heart attack on October 13, 1966, a little over a month shy of his 75th birthday. Besides being remembered for his many prissy and snobbish acting roles, one interesting legacy that Webb has left behind is the inspiration for the cartoon character of Mr. Peabody from the *Rocky and Bullwinkle* cartoon show. The 1960s character was based entirely on Webb's persona.

Oleg saw many comparisons between Gene's festering illness and her role of Laura Hunt. He explained, "When I think of Gene's illness, I think more of Laura, which was her most famous role. It is ironic that through much of the film she played a girl presumed dead who was actually alive, in some ways, Gene was quite the opposite. After Daria's birth, she seemed to die inside. There was a ghostly quality, an evanescence, to both Laura and Gene. Even after Laura is found to be alive, she has a certain mystery, an aura, that permeates the film and gives it much of its magic. And Gene? After Daria, there was a distance I never seemed able to bridge. I don't think she was ever truly happy again. She played at happiness, pretending to laugh when the occasion called for it, but it was a role she performed so as not to disappoint or alarm others. That distance was a wound that crippled our marriage."

At least professionally, *Laura* proved to be a success for everyone involved. Zanuck was right. *Laura* was the ultimate comeback film for Gene, and it didn't end there. It seemed to be the stepping stone to a succession of unforgettable roles for her.

9

Heaven and Heartbreak

It was now 1945 and Gene had just accepted a part in a film to be directed by Henry King. It was *A Bell for Adano*. For the first and only time and against her contract stipulations, Gene dyed her hair a platinum blonde for the part of Tina. With the exception of a little lipstick, Gene wore no other makeup for the role. John Hodiak starred alongside her as Major Joppolo, as did William Bendix as Sergeant Booth. *A Bell for Adano* seemed to be the one so-so film that was scattered among the classics during this period of Gene's career.

Her next role was once again handed to her on a platter by none other than Darryl F. Zanuck himself. Fox had just bought the rights to the book written by Ben Ames Williams, and he felt that Gene could play the part better than anyone else. The film was *Leave Her to Heaven*, and Zanuck wanted Gene to play the part of Ellen Berent. This was a role much different from any she had ever played before. The personality of Ellen was a long way from the real life personality of Gene Tierney. For her to pull off this role the way it was intended, she would really have to be acting.

It didn't take much convincing by Zanuck this time. He had proved his hunches were right with *Laura*, and this time the script read brilliantly on paper. The part of Ellen called for Gene to play the bitchy, psychotic wife of Cornel Wilde's character, Richard Harland. Jeanne Crain was cast as Gene's younger sister, Ruth Berent. Vincent Price was again alongside Gene, playing the role of Russell Quinton.

Ellen (Gene) lures the handsome Richard (Wilde) into marriage after knowing him for little more than a few days. At first his alluring new bride besots Richard, but he soon learns from her sister and mother that Ellen's jealous, possessive love has ruined other people's lives before him. When his crippled brother drowns while in Ellen's care and she has an accident that kills their unborn child, Richard starts to grow increasingly suspicious of her intense devotion. For her finale she decides to kill herself with poison but sets up enough clues to suggest that her husband and adopted sister murdered her.

Gene Tierney

A hardly recognizable platinum-blonde Gene looks defiant as two curious soldiers ask her a question or two in *A Bell for Adano* (1945).

From beyond the grave, Ellen still has the power to destroy the lives of the people around her. Her intense beauty masks the evil of her character. The bright sunny setting among breathtaking scenery masks the darkness of the unfolding story line. As the story plays out it sends chills up the audience's spine, especially when it's quickly realized that the devil can be disguised in such beautiful form. Highly acclaimed for its breathtaking Academy Award winning cinematography, the film was shot in several locations, including New Mexico and Wyoming. The famous lake scene was shot on Bass Lake in Madera County, California.

Although her role called for Gene to be a nasty and vindictive character, her humor never wavered on set. In between shots at the end of a very long day she would say, "Now, I'm getting very nervous and tired and I might just collapse and cost the studio millions of dollars." She had a fantastic sense of humor, and everyone laughed when she put on the drama queen act. Her mocking of the typical movie star attitude made for a much-needed break in concentration on set for

9. Heaven and Heartbreak

Gene as the beautiful yet evil Ellen Berent in *Leave Her to Heaven* (1945). Her unsuspecting, trusting husband, Cornel Wilde, stands beside his bride in this shot, but not for long. Gene received an Academy Award nomination for Best Actress in *Leave Her to Heaven*, only to lose out to Joan Crawford for *Mildred Pierce* (1945).

everyone involved. As funny as it was, that comment would often shake everyone into reality and get them thinking, "Gene's right. It's time to call it a day."

The role of an actor, any role, is to do the job well enough for us, the audience, to believe the actor to be *that* person. Gene Tierney portrayed Ellen so well that a cook employed by friends of hers in Cape Cod threatened to quit when she found out that Gene was coming to dinner. Gene's friends persuaded her to stay until Gene arrived. When Gene got there they told her their cook had just seen *Leave Her to Heaven* and was not going to stay under the same roof with such a ruthless, nasty woman. Gene laughed and went straight to the kitchen to say hello. After a few minutes of chatter the woman smiled and said, "Oh, ma'am. You sure were mean in that picture. Now that I've seen you, you are real nice." *That* is how convincingly Gene played the role of Ellen in *Leave Her to Heaven*. She was also convincing enough to be nominated for Best Actress, the only Academy Award nomination of her career.

Gene Tierney

Top: The gothic thriller *Dragonwyck* (1946) teamed the masterful screen villain Vincent Price and Gene Tierney, together once again in the lead roles. As in two of Gene's other films, *Laura* (1944) and *The Ghost and Mrs. Muir* (1947), the painting in this scene plays a prominent role in *Dragonwyck*'s plot. *Below:* Gene comforts her young co-star, Connie Marshall, in a scene from *Dragonwyck*.

The film was released on December 20, 1945, and grossed $5.5 million in U.S. ticket sales alone. After the success of *Laura* the moviegoing public flocked to see if Gene Tierney could produce a back to back hit, and they were not disappointed. Gene lost the 1946 Academy Award for Best Actress to Joan Crawford, who won for her role in the equally suspenseful *Mildred Pierce*. Although Gene lost the Academy Award, her nomination was enough to say she was finally accepted

9. Heaven and Heartbreak

as a serious actress. Another indication that you've made it in Hollywood is being asked to put your footprints, handprints and signature in the cement at the forecourt of Grauman's Chinese Theatre. By the end of 1946, Gene Tierney got her invitation to do just that. She had officially made it!

It seemed the same driving ambition that Gene had earlier in her career, before Daria's birth, had re-emerged. Her next film was the gothic thriller *Dragonwyck*. She was cast as Miranda Wells. Again she was teamed with Vincent Price, who was to play the role of Nicholas Van Ryn. Walter Huston played Gene's father, Ephraim Wells. Based on Anya Seton's book of the same name, *Dragonwyck* falls into the category of a classic 1940s thriller.

Vincent Price plays the main villainous character who sets the tone for his many horror roles to come. The picture is set in the mid–1800s. Nicholas van Ryn (played by Price) is a wealthy Dutch immigrant now living in Hudson Valley, New York. Living a bitter and hateful existence with his wife because she bore him a daughter instead of a son, he becomes infatuated with Miranda Wells (Gene) after she comes to live at his estate as an au pair. He soon plans to poison his wife so that he and Miranda can marry. He succeeds, and after Miranda gives birth to the son he has been waiting for, all seems to be perfect.

The boy is a sickly child and fails to reach adulthood. His death sends van Ryn into a world of madness. He moves into the attic of his mansion, experimenting with and succumbing to all sorts of drugs. Feeling helpless, Miranda seeks help from the local doctor, Dr. Jeff Turner (played by Jeff Langan). Falling in love with Miranda himself, he eventually figures out that Van Ryn did in fact poison his first wife, and just maybe, Miranda is soon to be his second victim.

Joseph Mankiewicz was a noted screenwriter and producer at the time, and *Dragonwyck* was his directorial debut. It was a film that held a personal memory far greater than any professional memory associated with the making of the picture itself: a memory that Gene would never lose. One day while filming a scene with Walter Huston she was told by director Mankiewicz to turn and look directly into the camera. Just as she made the pivot to turn, right there just beyond the camera stood a young man in a Navy lieutenant's uniform. He smiled at Gene and her heart skipped a beat. She was still in the middle of a scene so she couldn't acknowledge his smile until Mankiewicz yelled, "Cut."

The moment she heard that word she stepped forward and was introduced to Lieutenant Jack Kennedy. She later said, "Jack had the most perfect blue eyes that I had ever seen on a man." She was mesmerized by him. She swiftly wrote a letter home to younger sister Pat to tell her all the details. With Gene still being a married woman, she wrote that Pat must meet this man from Boston. Pat wrote back confused: "And just who is meant to fall for him, you or me?"

Between the time that Gene wrote to Pat and Pat wrote back, Gene had already met up with Jack Kennedy again at a party at Sonja Henie's house. Gene had a date for the evening. She and Oleg were now separated and both were openly dating other people. She was unaware of Jack even being at the party until he politely cut in on her while dancing. Something happened right then and there. Gene danced with Jack for the rest of the evening, totally unaware that she had been escorted to the party by another man a few hours before.

By the spring of 1946, Jack Kennedy and Gene Tierney had become something of an item. Gene and Oleg's marriage had been rocky for some time. They were now officially separated and talking of divorce. They seemed doomed from the very beginning. Daria's birth had caused a strain that was hard to overcome. Gene's constant hoping that a cure would be found was the total opposite of Oleg's acceptance of his daughter's disabilities. It had become a tension that couldn't be argued about anymore. On both sides, there was no sense fighting opinions that couldn't be changed.

Oleg's moments of infidelity caused more heartache for Gene. She had stayed faithful and believed that Oleg would do the same. Unfortunately, he was of the mindset that if you did have certain indiscretions with women other than your wife, it was okay as long as your wife was not publicly shamed in the process. Public shame had nothing to do with it. Gene felt betrayed, and the trust that existed between them as husband and wife was broken beyond repair by the first of many affairs that Oleg had. He would often accuse Gene of being suspicious, insecure and jealous. If she was, there was reason to be. Even as his wife she could not keep the Cassini wings from spreading and flying in another direction. The constant separations due to work commitments saw both of them drift apart. It was inevitable that the marriage would break down. With all of these factors involved, it soon did.

With Kennedy now out of the Navy, he was on his way to becoming the president of the United States. Now running for Congress in Boston, he was well on his way. They dated constantly. Gene was happier than she had been in a very long time. She wrote back home that she had met a wonderful young man "who one day will be our president." How right she was.

At age 29, Jack Kennedy was elected to Congress with a margin of 78,000 votes between him and his next competitor. Jack visited Gene's family home and met with Belle Tierney and Pat and Butch. Butch was particularly horrified that his sister was dating an upper crust Democrat. With the Tierney's being staunch New England Republicans, he was reluctant to even let Jack in the front door. Not pleased with having him under the same roof, Butch left the house ahead of Gene and Jack, passing them on the way down the driveway. He waved and spent the afternoon at the golf course. He was not impressed with Gene's choice in boyfriends.

With Kennedy not yet being a national figure, there was little press interest

9. Heaven and Heartbreak

A shot of Gene from the gothic thriller *Dragonwyck* (1946).

in this new relationship. Eventually it leaked out and the media showed some interest, but more often than not they were let alone. As the relationship became more intense Gene knew it was time to tell Oleg the divorce papers should be filed. Gene wanted to be free to live her future the way she wanted without being legally bound to a relationship that had now ended. Jack Kennedy seemed to be part of that future. The filing of the divorce papers was the first step in the direction to ensuring that he was.

It was a small world. Oleg also knew the Kennedy family and knew Jack. Genuinely concerned for Gene's future and not wanting her to get her heart broken, he sat down with her to talk about her new relationship. "Gene, don't you understand?" he pleaded, "Jack can't marry you. No Catholic is going to marry a divorced woman. His family won't stand for it. Just be sure you know what you are doing." Gene didn't want to hear any of it, "Oh, he'll marry me, he'll marry me," she said, beaming.

Many Hollywood columnists at the time were pushing for Gene and Tyrone Power to become an item. They were, after all, two of the most "beautiful" people in Hollywood at the time. Their being paired together seemed an ideal match. The fact they had just started working together on a film called *The Razor's Edge* also had people holding their breath thinking that maybe, just maybe, they would come out of this picture more than just friends.

Tyrone Power was *the* matinee idol of his day. Recently divorced from his French movie star wife, Anabella, he was now a free agent. It was openly apparent that Power wanted something more than just a friendship from Gene. He too believed the press to be right about him and Gene being the perfect couple, and he set out to give them exactly what they were hoping for. The studio's manipulation no doubt fed the press certain pieces of hot on-set gossip. It was their job to keep the rumor mill spinning, even if the rumors never proved true. It was the perfect publicity for Fox, two of their leading stars in the throes of a hot and steamy affair. Everyone was disappointed, however. The only sparks between the two of them were scripted and on film.

As much as Gene hated the fact that the studio would fabricate stories to the media about supposed affairs on the side, and as much as Oleg knew it was nothing more than studio hype, it did not stop him from going crazy when he came looking for Gene on the set one day. Oleg thought it would be nice to go over and pick Gene up after shooting had finished. After looking everywhere without any luck, he decided to try looking in Tyrone Power's dressing room. As he walked in he found three men playing cards. One of them was Bill Gallagher, Power's secretary. "Do you know where Gene is?" Oleg innocently asked. One of them smiled and with the boldest of tone said, "She's probably in the shower with Tyrone."

Well, if ever there was a red-flag-to-a-bull comment, that was it. Oleg was the bull and that comment was the reddest of flags. Oleg flew across the room, ripped

9. Heaven and Heartbreak

the guy from his chair and threw him against the wall. He then proceeded to destroy Tyrone Power's dressing room. He was picking up chairs and swinging them above his head, sweeping items from tables and throwing anything he could in an uncontrolled rage. He himself said of the incident, "I was out of my mind."

The Razor's Edge was a cast of brilliance. Gene played Isabel Bradley, another catty and bitchy role that would go down as one of the best performances of her career. This was Tyrone Power's comeback film. He had just returned from the U.S. Marine Air Corps. He was one of the first pilots to fly supplies into Iwo Jima during the actual battle. On January 14, 1946, he was discharged as a first lieutenant, and soon after he was cast as Gene's love interest, Larry Darell, in *The Razor's Edge*. John Payne played Gray Maturin, Anne Baxter played Sophie Nelson, and Clifton Webb played Elliot Templeton.

Larry Darell (Power) is a returning World War I veteran who discovers upon his arrival home that he can no longer fit into the world of upper-class society that his fiancée Isabel (Gene), lives in. He decides to embark on a soul searching tour of the world, shunning the responsibilities of his career and his intended marriage to Isabel. With Isabel never really understanding Larry's need to "find himself," she continues her life in the social world that she thrives in. She eventually seeks comfort in the arms of Gray Maturin (Payne).

Power did his best to seduce Gene, and she genuinely liked him, just not romantically. She had no romantic intentions of any kind. The fact that Jack Kennedy was still in her life may have closed down any thoughts of a romance with Power. That we will never know. On one of Gene's day's off from shooting, a note arrived at her home. It was sent by Power. It read: "There is no sunshine on the set today, Ty."

On another occasion, during the party scene of the film, he persuaded the prop man to fill his and Gene's champagne glasses with real champagne. Usually in pictures colored water is substituted for champagne. One or two takes wouldn't do any harm, but repeated takes of a scene involving alcohol would make for a very tipsy cast. The colored water was a safe substitute. Power eventually persuaded the prop man to lose the water and pop the cork on a real bottle. After several takes both he and Gene were very relaxed, without a care in the world. Luckily, no dialogue was called for in the particular scenes involving the alcohol. It was simply the two of them touring Paris, with musical overtones.

Although Oleg and Gene were on the verge of divorce at the time *The Razor's Edge* was filmed, Gene still pushed for him to design the film's costumes. This time it was an open battle with Zanuck. "I want Oleg to do the costumes," she yelled as she stormed into Zanuck's office. He simply replied, "No," then added, "Costumes are very important to this picture. They have to be right. Your husband has been out of touch for too many years. I can't take the chance."

Gene Tierney

There was nowhere for Gene to go but to the level of extreme. "Very well," she said, "then I won't do the picture."—"Very well," he replied, "then I'll put you on suspension." Gene stormed out of his office and back to Oleg to tell him what had happened.

"You're crazy," he told her. "I wish you wouldn't do that for me." Gene didn't back down. Zanuck did suspend her, but the ban lasted only two weeks.

Zanuck called Gene back into his office and told her that Oleg could design her clothes and the clothes of Anne Baxter, the two leading women. The other studio designers would take care of the rest of the cast. It was a compromise good enough for Gene, and for Oleg. He was given a cottage at the studio to work in and a reasonable salary for his work. Upon completion of the picture, Oleg received a note from Zanuck saying that he'd been wrong about him and he had done a superb job. He promised to give him other special projects in future pictures. For Oleg, after being in the Army for so long, this was the start that he needed to get back into designing. If not for Gene's insistence and stubbornness, *The Razor's Edge* would never have had the Cassini name attached to the credits.

Interestingly, the wedding dress that Gene wore in *The Razor's Edge* was actually designed for her by Oleg to be worn at *their* real life wedding. Because of their hasty elopement she was unable to be married in it. Some five years later she made up for it. The wedding dress that we see in the picture was actually *her* wedding dress.

On November 19, 1946, *The Razor's Edge* premiered at the Roxy Theatre. It coincided with the birthdays of two of the main stars of the picture, Clifton Webb and Gene. There was a party at the Plaza Hotel after the screening to celebrate both birthdays and the enthusiastic reception that the film got at the premiere. Everyone involved knew they had a hit with this one. There was definite reason to celebrate. During the celebration, Tyrone Power approached Gene, asking her if she would mind if he stopped by her suite after the party. He went on to tell her that he had a gift for her. Gene agreed that it would be okay if he stopped by once the party was over. He kept his word, arriving at Gene's suite shortly after she had returned.

Both Belle and Pat Tierney were in Gene's suite when he knocked on her door, but both hurriedly ran into the bathroom before Gene let him come in. He handed her the gift, and she casually mentioned leaving for Cape Cod the next day to meet with Jack Kennedy. That was enough of a clue to tell him that he'd lost the battle to win Gene's heart. He had certainly tried his best, but Gene was already in love. No man would come close to living up to Jack Kennedy, not even Tyrone Power. The gift was a silk scarf with the word "Love" embroidered near the bottom corner. It was a gift that Gene treasured for many, many years.

Everyone's predictions for the movie's success came true. The film received

9. Heaven and Heartbreak

several major Oscar nominations, including Best Picture of 1947. Clifton Webb received another career Best Supporting Actor nomination. Anne Baxter was nominated and won for Best Supporting Actress of 1947 for her role as Sophie Nelson.

Gene went to Cape Cod and met Jack the next day. Their romance was still going strong, and Gene honestly thought that she and Jack had a solid future together. A few weeks later while having lunch in New York, Gene realized that she and Jack had been on a very different wavelength. Jack was due back in Washington, and they decided to have a farewell lunch of sorts with a few close friends. Gene and Jack had arrived first and were sitting at their table chatting while waiting for the rest of their party to arrive. Right out of nowhere Jack blurted out, "You know, Gene, I can never marry you."

That one line ended everything. Before Gene had a chance to respond the rest of the people started to arrive. Jack got up to greet everyone, but Gene just sat there, stunned. The chatter and countless hellos and kisses and shaking of hands were all happening around her. She could only hear that in echo. The only clear words that she repeatedly heard were the ones that Jack had spoken to her just moments before.

Gene sat mostly silent throughout the luncheon. When it was time for Jack to leave for the airport to catch his plane back to Washington, he moved his chair back from the table and got up to leave. In a voice barely above a whisper but loud enough for him to hear, Gene said, "Bye, bye Jack." He continued to get up and move away from the table as he walked toward the door. Before he left he turned back around and said, "What did you mean by that? That sounds kind of final." He gave a half smile as he waited for Gene's response. "It is," she said. "It is."

There was nothing more to say; they stood and looked at each other from a distance for a long moment. With the noise of a crowded restaurant still bustling in the background, Jack broke their gaze and turned and walked out of her life.

Gene would cross paths with Jack on a couple more occasions. A few years after the restaurant incident they crossed paths in yet another restaurant, Maxim's in Paris. Jack was still a bachelor and preparing to run for the Senate. Gene was lunching with friends, as was he. He approached Gene's table and asked her to dance. Gene politely accepted. This time he blurted out another line. It was far more positive than the last time they exchanged words. "Gene, isn't it time we started seeing each other again?" he said with a smile, hoping that she would succumb to the Kennedy charm once more. Gene stayed strong. "No Jack, not for me."

It would have been easy to say yes, but this was a relationship that had no future. His political aspirations were high. He was climbing the ranks of politics toward the presidency, and just as Oleg said, he would not risk the loyalties of his family or destroy the ambition of becoming the leader of the free world for her.

There is no doubt that Jack Kennedy was torn between love and career. A little under six months after Gene's rejection, Jack married Jacqueline Lee Bouvier.

Gene Tierney

Gene and Tyrone Power play out a scene in *The Razor's Edge* (1946).

9. Heaven and Heartbreak

Gene in a promotional shot for *The Razor's Edge* (1946), appearing here in the wedding gown she was supposed to wear in her wedding with Oleg Cassini. Their hasty elopement changed all that, but she did get to wear the stunning dress on film (photograph courtesy Oleg Cassini).

Gene Tierney

She was the perfect bride for a soon to be president. By 1960 Jack Kennedy was elected to the White House as the youngest ever president of the United States. The world knew him as President John F. Kennedy. Gene had voted for Richard Nixon, but not out of bitterness or spite for a relationship lost. It was a vote influenced by her conservative upbringing. She did, however, send Jack a telegram of congratulations. It repeated exactly what she had predicted years before, simply, "Congratulations, I knew you would make it — Gene."

She was to see Jack one last time much later in life. There was a luncheon at the White House for Gene's newest picture, *Advise and Consent*. It was 1962, Jack's second year in office. Gene was now happily married to her last husband, Howard Lee. They both attended the luncheon with several other members of the cast of the film, and Gene was, maybe purposefully, seated next to Jack.

By the time of this meeting, Gene had been in and out of mental institutions, had undergone an excessive amount of electric shock therapy treatment and had even attempted suicide. Both Gene and Jack had now grown into two very different people from the early days of their courtship. Gene's mental illness had been widely covered by the press, and with this meeting between the two of them, it must have been a hard topic to bring up. Jack did, and he did it as tactfully as he possibly could. With a concerned look, he leaned across to Gene and asked, "How have you been Gene?"

Gene looked at her husband, Howard, and gestured toward him with her hand. "I'm a very lucky woman, Jack. You see, I have a husband who loves me, even when I am crazy." They both laughed. That was the moment that broke the thick layer of ice that had built up over a relationship that once held so much hope. They were both at a time in their lives that was individually satisfying. Even without each other, they were both content with the knowledge that they were both getting exactly what they wanted out of life. That was *their* moment of closure.

During her time as first lady, Jacqueline Kennedy chose Oleg Cassini as her White House fashion designer. The eyes of the world were on the first lady, and her Cassini designs changed the face of fashion overnight. It was a strange web that linked Oleg, Gene and the Kennedys, but eventually everything worked out for everyone, albeit briefly. In November of 1963, President John F. Kennedy was assassinated.

The loss of hope, that of a promising future, was felt not only in the United States, but throughout the world. Gene felt the loss a little more personally than the rest of us. He was not only her president. He was also her Jack.

10

The Ghost and Mrs. Muir

Here, I must turn the hands of time back to 1947. In 1945 Fox had just secured the rights to a book by R. A. Dick. Interestingly, it was a book that was only in British release. It had not yet hit American shores, but it was good enough for Fox to know it deserved to be made into a motion picture. That picture was *The Ghost and Mrs. Muir*.

Filming began in the early months of 1947, and it has proved itself to be a timeless love story. During the filming, in fact right at the very beginning, Gene was rushing up a flight of stairs, hurrying to see a friend's new baby. She tripped on a step and hobbled to the top of the stairs in excruciating pain. Her friend thought she was joking. "Oh, get up Gene, you're all right." Her friend thought Gene was acting a fool. Gene tried to convince her that she really couldn't walk on the foot. "It really hurts," she said. "Oh stop being such a sissy and come see the baby," her friend said as she helped Gene to her feet.

On the drive home, still in pain and with a picture to make, Gene decided to stop off and see her doctor. An X-ray showed that she had done some serious damage. She had broken a bone in her foot. Needless to say, the first person she called when she got home was her friend. It was the best "told you so" of Gene's life.

There was a slight delay in filming because of Gene's wearing a cast. Even shooting her scenes from the ankle up would prove to be useless. Whenever she was required to walk, the cast would cause her to hobble. There was nothing to do but to shoot around her best they could and to wait for the cast to come off before continuing. Out of frustration Gene pleaded with the doctor to take the cast off two weeks earlier than planned. Her foot was not yet mended properly, but the slight pain was far easier to put up with than lugging around a foot enveloped in heavy plaster.

Filming continued with Gene playing the part of Mrs. Lucy Muir, a widow, who with her daughter (played by an eight-year-old Natalie Wood) moves to the serenity of the British seaside and into Gull Cottage. The quaint little cottage seems

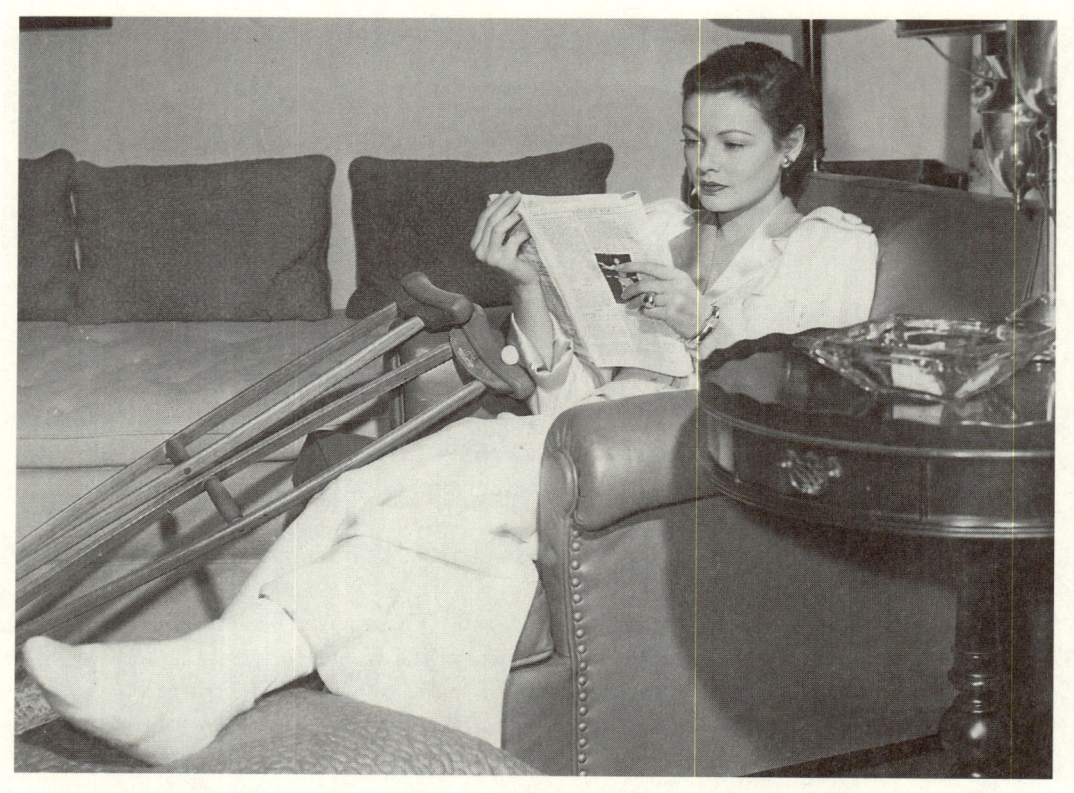

Top: February 10, 1947. This broken toe kept Gene off her feet and off the set of *The Ghost and Mrs. Muir* (1947) for several days. When she did return to work, filming resumed around her plaster cast. With a combination of long dresses, shooting above the waist and tricky camera angles, the film was completed on time. *Left:* Gene in her widow outfit from the ethereal love story *The Ghost and Mrs. Muir*, also starring Rex Harrison as the crusty sea captain, Captain Daniel Gregg.

like the ideal piece of real estate. The only problem is that it's haunted! The thought of the cottage being haunted doesn't faze Lucy Muir at all. She agrees to rent the cottage, being nothing more than intrigued by the tales of a ghost residing there.

Rex Harrison plays the ghost of Cap-

10. The Ghost and Mrs. Muir

Gene looks startled as she poses in front of the famous portrait of Rex Harrison as Captain Gregg. He plays the harmless, mischievous, yet cynically charming ghost who haunts the newly rented cottage of Mrs. Lucy Muir, played by Gene. A romance between a ghost and a widow? Yes indeed! *The Ghost and Mrs. Muir* (1947) is a timeless love story.

tain Daniel Gregg, the crusty sea captain who does his best to haunt Lucy Muir, just as he did the occupants of times past. He comes to realize that she isn't a woman to be messed with and starts to enjoy having her around. They begin to have conversations and soon develop a romantic friendship. When money starts to dwindle, Captain Gregg gets the idea of reciting his many tales of the sea to Mrs. Muir. She in turn will write a best selling book, and with the money she gets from having it published, well, all of her monetary problems will be solved.

Once the stories are written, Mrs. Muir heads into town to the publisher. There in his office waiting room she meets up with the always sneaky George Sanders, playing the role of a children's book publisher, Miles Fairley. He sets out to romance Mrs. Muir, despite the fact that he is married. Mrs. Muir learns of his sneaky ways. Like most cinematic villains, sneaks and scoundrels, Miles Fairley gets everything that he deserves by the end of the picture. Edna Best plays the lovable but outspoken Martha, the housekeeper with a big mouth and an even bigger heart.

November 14, 1949. Gene and her one-year-old daughter Christina arrive home on the SS *America* after the completion of location shooting in England for Gene's role in *Night and the City* (1950).

Since Captain Gregg is a ghost and Mrs. Muir is still among the living, their romance is destined for many problems. The feelings they have for each other could go nowhere. Besides, who ever heard of a relationship between a human and a spirit? It could not be, so Captain Gregg sets about releasing Mrs. Muir's love for him in the hope that she will find happiness with a man among the living.

One night while she's sleeping, Captain Gregg appears and, with a tear in his eye, he wipes all memories of him from her mind. He tells her any memories she has of him were only those of a dream. Lucy Muir awakes and goes on to live her life, with the film then winding forward to the point of the audience seeing her as an older woman, a tired woman no longer willing or able to be part of the living. We watch as she falls asleep in a chair in her room. There she dies peacefully in her sleep.

Suddenly Captain Gregg reappears. He holds out his hand as we

10. The Ghost and Mrs. Muir

watch an amazing transition. Through many, many tears, we watch the spirit of a young Mrs. Muir suddenly materializes from her lifeless body in the chair. Together they walk hand in hand out of the room and down the stairs, two ghosts reunited, living happily together, forever, in the hereafter.

Joseph Mankiewicz once again directed brilliantly, but the picture received only one Academy Award nomination, that of Best Cinematography for Charles Lang. Mankiewicz would make up for his lack of Academy Award nominations three years later. By 1950 he not only wrote and directed the cult classic *All About Eve* but also set a record for the greatest number of nominations for a single picture. His impressive 14 nominations stood as a record until *Titanic* equaled it in February 1998.

At the time of its release on June 26, 1947, *The Ghost and Mrs. Muir* was received only fairly by the public. Like many other pictures of times past, the audience at the time may not have been the best judge. Like fine wine, *The Ghost and Mrs. Muir* has most certainly gotten better with age. Its cult following developed years after its original release. There is no doubt it will continue to gain in popularity for generations to come. That, after all, is what classic films do. The movie spawned the television series of the same name. *The Ghost and Mrs. Muir* ran from 1968 through 1970 with Hope Lange playing Gene's role of Mrs. Lucy Muir.

With Oleg being employed as the exclusive costume designer for Gene's clothes on *The Ghost and Mrs. Muir,* by filming end it was reported that Oleg Cassini and Gene Tierney were once again an item. The reports proved true. They had agreed to give their relationship one more chance. Throughout their separation they had remained friends, never having a bad word to say about each other to anyone. The press had a field day, hounding both of them in the hope that one would attack the other. Oleg played a game of verbal tennis with one reporter when he was asked, "How would you describe Gene Tierney?" Oleg's reply was not what the reporter had hoped for, "Gene is the greatest girl in the world," he replied. The reporter, not wanting to give it up there, pressed him further. "If she's the greatest girl in the world, then why are you getting a divorce?" Oleg's reply was perfect: "You'll have to ask her," he said. "Maybe I'm not worthy of the greatest girl in the world." With that said, he walked away.

At the time of reconciliation, their divorce was almost final. Gene had already received an interlocutory decree. It was an almost-divorced situation. There was just the compulsory 12 months to wait before it was final, and that date was looming. By March 10, Gene's lawyer phoned to tell her the papers were in his office and ready for signing. He laughed when she told him to hang back a little. She was hopeful there might be a chance that he could put those final papers through his shredder and forget about the whole thing.

Oleg had now set up his own designing business in New York. He could no

Gene Tierney

longer travel around with Gene, and with her working in California the terrible weeks of separations would again be a main hurdle to overcome the second time around. They agreed to at least try and make it work, and they did, at least for a little while. Gene wanted another baby, desperately, and not a child to replace Daria. She just wanted a healthy child to love and care for. It didn't seem much to ask. During the making of *That Wonderful Urge*, yet another picture with Tyrone Power, Gene found out she was pregnant.

Gene was cast as Sara Farley and Tyrone Power as Tom Tyler. It was a simple story of a mismatched couple who end up stranded together. Their isolation from the world eventually makes them realize they were made for each other. Oleg once again designed Gene's costumes. The picture was a remake of a 1937 comedy, *Love Is News*, with Loretta Young playing Gene's part of Sara Farley.

The making of *That Wonderful Urge* held great personal memories for Gene. Her life seemed to have finally gotten to a point of calm. She was married, pregnant and working once again with her friend Ty Power. Although his death wouldn't occur until a decade later, without either of them realizing it, *That Wonderful Urge* would be their last professional pairing. Ten years later, while working on location in Madrid, Spain, on the film *Solomon and Sheba*, Power complained of severe chest pains in the middle of filming a dueling scene with George Sanders. Thinking he had strained himself and only needing a break, he went to his dressing room to rest for a while. Moments after he entered his dressing room, he collapsed. There was nothing anyone could do for him. On November 15, 1958, Tyrone Power died en route to the hospital. He was just 44 years old. The tragedy of Tyrone Power's death would devastate Gene when it occurred, but for now, life was dealing her a good hand.

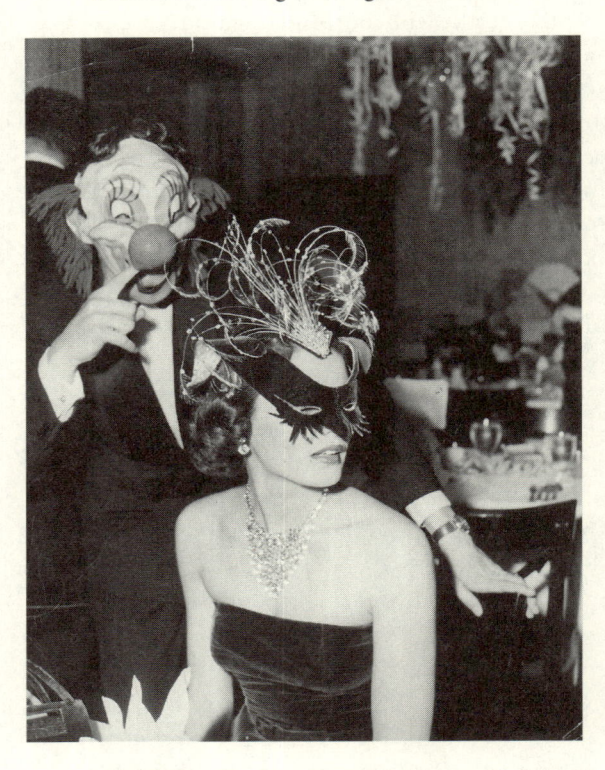

February 8, 1950. Disguised as a clown, Oleg Cassini sneaks up on his unsuspecting wife, Gene Tierney, at a masquerade ball.

Gene completed the picture, and within a year of Oleg and Gene's reconciliation, on November 19,

10. The Ghost and Mrs. Muir

1948, on Gene's 28th birthday, Christina (Tina) was born, a perfectly healthy little girl. They were both thrilled. Life seemed to be taking a turn for the better and it was about time. Their new arrangement seemed to be working. Both were trying hard to mend the cracks that had brought their marriage down before. Oleg would fly out to see Gene between assignments, and Gene would fly to Oleg when she had a break in production.

Right: A portrait shot taken for publicity on *The Iron Curtain* (1948). This was Gene's first film after the birth of her younger daughter, Christina. *Below:* Gene takes to the dance floor with Tyrone Power (right foreground) in *That Wonderful Urge* (1948).

Gene Tierney

Gene went back to work soon after Tina's birth. Her first post-pregnancy film was *Iron Curtain*. She was to play the part of Anna Gouzenko in a story of a Russian defector of the Cold War. It was an unusually serious role for Gene. The picture was based on the true story of Igor Gouzenko, played by Dana Andrews. He is a Russian decoder clerk who is stationed in Canada by the Soviet Embassy agents. He defects after the war with secrets about the Communist spy operations that were carried out during that time. The Canadian people embrace him and his family, but they are forced to live the rest of their lives under police protection. The harsh reality of the story is tempered by the love story between his wife, Anna (Gene), and their baby son.

Soon after *Iron Curtain*, Gene went to work on *Whirlpool*, another production under the watchful eye of Otto Preminger. The movie was based on the novel by Guy Endore. Gene was to play the part of Ann Sutton, a kleptomaniac. Richard Conte played Dr. Bill Sutton, Jose Ferrer played David Korvo, and Charles Bickford played Lt. Colton.

A dramatic scene from *Whirlpool* (1949). The confinement of a cell would soon be a reality when Gene is institutionalized as an inpatient for treatment of her mental illness.

10. The Ghost and Mrs. Muir

On one of her many shoplifting experiences, Gene's character, Ann, gets caught, but she's eventually saved by hypnotist Korvo. She becomes entangled in his life and the lives of his friends, Tina Cosgrove, played by Constance Collier, and Theresa Randolph, played by Barbara O'Neil. The latter character is a focal point in the story after her murder points toward Ann as the major suspect. David had a major operation just before the murder took place and he was immobile. His alibi is airtight. Ann's fingerprints are on the glass found in the murdered woman's library along with Ann.

The mystery deepens when the investigating officer discovers that the dead woman was a patient of Ann's psychiatrist husband. It really is a *Whirlpool* of intrigue and suspense, the classic on-the-edge-of-your-seat whodunit. In a scene where Gene's character, Ann, is arrested in the store she has just stolen from, she is taken by elevator to the manager's office. While in the elevator, Ann faints with despair. The rehearsal for this particular scene was an afternoon of headaches for everyone. During the first rehearsal Gene went limp on cue and fell perfectly to the floor, the only problem being that her skirt had risen too high. So it was time for take two. Once again she went limp and fell to the floor, but this time she hit another elevator patron on the way down. Too clumsy. On the third take, she hit the mark perfectly. Her skirt stayed at a respectful level, and she cleared the rest of the elevator patrons.

With Preminger being a stickler for detail, he insisted that she try it one more time, just to be sure she had it. Gene sighed, got up from the floor, rubbed her aching back, looked at Preminger and said, "Hey! Do I get a stunt check for all these falls?" Otto, with a wit to match Gene's, shot back, "It's quite a stunt just to earn what you do, Gene."

With the banter out of the way it was time to do it again. On this take Gene fell too far back. She hit her head with such force on the way down that everyone thought she must have knocked herself out cold. Just as Preminger rushed over to help her, she propped herself up on her elbows and with great concern said, "Did I ruin the hat?"

"I worry about your head and you worry about the hat?" Preminger responded with a shake of his head. "I'm so crazy about it," said Gene, "I want to buy it from wardrobe when the pictures finished."

"I'll give you the hat," said Preminger, "If you'll promise to do this scene without injuring yourself."

"This is a profitable day for me," Gene said. "I'll have to play more kleptomaniac rolls!"

Gene got through the take without bumping her head a second time. They finished the movie, and just as Preminger had promised, he gave her the hat.

The media did not let up on Oleg and Gene. They had succumbed to an almost-divorce once before, and the media, like sharks, were circling and waiting for it to happen again. When Gene was working in California she would fly back east to meet Oleg once her filming was complete. The media would call her a traitor for leaving California. If California was good enough to pay her and keep food on her table, then why isn't it good enough to live there? they'd ask. On the other hand, if she stayed in California and did not fly back east to meet Oleg, the press would attack her for being the uncaring wife. Questions were asked and eyebrows were raised about the solidity of the marriage. When it came to the press, it was a lose-lose situation.

By 1950, Gene's work would take her a lot farther from Oleg. This time she was to work on her new picture, *Night and the City*, in London. Tina would have to fly over with her, and Oleg would have to be content with making the trip over amid his own schedule to see both of them. With Tina still only six months old, Gene hired a nurse to travel with her on the trip. She would take care of Tina while Gene was busy with the film.

There was much socializing for Gene in London between shooting. She had always held a special place in her heart for England. No doubt, that affection stemmed from her boarding school days. This was the country that had saved her that very first Christmas away from home. Sylvia's invitation to spend the holiday with her and her family had made the homesick feelings almost bearable for her. She of course would visit with Sylvia again.

Now married, Sylvia was Mrs. Sylvia Hambro, a proper English lady, and she was Gene's savior yet again. With London still not yet recovered from the war, rationing was still in place. Sylvia would make regular trip to Gene from her country property with fresh eggs for her oldest best friend. Richard Widmark and his wife supplied Gene with canned milk they had packed up and brought with them from the U.S. At least with eggs and milk there was an omelet never far away from the dinner table.

With Clifton Webb now working in the West End in London, he would often call on Gene to escort her around town. One night he asked Gene if she would have any interest in meeting playwright Noel Coward. Gene didn't know what to say. She had read his plays and heard a lot about the man himself. One personal account of a meeting with him was from her Aunt Leila. She had met Coward years before and always told stories about how he was the only man who ever terrified her. Gene's instant thoughts spiraled back to Aunt Leila's horror stories, but she was intrigued by the man and agreed to have Webb arrange a dinner meeting.

Gene was staying at the Dorchester in London. Webb arrived to pick her up for their evening out and informed her that another guest would also be joining them. "Who?" Gene asked, not really paying much attention to her own question. "It's Marlene Dietrich," Webb said. Gene was already nervous, and now she was

10. The Ghost and Mrs. Muir

A scene from *Night and the City* (1950) with Richard Widmark.

terrified. On her way to dinner she thought she at least could talk about Marlene's daughter, Maria, if they got stuck for conversation. She had, after all, been a best friend with her daughter in boarding school. That had to count for something.

As for Noel Coward, she went in with the thought of saying very little. At least, then she wouldn't make a mistake. She did not want to be embarrassed by this brilliant man with a wit to outwit anyone. If the conversation was of minimum level then he would have nothing to challenge her about. She would leave the evening unscathed. It was a plan, her plan, and she was sticking to it.

As they approached the table at the restaurant, Webb first introduced Gene to Marlene Dietrich, almost 50 at the time. Gene remembers her still looking as stunning as a woman much younger.

Next was the moment of dread and fear, probably more fear than dread. She *was* excited at meeting Coward, just terrified at the thought of it. His opening comment went a lot further than a mere "Hello, how do you do." He stood up and paid Gene a compliment that almost floored her. "I want to tell you, Miss Tierney, you gave me one of the most memorable evenings I ever had in the theater in your film *Leave Her to Heaven*. When I saw the expression on your face in the sequence in which you drowned the boy, I thought, "*that is acting!*" After that almost dreamlike compliment from one of the most notable and respected playwrights in history, the evening flew past without a terrible word being said. Gene had singlehandedly elevated the Tierney name with that dreaded beast, Noel Coward. Aunt Leila would have been most impressed with her niece's hold over the man that had once terrified her.

As promised, Oleg flew to London the first chance he could to spend time with Gene and Tina. Whenever Gene was on a break they'd all pack up and head across to Europe for a brief getaway. They visited Paris and Deauville. The last scenes of *Night and the City* were shot in Europe. It gave the three of them even more of an opportunity to spend time together.

At one point Oleg was booked on an Air France flight back to New York. It was near the end of shooting for Gene, and she would soon be meeting Oleg back in the States. She pleaded for Oleg to stay on with her and Tina for another week. If it wasn't a whole week then she at least wanted him to stretch his stay for another few days. Oleg explained to her that he *must* get back. He too had business commitments, and he had to be in New York to oversee them.

Gene had a terrible feeling that the plane Oleg was booked on was doomed. She feared something terrible would happen. His staying on was not out of a need to have him with her; it was out of a need to keep him alive. She had to prevent him from boarding. On the way to the airport Gene became more and more agitated. "Please, Oly, if you have any feeling for me at all…" That was enough said for Oleg to turn the car around and go back to the hotel. Nothing more was thought

10. The Ghost and Mrs. Muir

about it until the next morning when Oleg picked up the morning paper. The very plane Oleg was booked on to go back to New York had crashed 60 miles off course in the Azores. Everyone on board had been killed.

Once Oleg brought the article to Gene's attention she began to shake and cry. "Gene, how could you know this?" Oleg pleaded. "I don't know," she said. "It was like a tremendous weight on my chest. I couldn't breathe. It was an overpowering feeling. I knew I had to force you not to go."

Whatever it was, a hunch, woman's intuition, a vision, it didn't matter. The only thing that mattered was that Oleg was still alive. If only Gene had had the power to stop the flight altogether, all lives would have been saved.

Gene began work on *Night and the City*, a film co-starring Richard Widmark. Widmark plays Harry Fabian, a petty hustler and con man who goes after the bigger dollars in the London underworld. Not content with making small amounts of money on two-bit scams, he takes up the idea of becoming a top London wrestling promoter. Gene plays his girlfriend, Mary Bristol, the woman he promises "a life of ease and comfort" after his scam takes off. Fabian eventually creates such a tangled web of lies, deceit and corruption that we see him on the run throughout most of the movie, proving there is no such thing as easy money.

Filmed mostly on location in London between July and October of 1949 and released in New York City on June 9, 1950, the film was shot in the classic film noir style of the late '40s and '50s. *Night and the City* was remade in 1992 with Jessica Lange and Robert De Niro playing the same roles as Gene and Widmark. Somehow the sneaky, hyena laugh of Widmark and the classic dark, oddly angled style of filming of the late '40s cannot be improved or even matched by the most recent version. As good as the original is, it wasn't good enough for Fox to make a profit on it. Its original release lost the studio money. As with many films before it, the style was probably ahead of its time. Only now is it considered a classic example of film noir.

Gene's next role was back in the States, and this time instead of Oleg being separated from her, he was working with her, not only as her designer but as her fellow actor. *Where the Sidewalk Ends* was Oleg's acting debut, and once again the film was to be directed by Otto Preminger. Since the film had Gene starring as a Seventh Avenue fashion model, it was the perfect script for Oleg to appear in as a designer. Preminger persuaded Oleg to make an appearance. He was to play New York designer Oleg Mayer. When Oleg saw the rushes of his first day as an actor, he slumped down in his seat and said, "As an actor I am a good designer!"

He was right, but as a designer he was better than good. He was brilliant. Oleg designed a spectacular red velvet dress for Gene to wear in the picture. Otto Preminger took one look at it, shook his head and said, "That dress is dangerous!" It was tight and figure-hugging with that mermaid silhouette that enhances every

Karl Malden (right) with Gene in a scene from *Where the Sidewalk Ends* (1950). Dana Andrews stands in the foreground between them.

curve. It had spaghetti straps and was low cut in the front, quite "dangerous" for its time. I guess Preminger found the right word, after all.

Gene complained that she couldn't walk six steps in it, but there was no need for her to walk any farther anyway. The dress served its purpose and Gene looked stunning. The dress was hers if she wanted it after production, but Gene found it to be totally impractical. She couldn't have worn it out anywhere. She couldn't even sit down in it. She sent it back to the wardrobe department without a hint of indecision. A few years later Marilyn Monroe would wear that same dress in one of her many photo shoots. Marilyn's curves were a lot fuller than Gene's ever were, so one would have to imagine just how restricted the "blonde bombshell" was in the creation. She was known for being sewn into her dresses, so I assume that this "dangerous" dress was one of those altered to fit. Marilyn always looked flawless from the front, but from behind, it was a whole other story. A photographer's secrets play a big part in making the subject look good, and Marilyn Monroe was no exception.

10. The Ghost and Mrs. Muir

May 20, 1950. An on-the-set shot of Gene with her co-stars, Craig Stevens and Gary Merrill. All three were starring in *Where the Sidewalk Ends* (1950), produced and directed by Otto Preminger.

July 3, 1950. A candid snapshot of Gene taking direction from Mitchell Leisen (left) on the set of *The Mating Season* (1951).

10. The Ghost and Mrs. Muir

May 26, 1950. Gene takes direction from Mitchell Leisen on the set of *The Mating Season* (1951).

Gene Tierney

February 1948. Gene gets a quick morning snack after her Sunday tennis game at the Beverly Wilshire Hotel tennis courts. She and husband Oleg Cassini were avid tennis players, playing whenever they could fit a game into their hectic schedules.

10. The Ghost and Mrs. Muir

Mike Mazurki, football star and actor, is the first to welcome Gene and her infant daughter, Christina, home after the long voyage from England on the SS *America*. Mazurki starred with Gene and Richard Widmark in the film, *Night and the City* (1950).

    Once again the threesome of Otto Preminger, Dana Andrews and Gene Tierney set out to recreate the magic of *Laura*. It was a tough task to live up to, proving that even the same ingredients cannot duplicate a certain magic that has been captured on a previous film. Andrews plays a tough New York City cop, Mark Dickson. He accidentally kills a murder suspect while giving him some roughhouse treatment. In order to protect himself he sets out to cover the killing up and pin the blame on a racketeer who has committed similar crimes in the past.
    Gene plays the role of Morgan Taylor. She's the girlfriend of Ken Paine, played by Craig Stevens. A model by day and an escort in a sleazy gambling club at night, Gene soon crosses paths and becomes emotionally involved with Dickson. Even as the corrupt cop, Dickson somehow gains the audience's sympathy as we slowly watch his conscience gets the better of him. *Where the Sidewalk Ends* proved to be

May 31, 1950. Gene has a costume alteration by her husband, fashion designer Oleg Cassini (left), on the set of *The Mating Season* (1951). Director Mitchell Leisen takes the opportunity to chat with Gene about an upcoming scene.

no *Laura*, but in its own right it had something else to give. It was and still is considered a perfect example of classic film noir.

The separations between Gene and Oleg were now becoming more and more frequent. The most telling observation on both sides was that the time apart was also becoming less and less painful. It was not unusual for them to go weeks at a time without seeing each other. Their phone conversations, although nightly, gradually became shorter. Eventually it got to the point where either or both of them chose to go out and socialize with others after work, neither of them overly concerned about missing the other's phone call.

Once again Gene was on loan to another studio. This time it was Paramount, for a comedy called *The Mating Season*. Gene played the role of Maggy Car-

10. The Ghost and Mrs. Muir

May 29, 1950. Gene in a casual shot on the set of *The Mating Season* (1951) with director Mitchell Leisen.

Gene Tierney

leton/McNulty, the innocent new bride of Val McNulty, played by John Lund. The always lovable Thelma Ritter plays the role of Ellen McNulty, Gene's new mother-in-law.

The story sees Maggy and Val setting up house after just being married. Ellen decides it would be nice to pay her son and new daughter-in-law a surprise visit, so she sells her New Jersey hamburger stand and makes the trip west. When Ellen arrives, her daughter-in-law, Maggy, mistakes her for the maid she's just hired to help out at the lavish party she's throwing for her husband's boss. Ellen goes along with the role of "maid" and persuades her son not to correct his new wife. At least not yet. The confusion makes for a very funny chain of events with Ritter's performance earning her an Academy Award nomination for best supporting actress of 1952.

Gene shone in comedy roles. She was funny in real life, and her comedic timing was perfect on film. Her career was hurtling ahead, but on a personal level, the cracks were once again opening in the Cassini marriage. Gene was about to begin work on her new picture, a comedy with Danny Kaye called *On the Riviera*.

Oleg was totally against the role, telling Gene that it was not the right comedy for her. He would be constantly frustrated with her for taking almost every role sent to her by the studio. She would feel bad about rejecting a script. Once again her constant need to please others, even the studio, did nothing to advance her career or eventually her own peace of mind. *On the Riviera* was the third remake of the story. The original film starred Maurice Chevalier and Merle Oberon; called *Folies Bergere*, it was released in 1935. In 1941 the second version, called *Night in Rio*, starred Don Ameche, Alice Faye and Carmen Miranda. This Kaye/Tierney version was the third. Their performances ensured it being the best of the three.

Gene holds her fingers to her ears as the large bell rings in the new year. The photograph was taken as a publicity still for Gene's film, *On the Riviera* (1951), co-starring Danny Kaye. The new year being celebrated is 1951.

132

10. The Ghost and Mrs. Muir

Kaye plays dual roles, those of Jack Martin and Henri Duran. His Duran character is married to Gene, who plays his very confused wife, Lili. It's the classic tale of two men, so identical in appearance (obviously with Kaye playing both characters) that even a wife can't tell them apart. Kaye once again sings three very animated and comical songs written by his real-life wife Sylvia Fine. His performance was good enough to win him the 1952 Golden Globe Award for Best Actor in a Comedy or Musical. The film itself grossed a respectable $2.5 million in U.S. ticket sales.

In a desperate attempt to hold on to what was left of the marriage, Gene persuaded Oleg to move to Connecticut. Gene reverted to her own happy childhood. She somehow thought that moving back to a place with happy memories for her would magically mend a relationship on the verge of ruin. Unfortunately, a change

Top: Gene introduces her five-week-old daughter Christina to the public. The healthy baby girl was the second daughter for Gene and her husband, Oleg Cassini. Tragically, their first daughter, Daria, was born severely retarded after Gene contracted German measles in her early stages of pregnancy. Gene was the classic example of a modern-day working mother. At the time of this photograph, she was appearing on screen at the Roxy Theater in *That Wonderful Urge* (1948), also starring Tyrone Power. *Bottom:* November 18, 1950. A candid shot at home, as Gene keeps her younger daughter, Christina, entertained in the kitchen.

133

Gene holds off a gang of escaped convicts in *The Secret of Convict Lake* (1951).

in scenery does not make for a change in a relationship. It was still two people who had drifted apart. Only now, they lived in Connecticut. Living there was a transportation nightmare for Oleg. He had to commute each day on the New Haven Railroad to work in the city.

Each morning Gene would drop Oleg off at the train station and then go about her day. Playing the role of suburban housewife was not for her. Gene was lost and it scared her. She would look for things to do around the house and not be able to find enough to occupy her day, let alone an entire week. Oleg would make the daily ride into the city, saying, that he would arrive at Grand Central Station with his brain feeling like a twisted pretzel. The "country life" was not for the Cassinis. They soon realized they were not cut out for that lifestyle. Before long, they moved back to the city.

By the end of 1951, Gene had completed four pictures. Oleg had tried to reason with her about continuously working, but she would hear none of it. As a businessman he would try to explain to her that at this stage in her career she should just sit back and read scripts with the intention of making one prestigious picture

10. The Ghost and Mrs. Muir

per year. On a financial level he would go on to tell her that the difference between making one picture and two pictures was a mere $17,000. At one time, early in their marriage, that $17,000 was needed to pay the rent and keep food on the table. Now, with Oleg successfully running his own design business, there was just no need for Gene to be so obsessive about taking every role that was thrown at her. Of course, the Tierney stub-

Right: A glamorous publicity still of Gene to promote *On the Riviera* (1951). *Bottom:* A lobby card from *Close to My Heart* (1951). Ray Milland and Gene play a married couple who adopt a baby only to find out (when it's too late) that their new child stems from a less than desirable family tree.

born streak once again kicked in. She had made up her mind already, and her decision overrode any sense that Oleg was talking.

In hindsight, he was right. The four movies that Gene threw herself into in 1951 are all quite forgettable. The third of those was *The Secret of Convict Lake*. Gene was to star with the legendary Ethel Barrymore. Working with such a screen legend as Barrymore was Gene's best memory of making that picture. The story is set in 1870s California. Jim Canfield (Glenn Ford) is convicted of a crime that he didn't commit. He plans an escape from his Nevada prison with several other inmates, and together they set out for the home of the man that framed him and the man who committed the crime. On their arrival they find that mainly women now occupy the small farming community. The men who live there have formed a posse and left the women behind while they search for the escapees. Jim soon falls for Marcia, played by Gene. The only problem is that Marcia is engaged to the man who framed him.

The last of the four films of 1951 saw her playing Midge Sheridan in *Close to My Heart*. Ray Milland plays Brad Sheridan, her husband, in what turns out to be a soppy melodrama about the adoption process. It does, however, have a twist involved. The happy couple finds out that their newly adopted baby's biological father is a convicted murderer. The question of whether or not such evil is a biological or environmental component is brought up. But not able to bear the thought of being separated from their baby, they decide it must be environmental, and they all live happily ever after. Unfortunately for Gene, "happily ever after" wasn't applicable in her real-life marriage.

11

Cassini vs. Hughes

By 1951, Gene and Oleg had technically been married for ten years. Five of those years were solid husband and wife years, with the other five consisting of separations, infidelities, an almost-divorce and a reconciliation. This was the classic roller coaster relationship with all of the love/hate emotions that prove destructive to the minds of both parties involved. As their relationship floundered it still didn't stop Oleg from being exceedingly jealous of another man showing his wife some attention. Oleg would often use his fists as his main tool to defend Gene's honor and mark his territory as *her* husband.

The most notorious was his "great chase" with Howard Hughes. During a time when Oleg and Gene were separated, Hughes had come back into Gene's life. Primarily it was to find help for Daria and then eventually to date Gene himself. One night, as Gene and Hughes drove into the driveway of her home, Oleg came running out of the darkness from behind a bush shouting, "What are you doing here, Howard? I'm going to beat the shit out of you!" Oleg was furious, and this time he wasn't about to use his fists. Hughes jumped back into his Pontiac just in time. Oleg was running straight for him with a piece of wood in hand! He had waited in the garage for at least two hours. He'd spent the first half-hour rummaging around looking for something to hit Hughes with, finally coming up with a piece of two-by-four. The rest of the time he paced and waited for those headlights to appear in the driveway so he could eliminate his rival once and for all. There was nothing that Gene could do. She stood in her driveway helpless as she watched Hughes speed off out of her driveway with Oleg in pursuit in his car not far behind him. She listened as tires screeched from blocks away.

Later she learned that they were both running red lights. Hughes focused on finding a retreat, and Oleg focused on ripping him from his car and beating him to a pulp. Hughes went straight for the Town House Hotel. He had a suite there and it was the closest safe haven that he had. That couple of minutes head start that he had on Oleg gave him just enough time to get out of his car and run for

A casual pose in the grass to promote *Way of a Gaucho* (1952).

the elevator. Oleg reached the elevator before the door had a chance to close, but Hughes was saved by two burly bodyguards who protected him from the enraged Cassini.

Beating on the door, Oleg was shouting, "Give me Hughes, I have an appointment with him." Eventually two more Hughes bodyguards wrestled Oleg to the floor and escorted him from the building. Realizing he was fighting a losing battle, Oleg's only tool now was his tongue. He had the last word as they escorted him out the front door. "Well give the bastard a message. Tell him to never walk alone in this town." With that said, Oleg was tossed out the front door. He at least felt proud of the last line he'd come up with. It sounded good and he meant every word of it.

The battle did not end there. Several weeks later Gene and Oleg went to a party. As they entered the hall, there in full view in the middle of the next room, as if he was put there especially for Oleg to see, was Hughes. He spotted Oleg just as Oleg spotted him, and they both started to run. Hughes went straight up the stairs with Oleg hot on his tail. He retreated to one of the bedrooms, locking the door behind

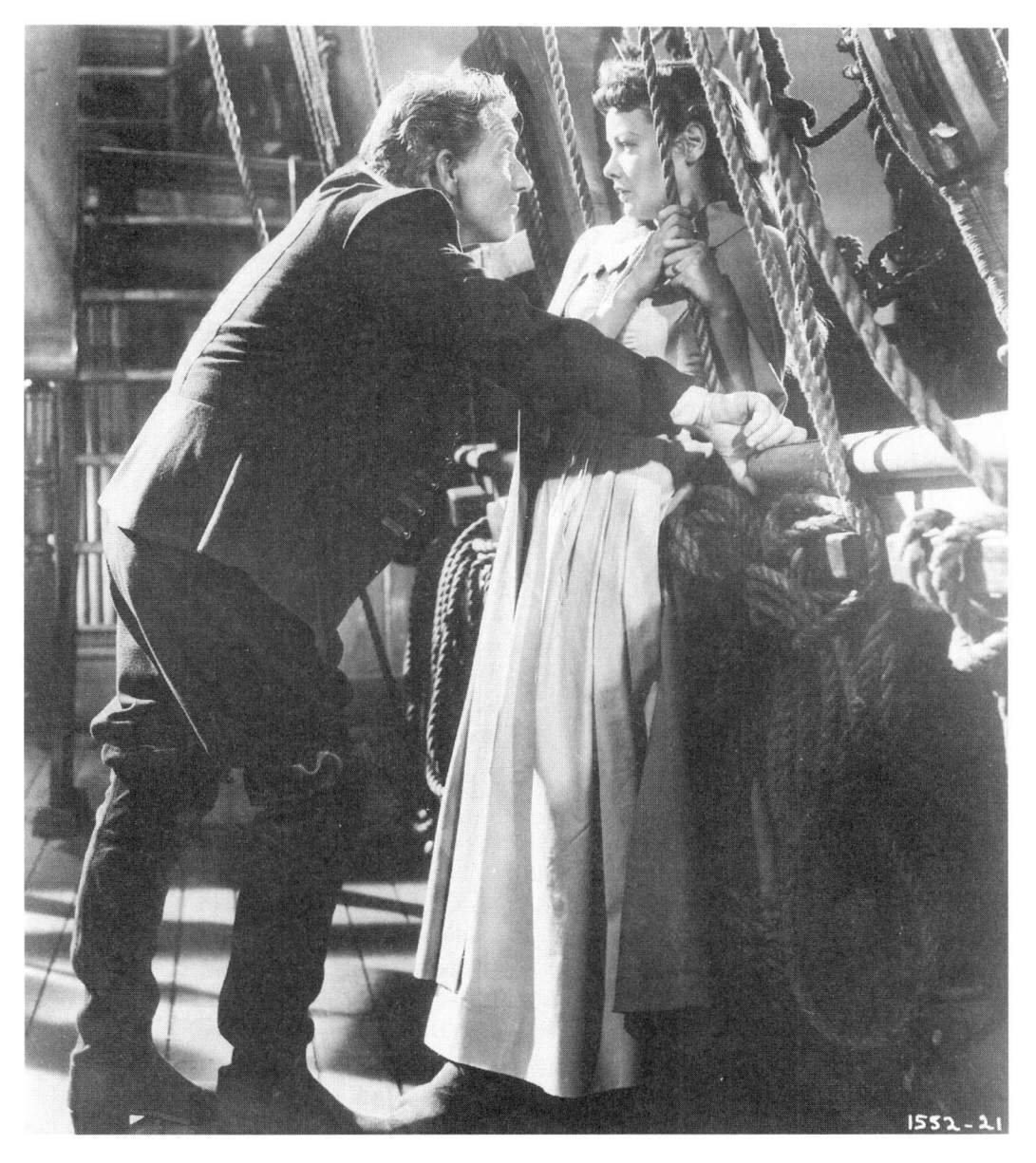

Gene is confronted by Spencer Tracy in *The Plymouth Adventure* (1952).

him. Oleg stood banging on the door, yelling, "Coward, coward," as he pounded harder and harder.

Oleg could hear Hughes talking on the telephone. Soon enough four burly bodyguards came to the rescue and escorted Hughes out of the bedroom and down the stairs. Oleg took the opportunity to taunt Hughes all the way down the stairs

Gene Tierney

Gene with Clark Gable in *Never Let Me Go* (1953).

until he was out of the building. Amazingly, perhaps stupidly, Hughes continued to pursue Gene, once telling her, "Do you realize you're married to a madman?!"

That same intense jealousy would also erupt in Gene. She would of course not react in the way that Oleg did, but the inner fire of jealousy brewed to the point of no return. Oleg now being the famous designer that he was, she would often see newspaper photographs of him with pretty girls and even prettier models. Opening up the morning paper and finding her husband photographed with a bevy of beauties did nothing but fill Gene's mind with thoughts of her husband's infidelities.

On both sides, the relationship would run hot and cold. Although each was still jealous at the thought of someone else being with the other, the trust between the two of them had obviously been eroded by life's temptations and misfortunes. It was time to say goodbye. They both knew it, years before. The finality of divorce is a hard prospect to face, especially when the two people involved genuinely *like* each other.

11. Cassini vs. Hughes

Gene studies her script for *Never Let Me Go* (1953), in which she plays a Russian ballerina in love with Clark Gable.

Gene Tierney

When Gene was cast in her next picture, *Way of a Gaucho*, to be shot on location in Argentina, she came to the realization that her marriage was coming to an end. She soon started to feel her grip on sanity, as she knew it, also coming to an end. This was the beginning of what would be the darkest of days. Nothing could prepare her for what lay ahead, nothing!

Shooting on *Way of a Gaucho* was to start in December of 1951. It would be a three-month location shoot in Argentina. The location choice paid off. The picturesque scenery of the Pampas and the Andes, along with the ancient Spanish buildings and churches, makes for a very enjoyable backdrop. Rory Calhoun plays Martin, the Gaucho outlaw, who Teresa, played by Gene, falls in love with. In short, this is another good girl falls for bad boy love story with breathtaking photography to complement the romance.

The studio agreed to pay for Oleg's plane ticket to enable him and Gene to be together. Even without the studio ticket, their finances at this point in life could easily have supported buying a ticket to Argentina. Even on the free ticket, Oleg did not make the trip. Instead he stayed behind in New York to work on his spring collection. Oleg had once again tried to discourage Gene from taking the role to begin with. "It's a silly picture and will do nothing for you as an actress!" he yelled.

She did not take his advice and once again agreed to do the picture. The marriage was already on the brink of collapse, and now a location shoot in another country was the final blow.

Gene continually insisted that Oleg join her in Argentina and Oleg continually argued that he must stay behind and work. "If you don't come, I'm going to divorce you," Gene said. Oleg stood firm and called her bluff. "That will be your decision, not mine," he said. "I'm not going." Oleg didn't back down, and Gene's threat was no bluff. She went to Argentina and upon her return filed for divorce, for a second time.

Gene's mental stability started to slip as she filmed *Way of a Gaucho*. She was working with newcomer Rory Calhoun. It was his first film role. For the first time in her career she was starting to become the "disagreeable actress."

Gene with José Iturbi at a Hollywood party, circa 1948.

11. Cassini vs. Hughes

Gene in costume as Marva, the Russian ballerina, in *Never Let Me Go* (1953).

Gene and Clarence Brown, producer of MGM's *Never Let Me Go* (1953), go over an album of stills taken for *Plymouth Adventure*, another movie he produced.

She was moody, brooding and jumpy with everyone around her. No one was spared from this uncharacteristic behavior. The hairdresser suddenly took too long to do her hair. The crew was talking too much between scenes, and the director was against her from the beginning. She felt that everyone was talking about her, and she wrote long and rambling letters home to Oleg about how disliked she was with everyone involved in the picture.

This was not the Gene that Oleg knew. He started to see a change that concerned him terribly. Gene was showing classic signs of neurotic behavior. Neuroticism was a word commonly used in the acting profession, but Oleg knew Gene well enough to know that she did not fit into the category of "neurotic actress." Yet what was he to do?

He considered leaving his business and flying to her, but then he would no doubt lose his business through sheer neglect on his part. His only attempt at keep-

11. Cassini vs. Hughes

November 6, 1952. During a break from filming on *Never Let Me Go* (1953), Clark Gable (left), Bernard Miles and Richard Hadyn (right) place bets on whether Gene will ever get through the sandwich the caterers have given her for lunch.

ing both his business and Gene was to write her equally long and rambling letters in return. He would plead with her to come home to him so they could work things out. He begged her forgiveness for his not being on location with her and again tried as kindly and as tenderly as he could to explain to her the importance of his spring collection. Tina had once again traveled with her nurse to Argentina to be with her mother on location. Three months of a child's life is a long time, and Gene wanted her daughter with her as often as possible.

The production broke after the first few weeks to celebrate Christmas. The holiday was spent in Buenos Aires. It was to be a Christmas without Oleg. During one of these holiday parties, Gene had her first encounter with Prince Aly Khan. She knew of his reputation. He was commonly labeled the "Playboy Prince" by the media. You would have to have been on another planet not to know of this man and his conquests. He had recently been featured in newspapers for his recent

Gene in the costume she wears for the Scheherezade ballet, one of the three that are danced in the film *Never Let Me Go* (1953). Because of the intense training for the grueling dance sequences, Gene's co-star, Clark Gable, bought her a cream to help soothe her aching feet during production.

11. Cassini vs. Hughes

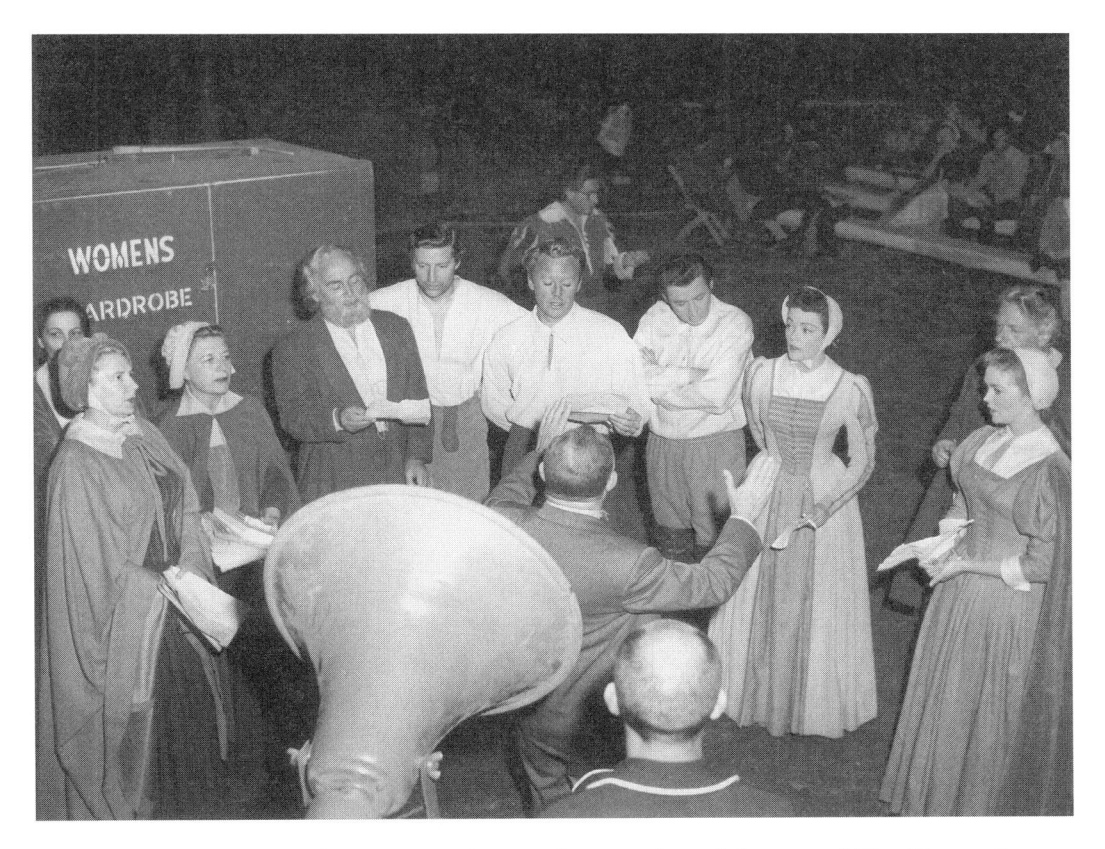

Studio voice coach Arthur Rosenstein gets the attention of the cast of *The Plymouth Adventure* (1952). ***Left to right:*** Elizabeth Flournoy (partially hidden), Kathleen Lockhart, Ivis Goulding, Barry Jones, Keith McConnell, Van Johnson, Leo Genn, Gene Tierney, Dawn Addams and Murray Matheson (partially hidden). Spencer Tracy, not pictured, is the lead actor in the film, which tells the story of the *Mayflower*'s voyage in 1620.

divorce from actress Rita Hayworth, with whom he had a daughter, Yasmin. Although Gene wasn't impressed with Aly (she thought him to look like a thinner version of Orson Welles), his impression of Gene was quite the opposite.

As was the case with most men in her company, she mesmerized him. His pursuit of her that evening did nothing to impress her, and she left the party alone. Being rejected by a woman was something new to Aly, and Gene's aloofness only caused him to want her more.

As soon as the holidays were over she went back to making her picture. Upon completion of the film in February of 1952, she returned to the United States and did as she had promised to do before she left for Argentina three months before. She filed for divorce. Gene's rocky marriage to Oleg was over. Even with the real-

Gene Tierney

In her dressing room for *The Plymouth Adventure* (1952), Gene entertains real life brothers Owen (left) and Jeffrey Pritchard, who play brothers in the film.

ization of her marriage ending and her own apparent erratic behavior, Gene continued to throw herself into her work.

Upon her return home she was loaned out to MGM for the making of *The Plymouth Adventure*. She was to star alongside Spencer Tracy. He was cast as a ship's captain with whom Gene's character falls in love. The story follows the English settlers of the 17th century who traveled from England to New England on the Mayflower. Spencer Tracy plays Captain Christopher Jones and Gene plays the pioneer woman Dorothy Bradford, who although married, falls in love with him.

The film was released on November 28, 1952. The special effects team of A. Arnold Gillespie, Warren Newcombe and Irving G. Ries all won an Academy Award for Best Special Effects in a Motion Picture of 1953. Producer Clarence Brown offered Gene a role in his next picture, *Never Let Me Go*. Having just finished directing Gene in *The Plymouth Adventure*, he thought her to be the perfect Russian ballerina in his next project.

11. Cassini vs. Hughes

A candid shot of Gene with her co-star of the moment, Clark Gable, on the beach at Gunwalloe Cove in England. With the help of their four-legged co-star, Juno, the Great Dane, they're taking a break from filming MGM's *Never Let Me Go* (1953).

Gene Tierney

Gene accepted the role and flew to London to begin shooting. It was to be one of the most demanding roles of her career. She endured six weeks of intense training, two hours of dance practice a day in order to master a few simple ballet steps to get her through the film as a "believable enough" ballerina. Her teacher was Anton Dolin, one of the great dance instructors. Gene had a new respect for the ballet after her grueling training schedule was completed. It took six weeks of training to master getting up on her toes and completing a few simple turns for close-up shots. Thankfully for Gene, the Russian ballerina Natalie Leslie doubled for her in long shots.

As filming began, take after take took its toll on Gene's feet. Before too long her feet were covered in blisters. Her ankles ached day and night. Clark Gable starred alongside Gene and was a very considerate co-star. One weekend he flew to Paris and came back with an ointment that he picked up on his travels to help her feet. Gene would try anything to relieve the pain, and the cream did give her some immediate relief. She was thankful for Gable's concern and would often listen to stories of how much he still missed his third wife, Carole Lombard. Gene described him as a kind, gentle man, guarded by a tough, macho exterior. He would exude those same real life characteristics in many of his on screen roles.

Never Let Me Go is the story of an American news writer, Philip Sutherland (Gable), who has been stationed in Moscow since the war. He falls in love with a Russian ballerina, Marva Lamarkins, played by Gene. After he finds out that she learned the English language in order to communicate after falling in love with him, they rush to the American embassy and marry. Life seems perfect for the newlyweds until Sutherland (Gable) tries to bring his new wife out of Russia and into the United States. Communist

September 26, 1953, Nice, France. In the midst of their whirlwind affair, Prince Aly Khan is photographed at a party with Gene. In an eerie echo of her earlier relationship with John F. Kennedy, the prince eventually chose duty over love, yielding to his father's threats to cut him off entirely if he considered marrying another actress. The prince was previously married to actress Rita Hayworth.

11. Cassini vs. Hughes

Russia holds her captive, and he is forced to temporarily leave her behind while he figures out a way of smuggling his bride into his country of freedom.

Gable's kindness toward Gene during her times of emotional and physical torment no doubt helped her complete the picture. In fact, during the pre-diagnosis of her mental condition she could not have been cast with a more sincere group of leading men. Her mood swings were still occurring, often triggered by memories that should have pleased her rather than angering her. During filming, Gene, Gable and Gene's mother (who was on location with her) walked into the dining room of the hotel where they were staying. In an honorary gesture the band started to play the theme song from *Laura*. Belle Tierney nudged her daughter, prompting her to smile at the kind gesture, but Gene stood cold. "Why are they making fun of me?" she asked. "They are only making fun of me," she said as she took her seat. Strange comments like that one were starting to become more frequent. What's more, Gene was aware of her mood changes, but she continued to go on working. Work was her medicine, or so she thought.

12

From Countess to Princess?

It wasn't long before Gene and Aly Khan would cross paths again, this time at a party at the home of her friends Fran and Ray Stark. The two were more or less thrown together. The Starks insisted they'd be perfect together and kept arranging double dates for the four of them. Aly was a charming man, then the son of the world's richest monarch, the Aga Khan. It seemed strange that Aly would fight for his independence from his father but at the same time draw on the half million dollar income that was provided for him.

His father's money supported his lifestyle. He loved the money and he loved the lifestyle, but he wanted his independence at the same time. Even when pushing for his own independence he would still look for his father's constant approval. It was a seesawing trait that would eventually force him to make a choice among money, power and love.

Gene and Aly soon became inseparable. They would travel everywhere together, all over Europe, back to the United States and on to London. This whirlwind romance was so intense that Gene would not make another picture in 1953. For the first time in a long time she was turning down scripts and enjoying the jet set lifestyle. Literally speaking, she had found her Prince Charming.

Months rolled by like days. Gene was in love, but she would still have a fight on her hands. Most people did not meet their relationship with approval. One of those people was Oleg Cassini. Although divorced, Gene and Oleg remained close friends. They still had a small daughter to raise, and unlike the majority of divorced couples, there was no animosity between either of them about their failed marriage. They stayed in constant contact, with Gene even calling Oleg for advice. Gene decided to confess her love for Aly during one telephone conversation. As usual, Oleg did not hold back in his criticism. "Look," he said, "you are destined for your doom. You are not going to transform this sybaritic Oriental prince into a good Connecticut Yankee."

Once again his advice went unheeeded. Oleg had not said what Gene had

12. From Countess to Princess?

wanted to hear, so she called the next person who she thought would support her. Finally, after hearing Oleg's concerns being echoed by others, she decided to just go with her own feelings and continue her relationship with the Playboy Prince, with or without the approval of her family and friends.

Gene returned to work in the spring of 1954. She would make the trip back to London for the location shoot of *Personal Affair* for United Artists. Aly went in his own directions on business, eventually flying back to London near the film's completion to be with her. The filming did not go well. Gene was a perfectionist; whether it was a good performance or a bad performance, the one thing that she could count on was remembering her lines. Suddenly, as if she'd lost the ability overnight, she just couldn't remember her lines. She would stare at her script, knowing what she had to say, but when it came time for the script to be taken away, there was nothing. Her mind was blank.

A publicity photograph of Gene to promote *Personal Affair* (1953).

Concerned, she called in a psychiatrist, the same doctor who had treated Vivien Leigh for many years. Gene told him of her problems. "I just can't go on," she said. After looking at her for several moments without a word, he all of a sudden said, "Tell me what *you* think the problem is." Her response was surprising. "I'm involved with a certain man," she said, "and ... I'm not happy about it." The doctor nodded and scribbled something down on his pad, and they continued to talk. After several minutes of small talk he got up and left the room. There was no explanation, no diagnosis, nothing. Gene had reached out for help and received no answers in return. It was a bizarre reaction for a doctor to have with a patient who was voluntarily pleading for answers.

She continued to struggle through the picture, but her memory was getting worse. Gene's maid, Ruby, who had traveled with her on previous pictures, would sit up with her into the night and rehearse her lines. "You are going to do it Miss Tierney," she would say. "We will go over these lines until you repeat them in your

A scene from *Black Widow* (1954). Gene is pictured here with Van Heflin.

sleep." Gene gave full credit to Ruby for getting her through that picture. Without her help she would have no doubt given up. Although she was still struggling to work and pushing herself to complete picture after picture, she was only putting off the inevitable. It would not be possible for her to break through this darkness without a doctor's intervention. Upon completion of the picture, Aly and Gene flew to France for a break. Their romance continued, now more serious, with talk of marriage.

Gene had spent 18 months in Europe. Part of the reason was Aly, and the other reason was monetary. The government had passed a bill making all wages earned during a set 18-month period tax-free as long as you agreed to live overseas. Gene needed to save as much money as possible. Taxes were high, and avoiding them was enough of a lure to leave the United States for a year and a half to qualify for the exemption.

Gene was paying for Daria's long term care, and she had calculated what she thought it would cost to maintain Daria in the institution. She had estimated it to be at least $280,000 to guarantee her lifetime care. Any money saved was to go

12. From Countess to Princess?

Gene in full costume for her role of Baketamon in *The Egyptian* (1954).

Gene Tierney

A beautiful outfit showcases Gene to perfection in this candid shot of her outdoors. Just look at those bare feet and red toenails, a daring statement for its day.

12. From Countess to Princess?

toward that amount, but upon her return to the United States after serving her 18 months in Europe, she was told a different story. During her time abroad the exemption dates had been adjusted in such a way that she now no longer qualified for the exemption. No money was saved, and all taxes had to be paid the following year.

Again, Gene went back to the safe haven of Connecticut to spend Christmas with her family. Aly had already presented her with a massive six-carat emerald cut diamond ring, flanked by masses of smaller stones. The Hollywood rumor mill was buzzing with reports of the future marriage of the prince and the movie star. After the holiday festivities Gene had agreed to start work on her new picture, *The Black Widow*; her co-stars would be Van Heflin and Ginger Rogers. Rogers was coincidentally the cousin of Aly's ex-wife, Rita Hayworth.

With Aly flying around the world on business, he would call Gene when he could and fly in and out to see her as often as possible. Gene was again having problems remembering her lines. Her mind would now go blank with the name of a person she had known for years. She would wake up after dreaming that Daria was with her and walk the house looking for her. Despite her mounting problems, Gene managed to hold herself together, reporting for work on time and getting through her days the best way she could. Her symptoms were now increasingly worse, but still she continued to soldier on.

She had once again no sooner finished one picture before moving on to the next. This time it was the exotic tale *The Egyptian*. When it came to work she would be no more than a shell of a person repeating lines that were programmed into her. She was falling apart, and she herself knew it. She recognized this change in herself, and it scared her. It was the people around her who were in denial. Aly refused to believe anything was seriously wrong. He would tell her she only needed to rest on a quiet farm somewhere for a few weeks. Her mother thought the only therapy she needed was retail therapy. "All you need are some pretty new French dresses," she would say.

Although Gene was openly wearing Aly's ring, it did not set their relationship in concrete. There was opposition from all sides. The most influential came from the Aga Khan himself. It was to be déjà vu for Gene. Just as her parents had opposed her marriage to Oleg, this time it was Aly's father, the Aga Khan, opposing Aly's marriage to Gene.

After Aly's divorce from Rita Hayworth, the Aga Khan lost all contact with his granddaughter, Yasmin. She was the first girl baby to be born into the Khan family for 200 years. Hayworth's preventing Yasmin from seeing her grandfather had given the Aga Khan a bad perception of all actresses. The thought of his son and heir contemplating marrying another actress was enough to threaten him with the absolute worst. The ultimatum hit both of them hard. If Aly married Gene, the Aga Khan would strip him of all money and future political power. He would cut him off completely. The Aga Khan refused to even meet with Gene. He did not want another actress entering the Khan family and that was that!

Their romance was a whirlwind. It was exciting while it lasted, but it was not real enough for Aly to choose love over responsibility. Prince Aly Khan lost the love of his life out of respect for his father's feelings and respect for a country that he would some day rule. Sadly, the sacrifice of love did nothing for Aly's future as leader. In 1957 when the Aga Khan passed away, he bypassed Aly completely in his will and gave the title to Aly's son, Karim, by his first marriage. After 45 years, Karim Khan still reigns as the fourth Aga Khan, the title meaning "Great Chief."

By 1960, Aly Khan was dead. Sometime between May 12 and 13, Aly's Lancia sports car careened out of control in Paris, France. He was killed instantly. His model girlfriend, Bettina, who was traveling in the car with him, survived the crash. Gene was eating breakfast with her mother when they read of the accident. She thought back to the many times that she had been a passenger with Aly at the wheel. He would often speed around corners on two wheels. She was saddened but not surprised to read of Aly's demise in this tragic way. After reading the article, Gene's mother put down the paper, looked at Gene and simply said, "You're lucky you weren't with him."

In her next picture, Gene could not have wished for a better co-star than Humphrey Bogart. *The Left Hand of God* was to be her fourth picture while fighting the troubling signs of an illness that was plaguing her every thought. Coincidentally, Bogart had a sister who suffered with a mental illness, and as much as Gene held herself together, Bogart knew the telltale signs, and he saw them in Gene. With nothing but concern, Bogart went to the studio heads and told them Gene needed urgent medical treatment. She was sick and she needed someone to intervene. Once again, thinking as studios do, they assured Bogart that Gene would continue through whatever demon she was battling because that's the professional that she was. Their only advice to him was to be gentle and understanding. He carried Gene throughout the film, helping her with her lines, even feeding them to her when needed. At the time of filming, Bogart had his own unknown demon to contend with. He had terminal cancer. It was yet to be diagnosed.

Upon completion of *The Left Hand of God*, Gene fled to New York. She was living in an apartment with her mother in the city. Belle Tierney was always quick with the exact word, and sometimes the not quite exact word to throw at any snooping reporter. It didn't matter; Gene was unfit to answer questions, so she gladly allowed her mother to deal with the prying phone calls and constant questions. Belle did a marvelous job at keeping the press under control, all while her daughter was losing control of her mind. Eventually it became too much; the phone would ring constantly. There was no other choice but to have it disconnected.

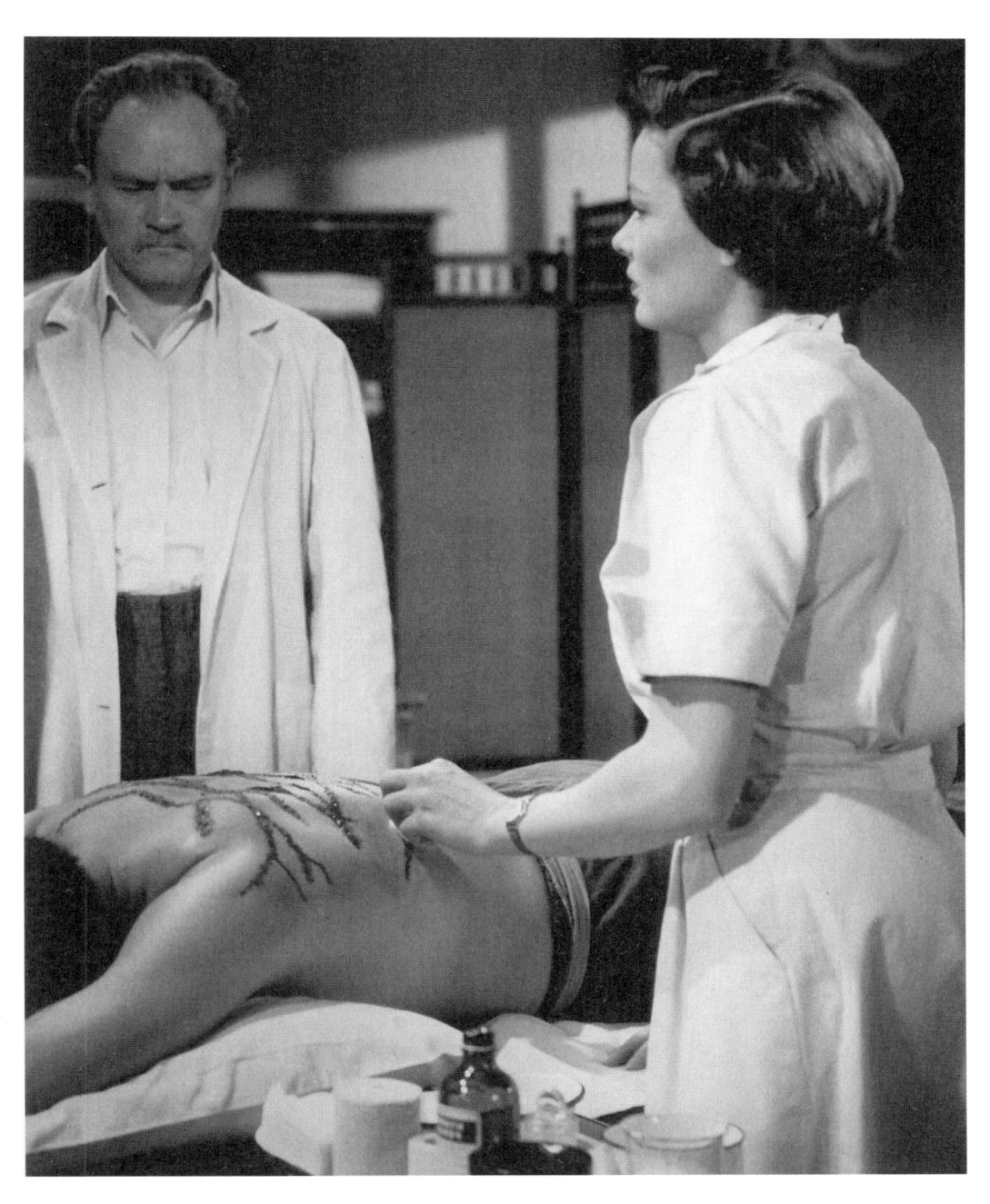

In a scene from *The Left Hand of God* (1954), Gene attends a patient in need. It was her last film before becoming a patient herself, for real. She later recalled her doctors going to see the completed film, just to see if they could spot her illness within her performance. They couldn't. She was flawless when playing a character. It was playing the role of Gene Tierney that she could no longer cope with.

Gene Tierney

The studio, showing no sympathy at all, put Gene on suspension. All of a sudden their agreeable, moneymaking star was turning down script after script, and they didn't like it. They refused to believe she was ill and decided her new attitude would have to be punished by a suspension. Gene didn't care. Work was the least of her concerns. At first, her family hoped that Gene's illness would be something she would just shake off, so the media were led to believe that she had a strong case of the flu and was simply finding it hard to regain her full strength. If only it were that simple. Gene's illness progressed to the point of her not stepping in front of a movie camera for seven long years.

13

The Darkest of Days

Days and nights were spent in the New York apartment. Gene would sit for hours in a chair with an unread book opened on her lap. It then progressed to hours and hours of sleep. At its worst she would sleep for two to three days on end. Gene did not have the energy to stay awake. Sleep was her salvation.

One New York paper reported seeing Gene sitting alone at a table in a nightclub. There she would sit, putting her gloves on and then taking them off again, one finger at a time, as if she were doing it for the first time upon entering the room. Over and over she would put the gloves on and take the gloves off. The idea that a columnist from a newspaper sat and watched Gene lose her mind in a public place and feel that it was his/her job to write the article as a news piece is beyond comprehension.

With the recent breakup with Aly Khan, the media soon blamed that as the sole cause of her mental collapse. It appeared to be the last "emotional" event before the collapse happened, but it was happening a long time before Aly had even entered Gene's life. Belle Tierney decided it was best to go back to their grass roots. Again it was time to return to Connecticut. It seemed almost ritualistic for the Tierney family to flock back to that state when trouble was brewing. Once there, Gene's family suspected that she was faking her illness. She may have been an actress, but this was no act. Gene's brother, Butch, honestly believed something was seriously wrong. Hoping the family minister could help, he immediately sent for him. The minister did not stay long. "The girl needs a doctor," he said, as he walked out the door.

The next day the family left for Cape Cod. A well-known psychiatrist had a summer home there, and he had agreed to see Gene, interrupting his vacation to do so. Gene recalls the meeting with the doctor being only minutes. In fact the meeting lasted most of the afternoon. Gene's sense of time was affected. Her entire memory was affected. She would have a conversation one minute and forget it moments after it occurred. The only recollections that Gene had of the meeting

Gene Tierney

was of him asking her who it was she trusted. She said she trusted no one. She had a terrible fear that the Communists were out to get her. She even stayed guarded when talking to the doctor. In her mind she truly believed that he was out to get her like the rest of them.

She would hallucinate and see things that weren't happening. She could look at a friend as they spoke and instead think she was watching the friend make a face at her. Everything of reality was distorted. This was the world that Gene Tierney's mind had entered. This strangeness was now her reality. The doctor in Cape Cod referred Gene to yet another doctor, who was right across the street from Gene's New York apartment. The family packed up and went back to New York, hoping that this new doctor would have some much-needed answers.

It took only one session with Gene for the New York doctor to admit her to a sanitarium. She was to go to the Harkness Pavilion. There she would undergo the first series of many electric shock therapy treatments. At the time, electric shock therapy was considered something of a scientific breakthrough. The doctors performing the treatments knew just as much about its effect on the brain as the patients they were performing it on. In other words, not much. It was developed in Italy in 1938 and commonly used there to treat severe depression, even schizophrenia. There was talk of long term harm, but since it was now an approved treatment the doctors were using it as flippantly as they would prescribe a pill.

The patient is strapped down on their back to a flat table. In the event of the patient vomiting the table can be spun upside down to prevent the patient from choking on their vomit. The patient is given a muscle relaxant. An electrode is attached to the patient's temples

An older, more pensive Gene in the 1950s. This photograph is a telling sign of the pain that Gene hid for so long. If the eyes are "the windows to the soul," Gene is a lost soul at this sitting. She genuinely looks sad.

13. The Darkest of Days

and an alternating current of 80 to 90 volts is passed between the two electrodes for a split second. The procedure sends the patient into a seizure triggered by the electric shock to the brain. Most patients awaken from the procedure with a severe headache and no memory of what has occurred.

During the early days of the procedure the muscle relaxant wasn't administered before the shock was given. The result was patients dislocating and fracturing bones with their violent seizures. The muscle relaxant before the procedure was developed to prevent the body from violently jerking around and doing the patient physical harm. With the muscles of the patient being in a relaxed state, the only way of knowing if the patient is convulsing is by looking at the twitching of the patient's toes. If the toes are twitching the patient is convulsing, a sure sign the treatment is working effectively.

The results have the patient coming out of the treatment in an amnesia like state. The theory is that you will cease to be depressed if you can't remember what you were depressed about to begin with. That line is true, but if the depression is triggered by a chemical imbalance in the brain, no amount of electric shock therapy is going to remedy the depression. The patient is depressed without knowing why. In such cases there are no bad memories to erase, only good ones.

More often than not patients would lose all memory of pleasant family events or happy times they had experienced, simply because it was erased from their brain through the course of electric shock therapy. There was no way of picking and choosing what memories would be lost or retained. It was random erasing of all memories. In some cases, where only one or two shock therapy treatments were given, certain memories that the patient once had would be lost forever. In Gene's case, after an unbelievably high number of 32 shock treatments, years of her life were erased from her mind.

As with most patients, Gene was not told of the aftereffects and possible long-term side effects of such a radical treatment. Even if she had been told, she was not in a fit mental condition to sign papers and agree to the treatment being performed. Gene's mother signed the consent papers. She would tell Gene she had no memory of signing them, let alone reading the fine print. Gene's aftereffects from her many treatments left Belle Tierney racked with guilt for many years. Gene's reaction to her treatment was strong. She had no memory of where she was, no memory of why she was even there. She recognized no one, not even her own family. It was now the job of the doctors and nurses in the sanitarium to tell her why she was there and whom she was supposed to recognize. As if she were a robot, they set about to reprogram her mind after erasing the memories of times past.

Temporarily the shock treatment worked — the key word being "temporarily." The shock treatment scrambles the brain to the point of the patient's not really knowing where they are. Gene's mother left the sanitarium after the first of Gene's

Gene Tierney

Although she initially had "no cheesecake" poses written into her first film contract, Gene did quite a few during her career. This photograph of Gene (probably taken in the late forties) in her leopard skin bathing costume with a real life leopard on a leash is one of the more risqué poses of her career. It was later realized that a contributing factor to Gene's illness was her lack of the ability to say no. She would say yes to everything, loading her life with more than she could handle. No doubt the swimsuit poses that she eventually agreed to was another example of her saying yes to something she once felt strongly about not doing. Studio pressure to do what the other starlets were doing made Gene reconsider.

13. The Darkest of Days

many shock therapy treatments and was prematurely pleased with the results that she saw in her. "I don't understand how Gene got better so quickly," she said to Gene's brother, Butch. "It was like the twinkling of an eye." Butch knew better. He had done his homework and knew that Gene's new outlook on life would not last. He was right.

The doctors had scheduled Gene for a series of eight shock therapy treatments, all a week apart. Each session gave her the same elated feeling after it was performed, and each left her feeling flat and depressed once they had worn off. It was a short-term solution with long-term side effects. The doctors prescribed cocktails of drugs for her to take in between the shock therapy sessions. She was introduced to psychotherapy, in which she was encouraged to talk and talk and talk some more, all while a doctor sat across from her and nodded, agreeing to her ramblings. The theory behind psychotherapy is to allow you to talk out your own problems, the result being you'll eventually talk the answer out for yourself.

The next step was taking Gene to the Institute for Living in Hartford, Connecticut. Gene's medical file had been transferred to the chief psychiatrist there. He met with Gene, Pat and Butch as they arrived on the morning of check-in. Belle Tierney could not bring herself to accept that her daughter was being institutionalized. She chose not to attend the day that Gene was admitted.

The psychiatrist asked Gene how she spent her time. "Cleaning the kitchen floor," she answered. That was no lie. Whenever she felt anxious or unnerved she would get down on her hands and knees and scrub the floor. Once that was done she would clean anything else in sight until she was so utterly exhausted she would just fall into bed and sleep.

He smiled and continued, "You know Miss Tierney, in order for us to help you, you must stay with us for a while."—

"You can't force me to stay," Gene said. "My family has already agreed that I will not be admitted against my will."

The conversation continued. "No one wants to force you," the doctor said reassuringly, "but your mother is tired. It would give her a rest while you relaxed with us. We can work on your problem and you might even have fun." His speech was good enough for Gene to agree to at least try it. Still maintaining her sense of humor as she signed herself in, she asked, "Do you have any floors I can scrub?"

As soon as Pat and Butch had left Gene alone, she began to panic. She wanted to go home with them. She wanted to go back to her mother and be safe in their Connecticut home, just as she was when she was a little girl. The doctors and nurses refused to let her use the phone. Gene sat on the inner steps of the building, crying and pleading for someone to call her brother to rescue her. Finally, she was pulled to her feet and led to her room. She was pushed through the door of her new home. One tiny room. She listened, terrified, as the key turned on the other side of the door, locking her in like a wild animal.

She was confined to a room no bigger than a standard prison cell. The doors were locked, and the windows were barred. She could manage only to get one finger underneath the window and raise it not more than an inch without the confines of the bar stopping it from going any farther. It was the middle of winter, icy cold outside and blazing hot with artificial heat inside. There was no in-between. Gene's claustrophobic feelings of being locked in were making her even hotter. She would sit, huddled by the window, lifting it to its one inch limit, as she sucked in as much of the cool air from the outside world that she possibly could. That was Gene's first night in her new home. This was the very same place that the check in psychiatrist told her she "might even have fun" in.

Over the next few weeks Gene wasn't allowed any contact with her family at all. She was not allowed to use the phone to call out, and she had no idea what her family would be told about her if they were to make a call in. When she asked if her family had called, she was ignored. During that time of isolation, she was given five more electric shock therapy treatments. Her psychotherapy sessions were still in progress, and she was required to swallow a daily pill, all while the nurse watched over her. Her mouth would be checked when she was finished to ensure she had swallowed each one.

During the last of that series of electric shock therapy treatments, a nurse took Gene for a walk around the grounds. She was drifting in and out of a dreamlike state but became aware enough at the right time to notice a gate was open in the distance. Gene somehow found enough strength to break free from the nurse, and she ran straight for the gate. This was her chance to escape. She ran and ran and ran. She heard voices yelling, "Stop!" behind her but she continued to run.

She had no recollection of how far away the shops were from the institute, but before long she found herself standing in the middle of a store. She had intended to plead with the sales assistant to call her brother for her, but before she could even speak her nurse appeared in the doorway. She was out of breath and moving toward her. Gene took a step back as the nurse took a step forward. "I'll go with you," Gene said, "but don't you touch me! Don't try to put a straitjacket on me. Don't put a hand on me!" It wasn't long before several other staff members joined the nurse. They all agreed to Gene's demands, not wanting to upset her for fear of a scene in the store. Slowly and calmly she was walked back to the institute and once again locked in her cell. The cell they called her *room*.

Gene all of a sudden became the topic of most conversations back at the institute. She was the one who had dared to escape the confines of this human zoo. Her daring escape attempt was after she had been there for three long weeks. At the six-week point, and with no more escape attempts, the doctors decided to allow

13. The Darkest of Days

Gene visitation with her family. She was thrilled at the thought of seeing everyone again. The hospital would arrange the visits. It would be a weekly treat, and something that Gene would look forward to more than anything she ever had done before.

Butch came first with his wife, Jane. Then it would be Pat's turn with her four children. They were allowed to take her to lunch in the outside world and then bring her back by a certain time. She would constantly plead with them to just take her home. Her stories of how she was treated were told to them in the hope they would see that taking her home was the best thing for them to do for her. In the most coherent manner she would talk to them about wanting to leave the institute. She felt she was well, she felt she could now function in the outside world again. Gene's family thought she was in the best place to treat her condition. Only when the doctors told them she could be released would they be willing to take her home. Then and only then.

For now, Gene had to be content with her weekly visits, something she would look forward to for the next eight months. During that time she underwent 19 shock treatments, a total of 32 in all. As her treatments progressed she would suffer with more severe side effects than her usual headache and vagueness of what had happened to her. She was now to the point of being physically ill, constantly vomiting after each treatment until she was as weak as a newborn lamb.

After coming out of one anesthesia, Gene got her revenge on the nurse that had put her under. The nurse was standing over her, looking at her closely to see if she had fully awakened. With the nurse's face being the first that she saw and recognized, Gene shouted, "How dare you let them do that to me!" She made a fist and with all the strength left in her, she whacked the nurse right in the eye. It was the first time she had retaliated with such violence. The always accepting Gene Tierney had suddenly struck back, and the revenge felt good, at the time.

The pleasure of that one brief moment was not worth the punishment. The nurse, a large burly woman, yanked Gene from the bed and pulled her along the corridors until she got to a large room with, of course, yet another locked door. She pushed Gene in and locked the door behind her. After just coming out of the anesthesia of the last electric shock treatment and now having to deal with her constant nausea, this was the last place she wanted to be.

The room was like a pit of madness, the place where the worst cases were kept and hidden from the world. There were men and women rocking back and forth on the floor. Some were pacing and others were twitching uncontrollably. Some were shaking, talking and screaming, all of them fearing their own demons, all of them having slipped far beyond the realm of sanity as we know it, all of them stuck in that world forever!

Gene was left in the ward for hours. That was the first stage of her punishment. The same nurse came back for her and once again grabbed her arm. "Now I have something else for you!" she yelled. Taking her once again down the corridor, she led her to another door, of course again locked. This could not have been called a room at all. It was nothing more than a dark hole. It was a cold damp box with a door. There was no window, no toilet, and no running water. Nothing!

It wasn't a place fit for an animal, let alone a human being, yet this was to be stage two of Gene's punishment. She was locked in and left. Gene pounded on the door, crying and begging for someone to let her out. Still having no real sense of time, she had no idea of how long it was that she was locked in "the box." Eventually she was led back to her own section, back to her own private cell. She never thought she'd be so happy to again see the place they called "her room."

After 18 long months of being prodded, poked, analyzed, tortured and experimented on like a lab rat, Gene was released into her mother's custody. With the help of her mother and Tina, Gene would try to rebuild her life in the New York apartment they shared on 57th Street. It was a long road ahead; the electric shock treatments even erased what foods she once liked from her memory. She would taste everything as if she were doing it for the first time. It was as though she had started life again. In some strange way it was like being reborn.

14

The Ledge of Insanity

Sadly, it was within those first few weeks of freedom that Gene gradually began to slip back again. Her days would be spent sleeping. She could not get up. She was exhausted. She wasn't medicated. Her lethargy was her way of not coping with the world, not wanting to cope or even being able to cope. It was all too hard, and sleep was her salvation.

Gene's mother would take care of Tina, get her off to school and do her best to wake Gene and get her dressed before Tina came home again. Belle Tierney would use guilt to motivate her daughter. "At least get up for your daughter," she would say. Gene would simply roll over and go right back to sleep again. Getting up and getting dressed was a task that seemed impossible. Even if she managed it she would just move to a chair and stare at the wall in front of her.

In an attempt to jolly Gene out of her depression, her mother thought of asking Gene to do something for her. To make her feel useful she asked Gene to go to the grocery store for her. "I can't," Gene said. "You mean you won't!" her mother replied. "Please, mother, I mean I can't," Gene responded. Frustrated and tired, Belle Tierney headed toward the door. "I'll do the shopping myself," she said angrily. Just before she closed the door, she hesitated and stuck her head back in for one last word. "What are you, Gene? Are you sick or just lazy? You know you're not being a good mother." With that she closed the door and left for the grocery store.

Gene was not responding. There was no way of conversing with her, but she could still hear, and she heard every word her mother had just said. The words struck her hard. She started to think she was useless. Yes, she was a bad mother and, yes, maybe she wasn't sick at all, just lazy. With every last drop of energy Gene sat up in bed, swung her legs around and touched her feet to the floor. She stood, put on her housecoat and slippers and walked, dazed, into the living room, where she raised the window.

The ledge was no more than two feet wide, but in an instant she was standing out there on it. Her arms were pressed to the wall behind her. Her fingers dug into the mortar. It was the only grip on life that she now had. As the wind brushed her face she looked down to the busy New York Street below her. She was 14 stories up from the world, out on a ledge and ready to jump. Within a few seconds her pain would be gone forever. The feeling of knowing she had that instant cure in her own hands gave her a sense of calm that she hadn't felt in a long time.

She looked down and watched as people bustled by. Some got into cabs, others talked, and there she stood 14 stories up and watched others plow through life without any one of those people looking up to see her about to end hers. She hadn't had one clear thought in months, but suddenly she remembered what her actress friend Constance Collier had once told her. "Sometimes, when you get up in a plane and look down, your troubles seem so insignificant compared to the vastness of the world."

She thought about that for a moment. She thought about the world continuing now, even when she was in such a desperate state of mind. She thought about the world continuing even if she did decide to jump. She thought about jumping and wondered what she would look like when she hit the pavement. Gene Tierney's life would end, splattered and broken on the concrete of 57th Street. If she was going to die she at least wanted to know she was going to look pretty in her coffin. This was definitely not the way to die and look pretty.

Suddenly she realized this was not the time to die. She edged her way back across to the open window and slipped back into the safety of the living room. No one had known of the risk that she had just taken. It was her secret, and the fear factor alone had enabled her to think clearer than she had in months. Her secret didn't last for long. Sirens squealed toward the building. Gene heard the urgency of the sirens' sound as they got closer and closer to the building. The sirens were for her. Apparently, she did have an audience after all. Someone had seen her out there on the ledge and called for help.

A closer, more posed portrait photograph of a still glamorous Gene in her late 30s.

14. The Ledge of Insanity

In the time that Belle Tierney had left and returned from the grocery store, the picture had changed completely. As she walked back into the apartment she found Gene sitting on the couch, talking, in between two police officers. As Gene watched the color drain from her mother's face she said, "Don't be alarmed Mother; I'm all right." The doorman had already filled Belle in on the details of what had just happened, and she had raced up to the apartment not knowing what she was about to find. She was thankful her daughter was still alive.

Gene was giving her best acting performance in a long time. "Mother, I was just convincing these two officers that I was only cleaning the windows. Where could anyone get such an idea that I would want to do such a thing as jump?"

"Oh, Gene, how could you?!" Belle said as she broke down in a flood of tears. Gene quickly went to her mother and whispered, "I wasn't really going to do it. I was only looking to see how far it was." She thought, or rather hoped, that she had convinced the officers that she was merely spring cleaning. She hoped that she had made sure her mother believed the story. The officers soon left. Luckily for Gene, her almost-suicide never made it to the newspapers.

Belle Tierney put Gene back in the safety of her bed and went to call the family doctor. He arrived shortly after, gave Gene a tranquilizer and arranged for Gene to be taken to her third mental hospital the very next day. It was now the spring of 1958, and the Menninger Clinic in Topeka, Kansas, was Gene's new home. Although she wasn't happy to once again concede defeat and be admitted to an institution, she was coherent enough to know she needed professional help beyond that of her family.

Gene was sedated for her flight to Kansas. Once again her brother Butch accompanied her. Butch now held Gene's power of attorney; he would maintain control of her money until she was well enough to maintain control of it herself. Upon finding out that Gene's treatment cost would run to $25,000 per year, he went directly to Dr. Karl Menninger himself and asked if there was any way of reducing the fees. Gene's finances were already mostly eaten away by ongoing medical bills. Any long-term stay at Menninger's was bound to take care of what was left of it. Dr. Menninger suggested the only way to cut costs would be to put Gene into a public institution. A private hospital was expensive, and with Menninger's having the reputation of being the best psychiatric facility in the world, it was going to be especially expensive.

Butch thought about it, but it didn't take long for him to realize that maintaining Gene's savings and having a sister who was mentally ill was pointless. If need be, her finances could support several years of full time care in the highly respected Menninger's. There was nothing else to be thought about. This was her chance to get well. She was admitted as a patient, and her treatment soon began. As the saying goes, "Money cannot buy one's health," but in this case, $25,000 a year would have to at least try to buy Gene's back.

Gene Tierney

Menninger's at least had a more pleasant atmosphere than most institutions. Gene's room consisted of a bed, a separate bathroom, a desk, a mirror and a window that wouldn't open. After a review of her medical files it was decided that no further shock treatment would be administered. It was not believed to have been beneficial to Gene's well-being in the past. Thankfully, she endured no more electric shock therapy treatments. The 32 treatments that she had undergone previously had already done irreversible damage. One morning she woke up and was told it was 1959. Her last real memory was of being invited to President Eisenhower's inauguration dinner in 1956. She had lost three years, just like that.

Menninger's gave patients a say (to a certain point) in how they wanted to be treated. Gene had decided she'd like to speak with a woman psychiatrist. She was listened to and assigned Dr. Ann Wilkens. Gene actually looked forward to her session with her. She would talk back and not just sit there and nod while Gene rambled on and on about nothing.

Dr. Wilkens would usually begin the session by asking Gene what she had been doing recently. The clinic would run several art and craft courses for the patients to participate in. Gene would always be working on a new bowl or making a table or knitting a sweater. Her discussion with Dr. Wilkens would always include an update on how she was progressing with such handiwork. It was an icebreaker of sorts, a lead-in to the more serious topics that might be the reason for Gene's being at Menninger's to begin with.

She would talk about her father, her failed marriage, falling in love with the wrong men, constantly. And of course, Daria. The one on one therapy sessions seemed to be progressing well for Gene. However, the physical treatments were still inhuman. Although her electric shock therapy treatments were a thing of the past, she was not exempt from receiving another form of treatment used to shock the brain back to some semblance of normalcy. It was called "the cold pack." It was a treatment that would entail Gene being wrapped from the neck down in icy wet bed

A sultry glamour portrait of Gene.

14. The Ledge of Insanity

sheets. She was wrapped like an Egyptian mummy, her arms were strapped to her sides, and her legs were tightly bound. She lay there shivering as she began to lose all feeling in her arms and feet. The treatment was supposed to have lasted an hour, but the doctor released her after 30 minutes. After seeing her face full of panic, they realized it was not a beneficial treatment for her to endure. The aftereffects of such a treatment had Gene not being able to straighten her arms for days. She would walk around with her arms bent at the elbows, hands out in front as if she were carrying an imaginary tray. It was an unconscious reaction to being bound in "the cold pack." She was now bending her arms simply because she could.

In early August of 1958, Gene was notified that she would be scheduled to appear before a board of medical staff for an evaluation interview. She would be assessed by a team of doctors who would question her on a variety of subjects. Based on her answers, she would either be released to her family or taken back to her room. It was as if she were applying for parole. The interview was set up in a cold manner, not face to face. Gene was led into a room with one-way glass.

The doctors would sit in the room opposite and watch her reactions to the questions they asked her. The questions would come through a speaker and Gene would give her answers into a microphone. Before too long, Dr. Wilkens appeared in the doorway of Gene's room. She was smiling. "Gene," she said, "you're going home."

Once again Gene was going home. She had done this before and it had failed. There were bittersweet feelings about having passed the test for release. Her world was the institution; she had a routine there. It was safe. She was now being released to the bigger world, the outside world. It was the place where her problems began, but the doctors felt she was ready. It was time to go back to life.

15

Home, Howard, Happiness…

Instead of the safe haven of Connecticut, Gene, her mother and Tina vacationed in Aspen, Colorado. In less than a week of being released Gene would meet her second and last husband, Howard Lee. Once again love came at a time when it was least expected. Gene wasn't thinking of having anyone new in her life, at least not yet. First, she wanted some peace of mind in her own life, but miraculously, peace of mind came in the form of a tall, quiet unassuming Texan.

Howard Lee was a millionaire oilman. His family had been in the business since he was a boy. It was expected that he follow the same route. He was distantly related to Robert E. Lee, with his family tree stemming from Virginia and branching into Texas. Having just separated from another actress, Hedy Lamarr, the last thing on Howard's mind was getting involved "with those actor types again." Mutual friends threw Gene and Howard together during Gene's stay in Aspen. It was a difficult task to convince both of them that "it's only dinner." Neither one of them wanted to start a new relationship, but they agreed it wouldn't kill either one of them to at least eat a meal together.

They talked for hours and saw each other right up until Gene's last night in Colorado. Gene invited him to visit her in Connecticut and he agreed to take her up on the offer as soon as his business was taken care of in Aspen. Gene had business of her own to take care of. Twentieth Century–Fox had kept her under contract during her absence (now four years), and Gene genuinely wanted to do what was right by the studio and go back to work. Under her old contract Gene owed the studio one more picture. In turn they owed her $100,000 for completing the contract. The money was very much needed. She agreed to begin filming in December.

As September rolled around, Howard kept to his word and visited Gene in Green Farms, Connecticut. He had originally wanted to commute between Gene's

15. Home, Howard, Happiness...

house and Yankee Stadium. His beloved Yankees were playing the Milwaukee Braves in the World Series. He was an avid baseball fan. Instead, he stayed with Gene and watched the games on television. Any man who passes up going to a baseball game to stay at home and watch the game on TV in order to be with a woman at the same time is definitely in love. And he was.

Gene was happy. Howard was a calming force in her life and she enjoyed having him around. She had described him as having the look of infinite kindness, the kindest face she had ever seen. Once again she was battling those bittersweet emotions. On one hand she loved and cared for this kind and gentle man, but on the other she felt she was unfairly burdening him with the ticking time bomb of her mental illness. She certainly hadn't hidden the fact that she had been institutionalized. Besides, everyone knew it—family, friends, colleagues, the press, everyone. That initial story of her not being able to shake off a bad case of the flu would not hold out for four years.

Gene with her second husband, oil tycoon Howard Lee.

The truth had to be told and Gene was happy to tell it. By being so up-front about her own mental illness, she hoped it would encourage a broader spectrum of people to be more accepting of others with similar diseases. After all, these were the days when people would lock family members who had "gone mad" in their attics and cellars. They were considered to be an embarrassment to the family, written off like outcasts. Destined for a life of darkness, they would be locked behind a closed door and never again talked about. The Charlotte Bronte novel *Jane Eyre* is a perfect example of how mental illness was addressed in those early days. The 1944 movie version with Orson Welles and Joan Fontaine is regarded as a classic in every sense of the word.

The story sees Jane (Fontaine) falling in love with the much older Edward Rochester (Welles) after being employed to tutor his daughter. Rochester soon proposes marriage and Jane accepts his proposal. As the wedding day approaches, their love affair is stifled by Welles' secret. A locked room on the third floor of Thornfield Manor is forbidden territory for Jane to visit. With curiosity getting the better of her she finally learns the secret and Rochester finally allows Jane to see what he's hiding. His wife has "gone mad" and he has her imprisoned and locked away from the world.

Gene Tierney

Mental illness was something of a little-understood area in medical circles. It was either radically treated or completely ignored. Gene's open attitude and honesty toward her own experiences would have most definitely progressed the understanding of mental illness, then and now. So, along with the rest of the world, Howard knew of Gene's problems. He didn't ask her about it. If it bothered him, he wouldn't be sitting in her living room. If Howard wasn't concerned about her medical history, then she had to learn not to be concerned for him. He loved her for herself and that was that.

It didn't take long for the "M" word to pop into conversations. Marriage was soon the topic of most of them. After three months they both knew things were serious. With Howard's divorce from Hedy Lamarr not yet final, to Gene any talk of marriage was just that, talk. No plans were made until he was free and clear to remarry, but it was a well-known fact that he had chosen Gene as the next Mrs. Howard Lee. It would be another two years before his divorce was final. And with Gene facing another personal battle ahead, the wait to become husband and wife was balanced. On both sides.

As December approached and Gene began to prepare for her comeback picture, things began to unravel. Gene recognized the signs. She felt she was starting to slip again. This time it was her decision to return to Menninger's before it was too late. She met with another psychiatrist, Dr. Holtzman. He had been one of her treating doctors during her previous stay, and he was shocked to see her return. He truly believed she was well when she was released. "Why are you here, Gene?" he asked with concern. "You know, you don't need to be here." But Gene knew she needed help. "I think I do. I want you to examine me. I'm scared and I don't know why." She was now aware of her own strange behavior, aware enough to ask for help on her own without being taken to an institution by a family member or doctor. She had come a long way.

After a long talk with Dr. Holtzman it was decided that she should be readmitted, but only under one condition. "If we admit you, Gene, I want you to give us one year. I don't think it helps you to be in and out of here after six or eight months. Will you promise me to stay a year?" Gene instantly thought of Howard and Tina. One year was a long time no matter how you looked at it. This was a hard condition to accept but she had no choice. She needed help and the safety of Menninger's to help her through this next battle. She agreed. It would be a one-year stay.

On Christmas Day of 1958, Gene Tierney signed herself into the admittance book once more. She knew as she wrote the year, nineteen fifty-eight, it was a certainty that she would spend the coming year there. Menninger's would now be her 1959. She had accepted that now. Once again she retreated to the safety of those high stone walls that shut the world away.

15. Home, Howard, Happiness...

She was allowed to speak with Howard for the first few nights but warned him that phone communication was about to stop. She would be allowed to receive mail, so he could at least write to her. Receiving her mail was the thing she looked forward to the most. Over the next few weeks Gene was assessed and Dr. Wilkens was again assigned to her as her treating doctor. It was apparent that Gene had gotten help just in time. Although she got to the safety of Menninger's at the onset of trouble, her mental state deteriorated even further once there.

Again she would sit for hours in a chair, staring at the wall. If she moved from the chair she would only go to her bed and again sleep away hours of life. The doctors were content to let her be, at least for a few weeks anyway. She was medicated and under a watchful eye. She really was in the best place to help her. Dr. Wilkens would bring her art and craft supplies. Realizing Gene was artistic, she would try to coax her out of her catatonic state with the temptation of painting or needlework, something, anything to give her some sense of purpose. A reason to get up. At first the painting brought interest, she would paint and paint and paint. Then it was needlework; this proved to be her favorite pastime. She was churning out piece after piece, her hands moving constantly. The only part of her that seemed to function normally were her fingers. If for nothing else, her brain was at least instructing her to knit, and knit she did. In only a few short months she had quite the collection of work stockpiled. She had knitted two large rugs, five pillows, 40 sweaters and three full-length knit dresses.

It was three months before Gene could receive visitors. In between knitting she would devour Howard's letters, reading them over and over again. By March he was allowed to visit her. He would fly in from Houston every other weekend, never missing one. He looked forward to the visits as much as Gene. He was a loyal and devoted man, the type of man Gene had been searching for her entire life. His unwavering confidence in Gene getting well was the motivation that she needed to get back to life.

Days and months rolled by. Gene would spend most of her time knitting or crocheting another Tierney original. She was progressing in her therapy sessions with Dr. Wilkens, and she had a man who loved her dearly waiting for her to get well. Seeing the intensity that Gene was putting into her knitting and needlepoint, the doctors offered her the opportunity to get a job. She was showing signs of motivation. The doctors wanted to act on it and so they set out to convince her that her getting a job would be the next step in her recovery process. She was asked what job she thought she'd like. "Well, I love clothes and fashions," she said. "I'd love to work in a dress shop, if one would have me."

Dr. Wilkens told Gene to leave the rest to her. She would make the phone calls. There would be no interview process with the normal impediments that other job seekers would have to endure. Rejection wasn't something she needed to deal with.

Gene Tierney

The job would be offered to her and it would be up to Gene to accept it or reject it. Eventually Gene was offered a job by a lady in Topeka, Kansas. Billie Talmadge ran her own independent dress shop and was willing to have Gene join the sales staff.

It was an exciting yet daunting prospect at the same time. The acceptance of the position would mean that Gene would now become an outpatient. She would work nine to five as sales clerk and report to the clinic two days a week for an assessment of how she was doing. It was too good an opportunity to pass up. She accepted the position and it was arranged for her to live with Marguerite Craig, the elderly widow of a doctor.

Marguerite was a lovable woman in her late 60s. Gene struck up a deal with her on who should do what in the house. Since Gene was no cook it made sense to leave that to Marguerite. Gene volunteered to wash all dishes and clean house. Marguerite agreed, and the arrangement had them both living in a spotless house and eating hearty meals. They were a good team. Howard would now come to the house to visit with Gene. It was a much nicer environment than the institute to receive him in, and Marguerite loved him. Gene apologized for his not talking much. He was a man of few words. "Tell you what," Marguerite whispered, "during the pauses you can just enjoy a good look at him."

Gene was genuinely content with life as a sales clerk. She was selling clothes, something she loved. She was getting just $40 a week. It was a long way from the money her contract had promised her at Fox, but she was happy. As she put away the new stock she would put her favorite things aside and try them on during her lunch break. The result was her ending up owing Billie Talmadge more than she received in wages. She was Billie's best sales clerk and best customer all rolled up into one package.

It wasn't long before the press got wind of Gene's new job. They swooped on Topeka, Kansas, looking for the movie star turned sales girl. Gene knew it would happen. She would often see women looking at her and whispering among themselves. Some of the bolder ones would ask her directly, "Are you Gene Tierney?" "Yes, yes I am," she would reply humbly. Gene turned out to be one of the best sales clerks Billie Talmadge ever employed. She could talk a woman into buying a new dress, even if she originally came into the store just to browse.

Gene continued to work successfully in the dress shop and report twice weekly for her sessions with Dr. Wilkens. By November of 1958, after she had been under the care of Menninger's for almost 11 months, Dr. Karl Menninger, the founder of the clinic, called Gene to his office. The patients referred to him as the "Great White Father." Being called to his office was like being summoned to Emerald City to see the Wizard of Oz. It was a big deal, and Gene knew something in her life was about to change.

15. Home, Howard, Happiness...

"Gene," he said, "I have been reading your reports. You will continue to have your ups and downs but you do know right from wrong. There is no reason you can't have a happy life. We are going to give you your release." He smiled and outstretched his hand to her. "Good luck," he said with a warm smile.

Once again she had made her parole, and this time it was almost a month earlier than planned. She suddenly realized she'd be home for Christmas—home with her family and home with Howard. For the first time in many years and for the first time since leaving a sanitarium, she felt no fear at the thought of being released. She was eager to leave and eager to go back to her outside world. Going home for Christmas was the best gift her family could have hoped for. She always knew Menninger's was there to fall back on if she needed it. That safety net may have been one reason for her progress. Whatever the reason, it is certain that the love of Howard, the love of her family and the acceptance and understanding of her own illness ensured that she would never, ever, return to Menninger's or any other sanitarium.

At the time of Gene's release, she and Howard had had an almost two year engagement. Circumstances on both sides prevented the length of time being shorter, but there was to be no more waiting. It was now time to make things legal. After all, they had waited long enough.

On July 11, 1960, Gene Tierney became Mrs. Gene Tierney Lee. She and Howard were married in Aspen, where they had met a little over two years before. Gene was 39 and Howard was 51. If there was to be only one story that deserved the ending "and they lived happily ever after," then Gene Tierney deserved it more than anyone.

On the very day Gene and Howard were married a reporter bumped into Oleg Cassini on the street in New York City. Only this time, Oleg started the conversation, "You know," he said, "my wife got married today." Oleg would never have initiated a divorce from Gene. His "European ways," for want of a better term, tripped him up in an American marriage. Of course there were many other factors involved in the breakdown of their relationship. Some people just make better friends than husband and wife. In this case, Gene and Oleg always were the best of friends.

Gene always wanted the fairy tale, and she looked in a lot of wrong places before she found Howard. With him she found what she had been looking for her entire life. At age 39, Gene was finally content with life. She had found her peace of mind.

She and Oleg remained close friends long after their divorce. While Gene was in and out of the sanitariums Oleg paid for Daria's care and shared custody of Tina with Gene's family in Connecticut. Although Oleg later became engaged to actress Grace Kelly, that was the closest he ever came to being married again. She broke the engagement and married Prince Rainier of Monaco after a rather brief courtship. It wasn't long before Grace Kelly turned her back on Hollywood and became Princess Grace of Monaco.

Gene was once quoted as saying, "Fortunate is the woman who has a loving husband and an ex-husband who remains her friend." In his autobiography, *In My Own Fashion*, published in 1987, Oleg explains the nature of his relationship with Gene after their divorce. "Gene and I still remain close. We speak frequently by phone. I will on occasion send her some clothes or a gift to brighten her day. Sometimes, though, she will slip a little. She once called and asked me to meet her at the house in Green Farms, the house we shared briefly in 1951 when I pretended to be a Fairfield County commuter. She told me that the key was on the ledge above the door, that she would meet me there. It was so sad. Our months there were a fleeting moment of calm in her life, an oasis from the pressures of Hollywood and the debilitating trauma of Daria. It is a place she still visits, it seems, when she needs to find peace. I do not disabuse her of this solace. We shared great joy and terrible heartbreak in our lives. There is a bond between us that will never be broken. We will always love each other in our own fashion."

Oleg Cassini still lives in New York City, having turned 91 years of age in April of 2004. He maintains that same Cassini spunk that he always had. Without his kindness in donating personal family photographs and his openness in the retelling of his own life stories with Gene, this book would not have been written. His tales, his stories and his memories of a life once lived with her have given the public an insight into a private Hollywood world that we don't often see. In the nicest possible way, Oleg Cassini is one of a kind.

In 1961, Howard and Gene were thrilled to find that they were expecting a baby. At the time Gene had signed to appear in *Return to Peyton Place*, directed by actor Jose Ferrer. She withdrew from the picture and unfortunately miscarried at four and a half months. It was yet another blow for Gene, and for Howard.

Gene was happy in Houston. She had taken to life in Texas and she and Howard had a good, strong and loving marriage. The pressures of filming were behind her; she no longer felt the need to consistently make back-to-back pictures. Even if she wanted to, she was facing a problem far greater than her own personal need to act. Her medical history had caused her to become uninsurable. No insurance, no picture, no work. It was as simple as that.

16

Back to Work

Once again, in stepped the lovable and loyal Otto Preminger. By 1962 he was starting to cast his new picture, *Advise and Consent*. Preminger had called Gene to offer her the part of Dolly Harrison, a Washington hostess who ends up having an affair with the Senate majority leader, played by Walter Pidgeon. Gene had not stepped in front of a camera for seven long years, not since *The Left Hand of God* with Humphrey Bogart in 1955.

All offers had dried up. It doesn't take long to be forgotten about in fickle ol' Hollywood. With Gene's mental illness so widely publicized she was considered too much of a risk to even consider. After being absent for seven years, "Gene who?" was a two word question that often came up in conversations. Only good friends and associates remember you in good *and* bad times. In Gene's life, Otto Preminger was one of those people. He had been Gene's friend for too many years to let such a thing as illness or the word "uninsurable" get in the way of him wanting her in his picture.

She signed to do the picture, but the insurance company would not budge. They simply would not insure Gene Tierney. Preminger called the insurance agency and basically blackmailed them into a corner. He told them if they refused to insure Gene for this picture he would in turn cancel all coverage for this and any other future production under his control. That very costly threat was enough for them to swallow hard, cross their fingers and agree to insure her. Just as Gene was affectionately known as the "GET" girl, Preminger should have equally been labeled the "GET" boy. He was a man with fierce loyalties and determination. Whether it was a battle with Darryl F. Zanuck or a lowly insurance company, he always got what he wanted.

Preminger was born in Vienna, Austria, on December 5, 1906. Known for his imposing bald headed appearance, he is recognized today as one of the all time great directors. He was a law student before making his move to America to direct Broadway plays after being earmarked as a "potentially good director." It wasn't long

Seven years had passed before Gene (left) was well enough to return to the screen in *Advise and Consent* (1962). She completed the film without incident.

before 20th Century–Fox signed him to the studio. His clashes with studio head Zanuck were almost constant, even earning him a suspension for one disagreement. Being suspended from directing didn't deter him. He may not have been able to direct but no one could stop him from acting.

After the outbreak of World War II, Preminger was in great demand to play Nazi roles. It was an ironic casting since Preminger was of Jewish heritage. His most notable appearance was the role of the commanding Nazi in the 1953 prisoner of war classic, *Stalag 17*. Preminger guarded his personal life with great secrecy, but his affair with stripper Gypsy Rose Lee was a commonly known fact. How could something of that magnitude possibly be hidden? Their union resulted in a son, their only child, named, Eric Lee Preminger.

Otto Preminger died of cancer in New York City on April 23, 1986. He was nominated as Best Director on two occasions. *Laura* won him his first nomination in 1945. It was quite a wait for the next time around, when in 1964 *The Cardinal* gave him his next and last chance of winning. It wasn't meant to be. Three career nominations without ever taking home an award. It just goes to prove

16. Back to Work

Despite being the same age, Dean Martin plays Gene's son-in-law in *Toys in the Attic* (1963). A little gray in her hair and a few extra pounds enabled her to pull off a sound performance in an interesting film about a neurotic Southern family.

that brilliance is not necessarily always recognized with a gold statue named Oscar.

Preminger always proved to be one of Gene's most supportive friends. She was his *Laura* and he loved her for that. There was of course no guarantee that Gene would see the new job through. She had no way of knowing whether going back to work would trigger a relapse or not. With Preminger's determination to go out on a limb for her, there was nothing for her to think about but doing her best work for her producer/director and friend, Otto Preminger.

She also had something to prove to herself. Going back to work was a major step forward and she was determined to succeed. The role, although small, was another milestone in Gene's career. She was to play the role of a mature woman. Now 42 years old, she had missed the slow transition between the mid–30s roles through to the present day. When she last appeared on film she was 34 years old. That was almost a decade earlier.

Gene Tierney

A 44-year-old Gene in a scene from *The Pleasure Seekers* (1965). It was her last feature film role before her early retirement to Houston, Texas.

For an actress in Hollywood terms, ten years is the difference between playing a goddess and a grandmother. Remember, this was Hollywood in "pre" cosmetic surgery days. Going under the knife was considered a drastic procedure in order to extend a film career. The best an actress could hope for was strong tape behind her ears (the temporary facelift), good lighting and soft focus!

Gene came through for Preminger. She completed her part without a mishap. Howard was with her throughout filming in Washington, even attending a White House dinner with her, thrown in honor of the cast of the picture. That was the last time Gene saw John F. Kennedy before his assassination. She had accomplished what she set out to do. She attempted a comeback and she had achieved it. She had no aspirations to work in the film industry full time, but she did want to remain "in touch," so to speak. She was happy being Mrs. Howard Lee. They would travel together, play bridge, attend dinner parties with friends and donate time and money to many Houston charities.

It would be another year before she would step back in front of the camera. This time it was Gene who approached director George Roy Hill. The picture was

16. Back to Work

Toys in the Attic, a strange tale of a neurotic Southern American family. After Gene approached Hill, telling him that she would like to work with him, he politely said, "But Gene, the only part I am yet to cast is that of an older woman." Without missing a beat, Gene said, "Fine, we'll dye my hair gray. You've just completed your casting." And so it was a done deal. Gene was to play the mother-in-law of Dean Martin's character. At the time of filming he was the same age as Gene. The gray streaks in her hair helped. She was transformed into a woman at least 20 years her senior. It made for a convincing role.

In another move away from doing big time features, Gene started work on an independent short subject on location in Spain. Although the featurette was filmed in English, it is commonly referred to in title as *Las Cuatro noches de la luna llena*. Although the word "Cuatro" should

January 14, 1956. Still looking good at 35, and in a swimsuit at that, Gene poses by the pool.

make the English translation *The Four Nights of the Full Moon*, it is commonly referred to in English as *The Seven Nights of the Full Moon*. Directed by famed science fiction director Sobey Martin, the featurette starred Dan Dailey, Analia Gade and Gene. It was reported in a 1963 fan magazine that all stars were on location and footage had been shot, but I have yet to find a print of the film.

Howard was the encouraging force behind Gene's tiptoe approach back into acting. On a personal level he was doing some encouraging of a different kind. He very much wanted to meet his new father-in-law. Gene had explained to Howard on more than one occasion why she had harbored such resentment toward her father. He didn't go through that phase of her life with her. He didn't see firsthand the pain that a father would actively cause for his own child. He understood her pain but he was the "let bygones be bygones" type.

Her father had written to congratulate them on their marriage in the beginning and mentioned that he hoped to someday meet his new son-in-law. Gene didn't answer the letter. With Howard's constant persistence about arranging a

Gene Tierney

Top: August 30, 1960. In an inspirational comeback after years of mental illness, Gene, now 40 years old, holds a script in her hands for the first time in seven long years. Fellow actor Jim Davis happily runs through her lines with her. On the day this photograph was taken, Gene enthusiastically stated, "I'm interested in seeing major motion picture scripts and I'm open to any and all offers." *Left:* A rare unretouched proof of Gene from *Toys in the Attic* (1963). In one of Gene's "comeback" performances, she dyed her hair gray. Despite being the same age as her co-star, Dean Martin, she approached director George Roy Hill, pleading with him to cast her in the role of Martin's mother-in-law. He eventually agreed, and her portrayal of a woman meant to be about 20 years older than Gene was brilliant.

16. Back to Work

meeting, she eventually gave in. She did it for Howard Lee, not for Howard Tierney. Gene knew only that her father was living in Pennsylvania. She had no address or contact phone number, so she called an aunt to get the details. When Gene told her aunt the reason for her call, the aunt broke down and cried. "Gene, I didn't phone you for fear of upsetting you," she said. "Your father is dead."

He had succumbed to cancer only a few days before Gene's phone call, but she felt no pain. She had grieved for her father many years ago. She had lost him then. When Gene told Howard, his eyes filled with tears. He had hoped to re-create a lost relationship between a father and daughter. He had come so close and now it was too late.

The death of her father in some way gave Gene a sense of closure to a past pain that she would sooner forget than remember. The many doctors who had treated Gene concluded she had a predisposition to her mental illness. Life's traumas would trigger her chemical imbalance, and there's doubt that Gene had her fair share of those. Her illness was like a seed in her brain that would grow only if she led an overly stressful life. Her father's abandonment of the family and his suing his own daughter for $50,000 in no way helped Gene's state of mind in those early years. His actions started the growth of that ugly seed. That was a hard thing to accept, let alone forgive. In her eyes, his acts were unforgivable, but she loved Howard even more for at least trying to help a hopeless situation.

On a professional level she was yet to complete her contract with Fox. The contract stated that she must complete ten films in seven years. She had now gone over the seven-year limit, but Fox stuck by her contract and agreed to cast her in *The Pleasure Seekers*. It was a take-for-take remake of the 1954 picture *Three Coins in the Fountain*. Gene's part was minor, almost a walk-on, walk-off role, but it did technically round out her contract with Fox. It was a sense of professional closure. Her Hollywood days were now officially over.

Gene explained her condition just prior to her permanent retirement from the movie industry. She had grown to understand what had triggered her illness to begin with, and as with anything, understanding and knowing what causes the problem is the first step in avoiding its reoccurring and curing it for good. "In my case," she explained, "it means not doing anything I feel I'm not up to. It means eliminating from my life people who affect me unpleasantly. I must not allow myself to get into situations where I feel trapped."

She had at last realized that it was impossible to please everyone in life. If saying "no" upset someone, then so be it. She went on, "I have learned that it is okay to say no every once in a while. I believe it's important to realize you can't please everybody all the time. You can't please anyone — or yourself — if you try to base every move on the feelings of others."

She spoke of her stay at Menninger's. "It takes time to get over a mental illness and few people can afford the best care." At the time of Gene's illness Menninger's was considered the best psychiatric institution in the world. "From now on," she said, "I'll do everything I can to help the cause, talk about it, help raise funds. You can lose an arm or a leg and it really isn't so bad. To lose your mind is the most dreadful thing — the mind is the most beautiful part of the body and to lose it is the greatest tragedy."

In the meantime, Howard Hughes, Gene's ex-love from many years before, was battling his own demons of the mind. In order to avoid paying taxes, Hughes hired an ex–FBI agent, Robert Maheu, as his right-hand man. Hughes knew that Maheu had been involved in many operations with the FBI and the CIA, including the much talked about assassination attempt on Fidel Castro of Cuba. If anyone could elude the IRS it was Maheu, and with Hughes having several dozen subpoenas over his head, he needed all the help he could get.

Hughes bragged that he never paid a dime of income tax in his entire lifetime. It was Maheu's job to hide and protect Hughes from being brought to justice. In 1966, Maheu decided to move Hughes to Las Vegas. So in the early hours of the morning he was transported by train to the Desert Inn in Las Vegas, Nevada. There were strict instructions for the hotel lobby to be cleared for his arrival. He moved through the empty lobby and made the penthouse on the 15th floor his home for the next six months. During this time he wasn't seen by anyone. In fact, during the last 20 years of his life he wasn't photographed at all. The last known photograph of him was taken in the mid–'50s.

After Hughes had lived in the penthouse for six months, the hotel management decided to evict him. They had many high rollers at the time wanting to stay in the penthouse, and with Hughes making it his permanent home it was unavailable to anyone who requested it. The competition in Vegas was too fierce to turn such people away. There was a good chance they'd gamble elsewhere if the penthouse was already occupied. There was nothing else to do but give Hughes his marching orders. Again it was time for Maheu to step in. Hughes instructed Maheu to ask the hotel owner how much he wanted for the building. The owner humorously plucked the ridiculous amount of $14 million out of his head. It was twice the casino's market value. Hughes sent Maheu down with a check for the full amount the next day. The owner almost died on the spot.

Hughes ended up residing in Vegas for the next few years. He slowly acquired a number of other casino/hotels including the Sands, the Frontier, the Castaway and the Silver Slipper. His real reason for buying the Silver Slipper was because the rotating neon marquee was annoying him when it shone through his window. Maheu once again asked the owner of the place how much he wanted for it and Hughes wrote him a check for the requested amount. After handing over the check Maheu turned off the irritating sign and Hughes was happy.

16. Back to Work

Top: Gene enjoys a cup of tea at the first Romantic Film Festival in Cabourg, France, where she was an honoree. *Bottom:* Gene, aka "Bama," with her two youngest grandchildren, Alexander and Cedric. (Both photographs courtesy Christina Cassini.)

Gene Tierney

After several years in Vegas, Maheu decided it was time to move his boss to another area. This time it was the Bahamas. Eighteen months later, on April 5, 1976, Hughes died en route from his penthouse in Mexico to a hospital in Houston, Texas. He was 70 years old. The Treasury Department insisted on fingerprinting the remains in order to confirm it was indeed Hughes. His 6'4" frame weighed a mere 90 pounds, his hair was wild and matted, and his toenails were so long he was unable to wear shoes. He was unrecognizable. Years of drug abuse had ravaged his body. X-rays revealed several broken hypodermic needles wedged in his arms. Despite several life threatening ailments, the autopsy listed renal failure as the official cause of death. Almost 400 people came forward to claim a piece of his two billion dollar estate. Twenty-two cousins were eventually deemed legitimate heirs to the Hughes fortune. You would have to say his death in midair was a fitting end. His plane crash years before should have killed him; he cheated death as an aviator on more than one occasion. The odds were the plane would win at some point. This time it did.

Gene commented on Hughes' death. "I was glad I knew him," she said, "although I do not recognize the description of the eccentric, withered, drug addicted recluse that he turned out to be. I can only wonder what really happened to the Howard Hughes we all knew during the Hollywood years."

Gene continued to work every once in a while. She dabbled in various television projects over the next few years. Her roles were scattered; she would pop up here and there as a guest on various popular television shows of the time. In March of 1969 she guest starred in an episode of *The FBI* called "Conspiracy of Silence." The series was based on real FBI case files. It ran from 1965 to 1974. In the same year she appeared as the crippled wife of Ray Milland in the made for TV movie *Daughter of the Mind*.

In April of 1975 she appeared in the long running television series *M.A.S.H.* As a scene from one of her movies appears on television, the Korean War medics cheer for her. Her last appearance was in 1980 at the age of 60. She played Harriet Toppingham, a ruthless fashion editor, in Judith Krantz's soap opera miniseries, *Scruples*. It was the end of a career that had spanned four decades.

17

The Final Curtain Call

Gene and Howard would spend a lot of time traveling together. A "must do" yearly trek was back to Connecticut in autumn for the changing of the leaves. From there, they would travel to New York to visit friends and catch up on any new Broadway plays that were in town. They would travel at least once a year to France to visit with Tina and her four children, and when back in Houston they would enjoy dinner parties with friends.

Their home was an elegant Houston town house. The living room was decorated in white and gold and furnished with antiques from Gene's many years of collecting. The glass-covered atrium and sunken pool were very well used entertaining areas, often used with friends.

In her retirement, Gene was active in many Houston charity organizations, gravitating toward causes that especially dealt with helping retarded children and people with mental illness, two causes that related closely to her own life. She still saw a doctor once a month, sometimes more often but only if she felt she needed it. She was prescribed regular medication, a modern day marvel, to correct the chemical imbalance that once caused her the darkest of days. Sedation was once the only form of prescribed medication for her condition. In the early days of her illness she was taking more medication than any other patient in the institution. None of it was beneficial to her condition.

As time progressed, so did medicine. Eventually Gene's condition was understood and kept under control. By living as stress free a life as possible, by seeing her doctor monthly and taking her pills daily, she had finally found a sense of calm that was missing for so many years.

Her 30 years in Houston were mostly incident free, but one night she dreamed that Daria was no longer in an institution but living in the home of some neighbors down the street from her. Howard woke up and saw Gene gone; the front door was open, so he ran outside, frantically searching for her. It was the middle of the night when he found her pounding on the door of the people she had dreamed

February 1983. A candid snapshot of a few of the actors who made Hollywood. *Left to right:* Vincent Price, Gene Tierney, Louise Rainer, Kathryn Grayson and Joan Bennett. The photograph was taken at the Hilton Hotel for the Texas Film Society Yellow Rose Awards. It was a rare reunion of old Hollywood greats.

Gene catches up with Vincent Price at the 1983 Texas Film Society Yellow Rose Awards. Gene shared a lifelong friendship with Price.

had Daria with them. Howard explained the situation and they were completely understanding of the scene she had caused. After looking at that main isolated incident, it seemed that within those last 30 years of her life in Texas, the main cause of Gene's illness was Daria's tragic birth.

She very rarely spoke of Daria's problems. In an interview in later years she reflected back to that ter-

17. The Final Curtain Call

rible night at the Hollywood Canteen. "It was such a tragedy," she said. "There was nothing I could do to that fan. She had no idea what she was doing to me. She thought she was doing the best she could by coming out to see me." She paused for a moment to regain her composure and continued. "But how can you forget something like that? It is always with me."

Gene would sometimes hesitate about going out and mingling with people even when she was well. She was unsure how she had acted around these same people when she was sick. She had no memory of those times but she knew they did. Finally, she accepted the fact that she was now well and must live. She accepted herself as she was and took comfort in knowing her true friends would do the same.

Sadly, by 1980 she and Howard would only have one more year together. He died in February 1981. They were a happily married couple for 20 years. In remembering her husband she said, "Howard was so attractive and dear. I would have attacks of my illness from time to time and I would say to him, 'You ought to divorce me. Nobody can put up with this.'" She continues with Howard's response: "I would be so unhappy if we were apart," he would say. "I would much rather stick with it." Theirs was a relationship of true love and dedication. Gene dedicated her 1979 autobiography, *Self Portrait*, to him, with lines from a Shakespearean sonnet: "But if the while I think on thee, dear friend, All losses are restor'd and sorrows end."

Gene considered going back to her home state of Connecticut after Howard's death, but after a visit to scope out the real estate she realized in that short time

A Laura *(1944) reunion. In 1984, some 40 years after the release of the film noir classic, the surviving cast members came together to celebrate. Dana Andrews (left) and Vincent Price join Gene at a function honoring the film.*

that she already missed Houston. She had made good friends there and decided the best thing to do was to move out of the home she and Howard had shared and relocate to an apartment in Houston. She settled on an apartment in the River Oaks area. She spent her time shopping, reading, playing bridge with friends and raising money for charity. She was invited to all the gala balls and benefits but preferred to spend her time with friends at small dinner parties instead. She would often be seen having lunch or afternoon tea at one of the local haunts such as Tony's, Rudy's and the Grotto.

The last ten years of her life were filled with friends and family. Tina's children were her pride and joy. They would affectionately call her "Bama," a name Gene had for her own grandmother many years before. As busy as she kept herself, she missed her beloved Howard terribly. She lasted only another ten years without him by her side.

Gene died in her River Oaks apartment on November 6, 1991, just a couple of weeks shy of her 71st birthday. Her years of smoking (probably a habit she would never have taken up had it not been for her attempting to lower her voice for the sake of her career) had taken its toll. She suffered with worsening emphysema during the last year of her life. Sadly, the disease won out in the end.

Her death was covered nationally by the Associated Press, and many major daily newspapers ran the story at the bottom of their front pages. It was overshadowed by the news conference in which basketball legend Magic Johnson revealed to the world he had contracted the Aids virus. Cable news networks ran the story of her life and death.

She was loved and admired by fans the world over, and after her death the people who knew her best spoke of a woman they were honored to know and would greatly miss. Oilman Johnny Mitchell and his wife, Alleyne, were good friends of Gene and Howard. In fact they were the couple who got them together in the first place. Alleyne Mitchell spoke of Gene with great admiration. "She was natural and unaffected. She never once acted like a movie star in all the years I knew her. She adjusted wonderfully to living in Houston. She had many friends here who loved her. She rarely spoke about her years in the movies at all. I think she felt her successful marriage with Howard was a far greater achievement than her movie stardom. She was a vivacious and loving person and I enjoyed knowing her," she said with a smile. Faustine McCarthy, Howard Lee's sister, commented, "I loved Gene because she made my brother happy." Glen McCarthy, Jr., Howard's nephew, said, "She was a lovely person. I know that she made my uncle very happy."

The owner of the Grotto, one of her favorite eateries, talked of her being a regular customer. "She used to come in here late afternoon," he said. "She was always by herself, always cordial, sweet and quiet. She spoke in slow methodical tones and seemed a bit reclusive to me. I really didn't even know she was Gene

17. The Final Curtain Call

Tierney until someone told me. She always went by her married name, Mrs. Lee." But it was Gene's ex-husband, Oleg Cassini, who I think summed her life up best of all. "Gene," he said, "was the unluckiest lucky girl in the world." There really is no better way to describe her life.

The funeral service for Gene Tierney Lee was held at the Church of St. John the Divine on Monday, November 11, 1991, in Houston. Her ashes are entombed in the Lee family plot at Houston's oldest cemetery. She is 600 plots away from the grave of her former love, Howard Hughes.

A few months later, Gene's daughter, Christina, sorted her possessions for auction.

Many of her mother's antiques and precious personal items were shipped to Tina's home in France. The remaining items were commissioned to Hart Galleries in Houston. Everything to be sold was cataloged for a three-day sale on February 7, 8 and 9, 1992.

Some 2,300 people attended the auction over the three-day period. More than 1,000 registered bidders took up standing room only. All were eager to take home a piece of Gene Tierney memorabilia. They had come to the right place. The auction took place in the upstairs room of Hart Galleries. The valuable jewelry on sale was locked away in various glass display cases. Other items were arranged on the floor section at the front of the seating area, near the auctioneer.

One of the lots that held particular interest was an oil painting of Gene. It was displayed on an easel and roped off toward the back of the room. During the two-hour viewing just prior to the auction, the room swelled with people, some writing lot numbers down for later bidding. Others just came to remember. Several large television monitors were positioned around the room; all were simultaneously playing one of her most loved films, *The Ghost and Mrs. Muir*.

Among the items on sale was a wax face mask that was sculptured in 1945 especially for a *Vogue* magazine photo shoot. It was one of three life masks that surrounded Gene in the original photograph. The mask was eerily lifelike with painted lips, brows and lids. It sold for $1,000 and came complete with the issue of *Vogue* that it was featured in. Most of the jewelry pieces on sale were lavish gifts from Prince Aly Khan. The most noteworthy was a rare South Sea pearl necklace, a 19-inch strand of flawless pearls graduating in size from 0.7 millimeters to 1.2 millimeters. The piece sold to a Houston jeweler for $8,250.

Other gifts from Aly Khan included a set of platinum clip-on earrings with 106 diamonds totaling 5.7 carats. The highest bid reached $8,800 with the reserve not being met. The matching 11-carat diamond dress clip set reached a high bid of $11,000, but again the reserve was much, much higher. An elegant 3.3 carat art deco Cartier watch sold for $9,350. Her modest 1983 gold Chrysler LeBaron convertible went for the bargain price of $3,600. With only 45,163 miles on the odome-

Gene Tierney

THREE-DAY ESTATE AUCTION

Antique Furnishings, Fine Art, Estate Jewelry, Decorative Accessories & Oriental Rugs

featuring

The Estate of Gene Tierney

February 7th, 8th & 9th, 1992

HART GALLERIES

Gene Tierney's estate auction catalog cover. Held at Hart Galleries on February 7, 8 and 9, 1992, this auction gave grieving fans the chance to own something that once belonged to Gene. Everything from an 8 × 10 photograph to her car was auctioned to a packed house (catalog courtesy of Hart Galleries).

17. The Final Curtain Call

ter, it sold to a part time Houston car dealer. Her four poster king-size bed sold for $935. Since it's illegal to sell a secondhand mattress in Houston the auctioneer gave it to the highest bidder for free.

An initialed leather travel jewelry case sold for $247.50, a silver cigarette case for $55, and a pair of simple gold loop earrings for $330. A beaver and white fox trimmed coat with matching hat sold for $880. A luxurious golden Russian sable coat received the unsatisfactory high bid of $5,500 and was passed in. The matching hat was sold for $192.50.

A 40 × 48 inch unfinished portrait painting was one of the highlights. Gene had fired the artist before it was finished; she didn't like the way it was looking. Ironically the painting hung above her couch in her drawing room for decades. The top bid was a disappointing $1,600, a long way away from the secret reserve set by Gene's daughter Tina. She was far from disappointed with the lack of interest in the work. "She's coming back to Paris with me," Tina said as she looked lovingly at the painting. Many other items went under the hammer within those three days—books, photographs, various tables and chairs, even two television sets. After her 30 years as a Houston resident, Hart Galleries gave Gene Tierney Lee her final curtain call. And what a success it was.

Gene Eliza Tierney was known as the "Hollywood 'GET' Girl." She did, in life, get a lot of what she wanted. In turn she was dealt a lot of unwanted blows that would scar her life forever. All of our lives have a balance of ups and downs, but Gene Tierney seemed to have her scales tipped to the side of tragedy more often than not. Yet through it all she kept going. She continued to live, and above all else, she survived.

In a book titled *The Man with Bogart's Face*, author Andrew Fenady wrote an inscription in Gene's copy that I feel is a fitting end to any story. There is no story more deserving of such an end than Gene's own. Fenady wrote, "Every man has a *Laura*, but there's only one Gene Tierney."

Filmography

The Return of Frank James. 1940, Twentieth Century–Fox.

Director Darryl F. Zanuck. *Producer* Darryl F. Zanuck. *Writing Credits* Sam Hellman. *Cinematographer* George Barnes. *Running time* 92 mins. *Location* Bishop, California; Lone Pine, California. *Production Dates* 24 April 1940–20 June 1940. *Release Dates* 10 August 1940, New York; Nationwide U.S.A., 16 August 1940.

Cast: Henry Fonda (Frank James, aka Ben Woodsen), **Gene Tierney** (**Eleanor Stone**), Jackie Cooper (Clem, aka Tom Grayson), Henry Hull (Maj. Rufus Cobb), John Carradine (Bob Ford), J. Edward Bromberg (George Runyan), Donald Meek (McCoy), Eddie Collins (Station agent at Eldora), George Barbier (Judge Ferris), Russell Hicks (Prosecutor), Ernest Whitman ("Pinky" Washington), Charles Tannen (Charlie Ford), Lloyd Corrigan (Randolph Stone), Victor Kilian (Preacher), Edward McWade (Col. Fentridge Jackson).

When his brother's killers are set free, Frank James (Henry Fonda) makes it his business to find the men who murdered him. He becomes a determined one-man posse out to avenge his brother's death. The young reporter, Eleanor (Gene Tierney), desperately wants to tell the story of Frank James so she can convince her editor father that, like men, women can be good reporters too. In between writing the story of Frank and Jesse James, Eleanor falls in love with the outlaw.

Interesting Trivia: Twentieth Century–Fox bought the rights to the lives of the James Brothers but took artistic license to the extreme and changed most of the facts for maximum entertainment value. The story's accuracy ends with the outlaws' names, Frank and Jesse. That's about as far as accuracy goes.

Hudson's Bay. 1941, Twentieth Century–Fox.

Director Irving Pichel. *Producer* Darryl F. Zanuck. *Writing Credits* Lamar Trotti. *Cinematographers* George Barnes and J. Peverell Marley. *Running time* 95 mins. *Release Dates* 9 January 1941, U.S.A.

Filmography

Cast: Paul Muni (Pierre Esprit Radisson), **Gene Tierney (Barbara Hall)**, Laird Cregar (Gooseberry), John Sutton (Lord Edward Crewe), Virginia Field (Nell Gwyn), Vincent Price (King Charles II), Nigel Bruce (Prince Rupert), Morton Lowry (Gerald Hall), Robert Greig (Sir Robert), Chief Thundercloud (Orimha), Frederick Worlock (English Governor), Florence Bates (Duchess), Montagu Love (Gov. D'Argenson), Ian Wolfe (Mayor), Chief John Big Tree (Chief).

This epic drama tells of the foundation of a long-standing Canadian institution, the Hudson's Bay Trading Company.

Interesting Trivia: A mere four years after making *Hudson's Bay* in 1940, Laird Cregar died suddenly at age 28, the result of a crash diet. Fellow actor and friend Vincent Price read the eulogy at his funeral.

Tobacco Road. 1941, Twentieth Century–Fox.

Director John Ford. *Producer* Darryl F. Zanuck. *Writing Credits* Erskine Caldwell (novel), Jack Kirkland (play), Nunnally Johnson (screenplay). *Cinematographer* Arthur C. Miller. *Running time* 84 mins. *Locations* Encino, Los Angeles; Sherwood Forest, California. *Release dates* 20 February 1941, New York City; 7 March 1941, nationwide.

Production dates November 1940–December 1940. *Box Office Take* As of 1973, *Tobacco Road* had grossed $1,900,000.

Cast: Charley Grapewin (Jeeter Lester), Marjorie Rambeau (Sister Bessie Rice), **Gene Tierney (Ellie May Lester)**, William Tracy (Dude Lester), Elizabeth Patterson (Ada Lester), Dana Andrews (Capt. Tim Harmon), Slim Summerville (Henry Peabody), Ward Bond (Lov Bensey), Grant Mitchell (George Payne, banker), Zeffie Tilbury (Grandma Lester), Russell Simpson (Chief of Police), Spencer Charters (County Clerk), Irving Bacon (Bank teller), Harry Tyler (Auto dealer), Charles Halton (Mayor).

In an earlier *Beverly Hillbillies* or *Ma and Pa Kettle* version of a family of dirt farmers about to be pushed off their land, Jeeter and Ada Lester (Charley Grapewin and Elizabeth Patterson) are the parents of a clan of 16-plus children. The rose among the thorns is a young Gene Tierney as the beautiful but dirty farmer's daughter. A comedic romp of downright hicks, this raunchy tale of a Southern family battling to keep their home is a gritty story of spirit and determination. Even with the strong religious overtones, it is simply a good story that will remain in the viewer's hearts long after the credits roll

Memorable Quotes: Jeeter Lester: "Why, Ada here never ... never spoke a word to me for the first ten years we was married. Heh! Them was the happiest ten years of my life."

Filmography

Lov Bensey: "I want a young wife. I ain't gonna take no 23-year-old woman for a wife, have everybody laughin' at me."

Lov Bensey: "I ain't tradin' turnips with nobody."

Interesting Trivia: Tobacco Road, the play, opened on Broadway on December 4, 1933. In its day, it set a record for the longest running play in Broadway history. For reasons unknown, except to assume it was a little too racy for its time, *Tobacco Road*, the movie, was banned in Australia.

Belle Starr. 1941, Twentieth Century–Fox.

Director Irving Cummings. *Producer* Kenneth MacGowan. *Writing Credits* Niven Busch, Cameron Rogers and Lamar Trotti. *Cinematographers* Ernest Palmer and Ray Rennahan. *Release Dates* 12 September 1941, U.S.A.

Cast: Randolph Scott (Sam Starr), **Gene Tierney (Belle Shirley, later Belle Starr)**, Dana Andrews (Maj. Thomas Grail), Shepperd Strudwick (Ed Shirley, as John Shepperd), Elizabeth Patterson (Sarah), Chill Wills (Blue Duck), Louise Beavers (Mammy Lou), Olin Howlin (Jasper Tench as Olin Howland), Paul E. Burns (Sergeant as Paul Burns), Joe Sawyer (John Cole as Joseph Sawyer), Joe Downing (Jim Cole as Joseph Downing), Howard C. Hickman (Col. Thornton as Howard Hickman), Charles Trowbridge (Col. Bright), James Flavin (Sergeant), Charles Middleton (Carpetbagger).

Another highly romanticized *Gone with the Wind* type tale set within the Civil War and its aftermath as Belle Starr's (Gene Tierney) family deals with the reality of their land being taken by the Yankees. Its stereotypical stance on the African Americans within the story makes a viewer cringe while watching it today. In a poor attempt to capitalize on the success of *Gone with the Wind* two years previously, the strong ensemble cast struggles to come within a whisker of the Rhett Butler/Scarlett O'Hara tale.

Interesting Trivia: After her extensive eye problems during the filming of *Belle Starr*, Gene tends to squint during the last half of this film. Although her eye allergy was later diagnosed as a nervous condition, Gene refused to wear eye makeup in future productions unless essential to the character's appearance. At the time, Ingrid Bergman was the only other actress beautiful enough *not* to wear makeup on screen.

Sundown. 1941, United Artists.

Director Henry Hathaway. *Producer* Walter Wanger. *Writing Credits* Charles G. Booth (adaptation), Barre Lyndon (screenplay/story). *Cinematographer* Charles Lang. *Running time* 90 mins. *Location* Acoma Pueblo, Acoma, New Mexico, USA; Bronson Canyon, Griffith Park, Los Angeles, California; Gallup, New Mexico. *Release Dates* Premiere: 20 October 1941–U.S.A.; 31 October, 1941–Nationwide.

Cast: **Gene Tierney (Zia)**, Bruce Cabot (Crawford, District Commissioner

Filmography

of Monicka), George Sanders (Coombes), Harry Carey (Dewey), Joseph Calleia (Pallini), Reginald Gardiner (Turner), Carl Esmond (Kuypens), Marc Lawrence (Abdi Hammud), Cedric Hardwicke (Bishop Coombes as Sir Cedric Hardwicke), Gilbert Emery (Ashburton), Jeni Le Gon (Miriami), Emmett Smith (Kipsang)

Adapted from a Barre Lyndon short story, *Sundown* is based in Africa during World War II. Major Coombes (George Sanders) is a British army major who has neither the time nor patience for the local Arab population or his district commissioner, played by Bruce Cabot. Gene Tierney plays the beautiful Zia, a woman who is initially suspected of being a Nazi sympathizer. Only after she's called upon and agrees to lead the British troops through dangerous territory is her loyalty trusted.

Awards and Nominations, 1942 Nominated Best Art Direction, Black and White, Alexander Golitzen and Richard Irvine; Best Cinematography, Black and White, Charles Lang; Best Music, Scoring of a Dramatic Picture, Miklos Rozsa.

Interesting Trivia: A very young Dorothy Dandridge portrays a slave extra.

The Shanghai Gesture. 1941, United Artists.

Director Josef von Sternberg. *Producers* Theo W. Baumfield and Albert de Courville. *Writing Credits* John Colton, Jules Furthman, Geza Herczeg, Karl Vollmoller and Josef von Sternberg. *Running time* 97 mins. *Release Dates* 26 December, 1941–U.S.A.

Cast: **Gene Tierney (Poppy Charteris)**, Walter Huston (Sir Guy Charteris), Victor Mature (Doctor Omar), Ona Munson (Mother Gin Sling), Phyllis Brooks (The Chorus Girl, Dixie Pomeroy), Albert Bassermann (The Commissioner, Van Elst), Maria Ouspenskaya (The Amah), Eric Blore (The Bookkeeper, Cesar Hawkins), Ivan Lebedeff (The Gambler, Boris), Mike Mazurki (The Coolie), Clyde Fillmore (The Comprador, Percival Montgomery Howe), Grayce Hampton (The Social Leader, Lady Blessington), Rex Evans (The Counselor, Jackson), Mikhail Rasumny (The Appraiser, Mischa Vaginisky as Mikhail Rasumni), Michael Dalmatoff (The Bartender as Michael Delmatoff).

Gene plays Poppy, a good-time girl out for all the excitement she can get in Shanghai, and she gets it! As she accidentally falls into the gambling empire of Mother Gin Sling (Ona Munson), we watch as Poppy gradually spirals into living within a world of gambling, men and booze. It is a sultry story of deception, lust and betrayal. Although not a masterpiece, it stands alone as a theatrical gem, if only for the interesting, if not laughable, style of Mother Gin Sling's hair!

Awards and Nominations, 1943 Academy Awards, Nominated, Best Art Direction, Interior Decoration, Black and White, Boris Leven; Best Music, Scoring of a Dramatic or Comedy Picture, Richard Hageman.

Interesting Trivia: Ona Munson (Mother Gin Sling) committed suicide on February 11, 1955. She took an overdose of sleeping pills. She was 52 years old. A note found next to her lifeless body read, "This is the only way I know to be free again.... Please don't follow me."

Son of Fury. 1942, Twentieth Century–Fox.

Director John Cromwell. *Producer* Darryl F. Zanuck. *Writing Credits* Phillip Dunne, Edison Marshall (novel). *Cinematographer* Arthur C. Miller. *Running time* 98 minutes. *Location* Busch Gardens, Pasadena, California. *Release Dates* 29 January 1942.

Cast: Tyrone Power (Benjamin Blake), **Gene Tierney (Eve)**, George Sanders (Sir Arthur Blake), Frances Farmer (Isabel Blake), Elsa Lanchester (Bristol Isabel), Kay Johnson (Helena Blake), John Carradine (Caleb Green), Harry Davenport (Amos Kidder), Dudley Digges (Bartholomew Pratt), Roddy McDowall (Young Benjamin Blake), Halliwell Hobbes (Purdy), Marten Lamont (Kenneth Hobart), Arthur Hohl (Captain Greenough), Pedro de Cordoba (Feenou), Heather Thatcher (Maggie Martin).

Tyrone Power stars as Benjamin Blake, an 18th century heir to an English estate, but having been double-crossed by his devious uncle, Sir Arthur Blake (George Sanders), who swindles him out of his rightful fortune, he flees to a remote desert island to regroup. There he meets the beautiful native island girl, Eve (Gene Tierney) and proceeds to think about seeking revenge for the loss of his stolen fortune. However, he soon amasses a new fortune pearl diving with his partner, Caleb Green (John Carradine).

Rings on Her Fingers. 1942, Twentieth Century–Fox.

Director Rouben Mamoulian. *Producer* Milton Sperling. *Writing Credits* Ken Englund, Robert Pirosh (story), Emeric Pressburger (adaptation) and Joseph Schrank (story). *Cinematographer* George Barnes. *Running time* 86 mins. *Release Dates* 20 March, 1942, U.S.A.

Cast: Henry Fonda (John Wheeler), **Gene Tierney (Susan Miller/Linda Worthington)**, Laird Cregar (Warren), John Shepperd (Tod Fenwick), Spring Byington (Mrs. Maybelle Worthington), Frank Orth (Kellogg), Henry Stephenson (Colonel Prentiss), Marjorie Gateson (Mrs. Fenwick), George Lessey (Fenwick Sr.), Iris Adrian (Peggy), Harry Hayden (Train Conductor), Gwendolyn Logan (Miss Calahan), Eric Wilton (Butler), William "Billy" Benedict (Newsboy), Sarah Edwards (Mrs. Clancy).

A wisecracking, romantic comedy that teams Gene Tierney and Henry Fonda for a second time. Gene is recruited as a novice con artist by old hands Mrs. Maybelle Worthington (Spring Byington) and Warren (Laird Cregar). When John Wheeler (Henry Fonda) shows up, his desire to buy a yacht with his hard earned cash proves to be the perfect opportunity for Gene to con him out of his money and

Filmography

not deliver the yacht he's been dreaming of his whole life. As the con begins, Gene realizes her sucker isn't such a sucker after all. Love blossoms and Gene and Henry set out to turn the tables on the longtime crooks who recruited her. A lightweight romantic comedy in the familiar Rock Hudson/Doris Day style that we all love.

Thunderbirds. 1942, Twentieth Century–Fox.

Director William A. Wellman. *Producer* Lamar Trotti. *Writing Credits* Lamar Trotti and Darryl F. Zanuck (story). *Cinematographer* Ernest Palmer. *Running time* 78 mins. *Release Dates* 19 October, 1942, U.S.A.

Cast: **Gene Tierney (Kay Saunders)**, Preston Foster (Steve Britt), John Sutton (Peter Stackhouse), Jack Holt (McDonald), Dame May Whitty (Lady Stackhouse), George Barbier (Grampa), Richard Haydn (George Lockwood), Reginald Denny (Barrett), Ted North (Cadet Hackzell), Janis Carter (Blonde), C. Montague Shaw (Doctor), Viola Moore (Nurse), Nana Bryant (Mrs. Black), Joyce Compton (Saleswoman), Bess Flowers (Nurse).

Another Technicolor film, in 1942 set during the height of World War II, about the flight training of pilots at Thunderbird field in Arizona. The aerial shots with the desert background are cinematic art at its grandest. Not entirely accurate in it's aviational dialog but the cast pulls it off to make it believable enough for the untrained ear to accept it.

Memorable Quotes: Peter Stackhouse: "I hope you're not angry?" Kay Saunders: "That you were interested in my legs? Why not at all. That's what they're there for."

Interesting Trivia: Peter Lawford has an uncredited bit part as a young cadet. Aviation ace Richard Bong is one of the pilots flying in the North American AT-6's formation in the film. He is uncredited but would soon gain fame as the real life "Ace of Aces" by shooting down some 40 Japanese planes. It was a World War II feat that no other U.S. pilot accomplished. Unfortunately, he died on June 6, 1945, in California in the seemingly low risk phase of taking off in a P-80 jet. The plane lost power and crashed, killing him instantly.

China Girl. 1942, Twentieth Century–Fox.

Director Henry Hathaway. *Producers* Ben Hecht, William Goetz (uncredited) and Darryl F. Zanuck (uncredited). *Writing Credits* Ben Hecht and Darryl F. Zanuck. *Cinematographer* Lee Garmes. *Release Dates* 9 December 1942, U.S.A.

Cast: **Gene Tierney (Miss Young)**, George Montgomery (Johnny), Lynn Bari (Capt. Fifi), Victor McLaglen (Major Weed), Alan Baxter (Chinese Boy), Sig Ruman (Jarubi), Myron McCormick (Shorty), Robert Blake (Chinese Boy as Bobby Blake), Ann Pennington (Sugar Fingers, the Entertainer), Philip Ahn (Dr. Young), Tom Neal (Haynes), Paul Fung (Governor), Lal Chand Mehra (Desk Clerk), Kam Tong (Doctor).

An American newsreel cameraman, Johnny (George Montgomery), is stationed in China just prior to the bombing of Pearl Harbor. With information that is crucial to the Japanese, he escapes from a concentration camp with the help of his newfound love, the beautiful Miss Young (Gene Tierney), an American-educated Chinese woman. Together they join forces and get involved in the war effort, relaying important enemy information back home, information that Johnny has learned from his Japanese captors.

Heaven Can Wait. 1943, Twentieth Century–Fox.

Director Ernst Lubitsch. *Producer* Ernest Lubitsch. *Writing Credits* Leslie Bush-Fekete (play) and Samson Raphaelson. *Cinematographer* Edward Cronjager. *Running time* 112 mins. *Release Dates* 11 August, 1943, U.S.A.

Cast: **Gene Tierney (Martha Strabel/Van Cleve)**, Don Ameche (Henry Van Cleve), Charles Coburn (Hugo Van Cleve, Grandfather), Marjorie Main (Martha's Mother), Laird Cregar (His Excellency), Spring Byington (Bertha Van Cleve, Mother), Allyn Joslyn (Albert Van Cleve, Cousin), Eugene Pallette (E.F. Strabel, Martha's Father), Signe Hasso (Mademoiselle), Louis Calhern (Randolph Van Cleve, Father), Helene Reynolds (Peggy Nash, Showgirl), Aubrey Mather (James, Jack's Butler), Tod Andrews (Jack Van Cleve, Henry's Son).

A classy ensemble cast of character actors makes *Heaven Can Wait* a charming film. Upon arriving in hell, Henry Van Cleve (Don Ameche) must convince the ruler, the devil, that he was sent to the right place. Upon telling his story, he retells his life to us, the audience.

We see his marriage to Martha (Gene Tierney), and he admits to his many extramarital interludes. We see his children, and the devil decides he was nothing but a kind-hearted father. We see his world, one that he's now left, but the devil concludes that he's lived well. With the evaluation complete the devil states, "If you'll forgive me, Mr. Van Cleave, we just don't want your kind down here."

We then see Henry being shown to the elevator, giving the operator a one-word command, "Up." Henry is instantly sent to the pearly gates, ready to be rejoined in heaven with his beautiful wife, Martha.

Memorable Quotes: His Excellency: "If you meet our requirements, we'll be only too glad to accommodate you. Would you be kind enough to mention, for instance, some outstanding crime you've committed?" Henry Van Cleve: "Crime? Well, I'm afraid I can't think of any. But I can safely say that my whole life was one continuous misdemeanor."

Mademoiselle: "In your papa's time, papa kiss mama and then marry. But this is 1887! Time of bicycle, the typewriter has arrive, soon everybody speak over telephone, and people have new idea of value of kiss. What was bad yesterday is lot of fun today. There is a wonderful saying in France: 'Les baisers sont comme des bonbons qu'on mange parce qu'ils sont bons.' This means: 'Kiss is like candy. You eat candy only for the beautiful taste, and this is enough reason to eat candy.'"

Henry Van Cleve: "You mean I can kiss a girl once.... Mademoiselle: Ten times! Twenty times! And no obligation."

Martha: "Oh, Henry, I know your every move. I know your outraged indignation. I know the poor weeping little boy. I know the misunderstood, strong, silent man, the worn-out lion who is too proud to explain what happened in the jungle last night."

Awards and Nominations, 1944 Nominated, Best Color Cinematography, Edward Cronjager; *1944* Nominated Best Director, Ernst Lubitsch; *1944*, Nominated, Best Picture, Ernst Lubitsch.

Laura. 1944, Twentieth Century–Fox.

Director Otto Preminger. *Producer* Otto Preminger. *Writing Credits* Vera Caspary (novel), Jay Dratler, Samuel Hoffenstein, Elizabeth Reinhardt and Ring Lardner Jr. *Cinematographers* Joseph LaShelle and Lucien Ballard (uncredited). *Running time* 88 mins. *Production Dates* 27 April, 1944–June 1944. *Release Dates* 11 October, 1944, New York City; November 1944, nationwide.

Cast: **Gene Tierney (Laura Hunt)**, Dana Andrews (Det. Lt. Mark McPherson), Clifton Webb (Waldo Lydecker), Vincent Price (Shelby Carpenter), Judith Anderson (Mrs. Ann Treadwell).

Det. Lt. Mark McPherson (Dana Andrews) falls in love with the murdered Laura Hunt (Gene Tierney) through the tales her friends tell him and through her alluring portrait as he tries desperately to solve her murder. As the movie progresses, Laura suddenly turns up alive. The investigation deepens, as everyone now tries to uncover why Laura was marked for murder. And if she isn't dead, who was it that died in her place?

Laura is considered a classic film noir example. The perfect recipe of great acting, clever direction and haunting music composed by David Raksin takes the viewer on a magical ride that satisfies the senses.

Interesting Trivia: The film was initially directed by Rouben Mamoulian, but Otto Preminger, who undertook the position of producer took over the direction, hired a new cameraman and started again. All of Mamoulian's footage was thrown away.

The numerous stories of Otto Preminger's battle to get *Laura* made are legendary, his five Oscar nominations for the film well deserved. Darryl F. Zanuck was against casting Clifton Webb as Waldo Lydecker because of his known homosexuality, but Preminger stood firm and the 54-year-old Webb, making his first movie appearance since 1930, was nominated for an Oscar.

Subsequently, all of this excitement caused Webb to admit himself to a mental hospital upon completion of the film. He felt he was in the throes of a nervous breakdown.

The portrait of Gene Tierney as Laura isn't a painting at all but a photograph done over with oil paint. The portrait was used on the set of another film, *On the Riviera*, also starring Gene. However, it's undetectable in the final cut of the film.

Both Jennifer Jones and Hedy Lamarr turned down the role of Laura before it was offered to Gene. It's now hard to imagine anyone but Gene in the title role.

Clifton Webb had a clause written into his contract that required no one refer to or comment on his homosexuality. If they did, there would be consequences, most probably instant dismissal.

It was a collaborative effort in all departments to make *Laura* the classic it turned out to be. As much as David Raksin praised Johnny Mercer's brilliant writing of the lyrics for the title song. He himself wrote the music for those famous lyrics in one weekend.

Awards and Nominations, 1945 Won, Best Cinematography, Black and White, Joseph LaShelle; Clifton Webb, Nominated, Best actor in a supporting role; Best Art Direction/Interior Decoration, Black and White, Nominated, Lyle R. Wheeler, Leland Fuller and Thomas Little; Best Director, Nominated, Otto Preminger; Best writing, screenplay, Nominated, Jay Dratler, Samuel Hoffenstein and Elizabeth Reinhardt.

Memorable Quotes: Waldo Lydecker: "How singularly innocent I look this morning."

Bessie Clary: "I ain't afraid of cops. I was brought up to spit whenever I saw one."

Mark McPherson: "OK, go ahead and spit if that'll make you feel better."

Waldo Lydecker: "Love is eternal. It has been the strongest motivation for human actions throughout history. Love is stronger than life. It reaches beyond the dark shadow of death."

Mark McPherson: "Yeah, dames are always pulling a switch on you."

Waldo Lydecker: "Will you stop calling her a dame!"

Waldo Lydecker: "I should be sincerely sorry to see my neighbor's children devoured by wolves."

Waldo Lydecker: "I don't use a pen. I write with a goose quill dipped in venom."

Waldo Lydecker: "In my case, self-absorption is completely justified. I have never discovered any other subject quite so worthy of my attention."

Shelby Carpenter: "I can afford a blemish on my character, but not on my clothes."

Mark McPherson: "I must say, for a charming, intelligent girl, you certainly surrounded yourself with a remarkable collection of dopes."

Filmography

Waldo Lydecker: "I'm not kind, I'm vicious. It's the secret of my charm."

Waldo Lydecker: "I cannot stand these morons any longer. Leave with me now or I'll run amok."

Waldo Lydecker: "You'd better watch out, McPherson, or you'll finish up in a psychiatric ward. I doubt they've ever had a patient who fell in love with a corpse."

Waldo Lydecker: "It's lavish, but I call it home."

Waldo Lydecker: "I shall never forget the weekend Laura died. A silver sun burned through the sky like a huge magnifying glass. It was the hottest Sunday in my recollection. I felt as if I were the only human being left in New York ... I had just begun Laura's story when another of those detectives came to see me. I had him wait."

A Bell for Adano. 1945, Twentieth Century–Fox.

Director Henry King. *Producers* Louis D. Lighton and Lamar Trotti. *Writing Credits* John Hershey (novel), Norman Reilly Raine and Lamar Trotti. *Cinematographer* Joseph La Shelle. *Running time* 103 minutes. *Release Dates* 21 June, 1945, U.S.A.

Cast: **Gene Tierney (Tina Tomasino)**, John Hodiak (Maj. Victor P. Joppola), William Bendix (Sgt. Borth), Glenn Langan (Lt. Crofts Livingstone, USN), Richard Conte (Nicolo, Italian POW), Stanley Prager (Sgt. Trampani), Harry Morgan (Capt. N. Purvis as Henry Morgan), Monty Banks (Giuseppe), Reed Hadley (Cmdr. Robertson), Roy Roberts (Col. W.W. Middleton, Provost Marshal), Hugo Haas (Father Pensovecchio), Marcel Dalio (Zito), Fortunio Bonanova (Chief of Police Gargano), Henry Armetta (Errante, Cart Man), Roman Bohnen (Carl Erba, Cart Man).

Another wartime movie based at the end of World War II. A small military detachment arrives in the village of Adano. They go about reorganizing the village after its previous fascist mayor has abandoned it and headed into hiding. With the people embracing this newfound freedom, along with fresh food and medical aid, their biggest wish is for the town bell to be restored in the bell tower.

The original bell has been sent away to be melted down for military weapons, so the villagers' search for a replacement bell becomes the task at hand. The military leader, Maj. Victor P. Joppola (John Hodiak), is soon captivated by the blonde (Gene Tierney is a blonde in this film) village girl, Tina (Gene Tierney).

He soon confesses that he is married, and she tells of the day that she awaits when her sweetheart returns from the war. The continued reorganization of the village develops, and a new bell is bought to rehang in the town hall. As the festivities develop and the party begins to celebrate the new bell, word arrives that the major is being relieved of his post and will be sent to Algiers. As the major says farewell to the villagers, Tina learns of her sweetheart's death in battle. The major follows his orders and leaves the village and Tina behind. The only memory of his existence there is a newfound hope among people and a photo of him in the Town Hall.

Leave Her to Heaven. 1945, Twentieth Century–Fox.

Director John M. Stahl. *Producer* William A. Bacher. *Writing Credits* Ben Ames Williams (novel) and Jo Swerling. *Cinematographer* Leon Shamroy. *Running time* 110 mins. *Filming locations* Bass Lake, California, the notorious boat scene; Granite Dells, Prescott, Arizona; Monterey, California; New Mexico; Sedona, Arizona; Wyoming. *Release dates* 19 December 1945, premiere; 20 December 1945, nationwide. *Box Office Take* including rentals, $5,500,000.

Cast: **Gene Tierney (Ellen Berent)**, Cornel Wilde (Richard Harland), Jeanne Crain (Ruth Berent), Vincent Price (Russell Quinton), Mary Philips (Mrs. Berent), Ray Collins (Glen Robie), Gene Lockhart (Dr. Saunders), Reed Hadley (Dr. Mason), Darryl Hickman (Danny Harland), Chill Wills (Leick Thome)

In possibly her best role ever, Gene Tierney plays Ellen Berent, a beautiful but evil woman with an insanely jealous nature. After a whirlwind romance and marriage, Ellen's husband, Richard Harland (Cornel Wilde), becomes suspicious of the tragedies that seem to be happening all too often since Ellen became his wife. First his brother becomes the victim of a drowning accident, or was it? Then he loses his unborn son through Ellen's miscarriage. Ellen's family begins to see her unbalanced behavior, and it's soon clear that Ellen will stop at nothing to keep her husband for herself, even in death!

Gene Tierney deserved her nomination for Best Actress of 1946. It can be argued that she even deserved to win the Oscar for Best Female Lead in *Leave Her to Heaven*. Joan Crawford took that accolade from her, winning her only Oscar for Best Actress of the year in *Mildred Pierce*.

Gene's cold, dark, evil character behind her mask of beauty makes the role of Ellen Berent even scarier. Back in 1945, when this film was released, audiences would have been completely stunned by the dark, sinister nature of this film. With a great supporting cast, including Vincent Price (coming back again to star along side his lifelong friend), this movie has it all. Even today, as we watch misery and evil lurk within the saturation of brilliant Technicolor, *Leave Her to Heaven* has the ability to give the viewer goose bumps over and over again.

Awards and Nominations, 1946 Best Color Cinematography, Won, Leon Shamroy; Gene Tierney, Nominated, Best Actress in a leading role; Best Art Direction-Interior Decoration, Color, Nominated, Lyle R. Wheeler, Maurice Ransford and Thomas Little; Best Sound Recording, Nominated, Thomas T. Moulton.

Dragonwyck. 1946, Twentieth Century–Fox.

Director Joseph L. Mankiewicz. *Producer* Darryl F. Zanuck, Ernest Lubitsch

Filmography

(uncredited). *Writing Credits* Joseph L. Mankiewicz and Anya Seton (novel). *Cinematographer* Arthur C. Miller. *Running time* 103 mins. *Release Dates* 10 April 1946, U.S.A. *Budget* $1,900,000.

Cast: **Gene Tierney (Miranda Wells)**, Walter Huston (Ephraim Wells), Vincent Price (Nicholas Van Ryn), Glenn Langan (Abigail Wells), Spring Byington (Magda), Connie Marshall (Katrine Van Ryn), Harry Morgan (Klaus Bleecker as Henry Morgan), Vivienne Osborne (Johanna Van Ryn), Jessica Tandy (Peggy O'Malley), Trudy Marshall (Elizabeth Van Borden).

This gothic thriller, set in 1844, tells the story of a pretty young farmer's daughter, Miranda Wells (Gene Tierney). She receives an invitation too good to refuse, an offer to live in a grand mansion as a companion for a rich distant relative's lonely daughter. Upon her arrival, the charming Nicholas Van Ryn (Vincent Price) seduces Miranda (Gene Tierney) while servants continually warn her of lurking spirits and visitations from the dead.

Van Ryn's hatred for his wife deepens when she is unable to bear him a son, and with his increasing infatuation with the young Miranda he poisons his wife with the leaf of a deadly plant. His wife's demise gives him the freedom to marry the innocent Miranda. When Miranda, now his new bride, gives birth to the son he's always longed for, Van Ryn is overjoyed. However, the infant is sickly and soon dies. It is a tragedy that spirals Van Ryn into a drug induced madness. He retreats to his secret tower room for days, sometimes weeks. The tower room is a mysterious place that nobody dare enter, not even Miranda.

Dr Jeff Turner (Glenn Langan) falls in love with Miranda, and her increasing fears of her husband's instability causes Dr. Turner to delve deeper into the mysterious death of Van Ryn's first wife. Everything points to Miranda being his next victim, so he vows to save her from her husband's evil, murderous intentions.

Memorable quotes: Miranda Wells: "But there's everything here you could possibly want!"

Ephraim Wells: "Everything is what no man should ever want."

Johanna Van Ryn: "What can you possibly do up there?"

Nicholas Van Ryn: "Possibly? Anything from pinning butterflies to hiding an insane twin brother. Actually, I read. I hope that my explanation satisfies you?"
Nicholas Van Ryn: "But I will not live by ordinary standards. I will not run with the pack. I will not be chained into a routine of living, which is the same for others. I will not look to the ground and move on the ground with the rest so long as there are those mountaintops, and clouds, and limitless space."

Interesting Trivia: Ernst Lubitsch was scheduled to direct the film, but illness forced him to back out and he was replaced with the brilliant Joseph L. Mankiewicz. It was a big break for him at the time, as it was to be his directorial debut. *Dragonwyck* was the fourth and final time that Gene co-starred with Vincent Price.

Their other films were *Hudson's Bay*, *Laura* and *Leave Her to Heaven*. Gene's first meeting with future U.S. President John F. Kennedy was on the set of *Dragonwyck*. She remembered his eyes being the most beautiful blue that she had ever seen on a man. Her heart skipped a beat when she saw him that first time. It was the start of yet another relationship that would only end in heartbreak for her.

The Razor's Edge. 1946, Twentieth Century–Fox.

Director Edmund Goulding. *Producer* Darryl F. Zanuck. *Writing Credits* W. Somerset Maugham (novel) and Lamar Trotti. *Cinematographer* Arthur C. Miller. *Running time* 146 mins. *Release Dates* 19 November 1946, New York City, premiere; December 1946, nationwide. *Budget* $1,200,000. *Box Office Take* $5,000,000.

Cast: Tyrone Power (Larry Darrell), **Gene Tierney (Isabel Bradley)**, John Payne (Gray Maturin), Anne Baxter (Sophie Nelson Macdonald), Clifton Webb (Elliott Templeton), Herbert Marshall (W. Somerset Maugham), Lucile Watson (Louisa Bradley), Frank Latimore (Bob Macdonald), Elsa Lanchester (Miss Keith, Princess' secretary), Cecil Humphreys (Holy man), Harry Pilcer (Specialty dancer), Cobina Wright, Sr. (Princess Novemali).

The rich, handsome Larry Darrell (Tyrone Power) suddenly breaks his engagement to the beautiful Isabel (Gene Tierney) and decides to travel the world on a search for enlightenment and the meaning of life. Not willing to wait for his return, Isabel marries Gray Maturin (John Payne). After an invitation to move to Paris to live with her rich Uncle Elliot (Clifton Webb), they all run into Larry on his way home after having fulfilled his goal of "finding himself."

While out on the town, the group runs into an old Chicago friend, Sophie (Anne Baxter). Shocked at what she has become after losing her husband and child in an accident, Larry volunteers to help the drug addicted, booze addicted Sophie get back on her feet.

Once again Gene Tierney plays a beautiful but deceptive character to eerie perfection. We watch as she sabotages Sophie's attempt at rehabilitation for her own selfish reason, a reconciliation with Larry.

Memorable Quotes: Elliott Templeton: "The enjoyment of art is the only remaining ecstasy that's neither immoral nor illegal."

Elliott Templeton: "If I live to be a hundred I shall never understand how any young man can come to Paris without evening clothes."

Awards and Nominations, 1947 Academy Awards, Won, Best Actor in a Supporting Role, Anne Baxter; Nominated, Best Actor in a Supporting Role, Clifton Webb; Nominated, Best Art Direction–Interior Decoration, Black and White, Richard Day, Nathan Juran, Thomas Little and Paul S. Fox; Nominated, Best Picture, Darryl F. Zanuck; 1947 Golden Globe Awards, Won, Best Supporting Actor, Clifton Webb; 1947 Golden Globe Awards, Best Supporting Actor, Anne Baxter.

Filmography

Interesting Trivia: The Razor's Edge was the second time that Gene co-starred with Clifton Webb. Their other film was *Laura*. Herbert Marshall, who plays the role of William Somerset Maugham, had previous experience with the character, portraying him in the 1942 film *The Moon and Sixpence*. *The Razor's Edge* was Tyrone Power's first major film role after serving time in the Marine Air Corps.

The Ghost and Mrs. Muir. 1947, Twentieth Century–Fox.

Director Joseph L. Mankiewicz. *Producer* Fred Kohlmar. *Writing Credits* R.A. Dicks (novel) and Phillip Dunne. *Cinematographer* Charles Lang. *Running time* 104 mins. *Location* Carmel, California, and Palos Verdes, California. Various scenery shots were of the Cornish (U.K.) coastline. *Release Dates* 26 June, 1947, U.S.A.

Cast: **Gene Tierney (Lucy Muir)** Rex Harrison (Capt. Daniel Gregg), George Sanders (Miles Fairley), Edna Best (Martha Huggins), Vanessa Brown (Anna Muir as an adult), Anna Lee (Mrs. Miles Fairley), Robert Coote (Mr. Coombe), Natalie Wood (Anna Muir as a child), Isobel Elsom (Angelica, mother-in-law), Victoria Horne (Eva, sister-in-law).

This is where Joseph L. Mankiewicz came into his own as a director. *The Ghost and Mrs. Muir*, although not considered a big hit of its day, has gone on to become a classic in every sense of the word. In the film, set in 1900, a strong willed widow, Lucy Muir (Gene Tierney), isn't deterred by the gossip saying that the enchanting cottage by the British seaside is haunted.

She and her daughter, Anna (played by a very young Natalie Wood), move in, and the ghost confronts Lucy that very night. A crusty sea captain by the name of Captain Gregg (Rex Harrison) soon realizes that his scare tactics aren't going to be effective on the feisty Lucy Muir, but he begins to find her spunk enchanting.

He realizes she'd be the perfect person to write his memoirs, a chore she agrees to do. Upon its completion, she visits a publishing house where she comes under the spell of children's book publisher, Miles Fairley (George Sanders), a sleazy, very alive but very married man whom Captain Gregg despises.

The impending real life relationship forces both Lucy and Captain Gregg into confronting their very real but somewhat impossible feelings for each other. Upon finding out that Miles is a married man, Lucy breaks off their relationship and is content to spend her life alone, with the companionship of a ghost.

Only in death can they ever be together. The film ends with Lucy dying in her chair, an old woman who has waited for the moment of joining her beloved sea captain in the afterlife. We see an extended hand pull a now young spirit of Lucy out of her chair, and we, wipe away our tears as they walk arm in arm down the stairs and into forever, together at last.

Memorable Quotes: Captain Gregg: "I've lived the life of a man and am not ashamed to admit it."

Filmography

Captain Gregg: "No woman has ever been the worse for knowing me."

Captain Gregg: "You must make your own life amongst the living and, whether you meet fair winds or foul, find your own way to harbor in the end."

Mr. Coombe: "In my opinion, you are the most obstinate young woman I have ever met." Lucy Muir: "Thank you, Mr. Coombe!"

Captain Gregg: "My dear! Never let anyone tell you to be ashamed of your figure."

Lucy Muir: "It's no crime to be alive!" Captain Gregg: "No, my dear, sometimes it's a great inconvenience. The living can be hurt."

Awards and Nominations, 1948 Nominated, Best Cinematography, Black and White, Charles Lang.

Interesting Trivia: The Ghost and Mrs. Muir was the third and final time that Gene co-starred with George Sanders. Their other films were *Son of Fury* and *Sundown*. In 1937, George Sanders told fellow actor and friend that he intended to commit suicide if he ever got to old age. He was a man of his word.

In 1973, George sold his house, checked into a Majorca Hotel and took five tubes of Nembutal. His suicide note was written in the familiar George Sanders fashion. It read, "Dear World, I am leaving because I am bored. I feel I have lived long enough. I am leaving you with your worries in this sweet cesspool. Good luck." Cynical to the end, George Sanders was just three months shy of his 66th birthday.

The Iron Curtain. 1948, Twentieth Century–Fox.

Director William A. Wellman. *Producer* Sol C. Siegel. *Writing Credits* Igor Gouzenko (story) and Milton Krims. *Cinematographer* Charles G. Clarke. *Running time* 87 mins. *Release Dates* September 1948, U.S.A.

Cast: Dana Andrews (Igor Gouzenko), **Gene Tierney (Anna Gouzenkova)**, Stefan Schnabel (Col. Ilya Ranov, embassy attache), Berry Kroeger (John Grubb, aka "Paul"), Frederic Tozere (Col. Aleksandr Trigorin), Eduard Franz (Maj. Semyon Kulin), Peter Whitney (Cipher Lt. Vinikov), June Havoc (Nina Karanova), Nicholas Joy (Dr. Harold Preston Norman, aka "Alec"), Edna Best (Mrs. Albert Foster. neighbor), Noel Cravat (Bushkin), Mauritz Hugo (Leonard Leitz, Member of Parliament), Victor Wood (Capt. Donald P. Class), John Shay (Lt. Pyotr Sergeyev), Reed Hadley (Narrator).

Based on the true-life story of the Soviet Embassy code specialist Igor Gouzenko, played by Dana Andrews. This is the story of his country, Russia, sending him under a cloud of secrecy to Canada to further espionage efforts in that country. After living within the Canadian system, he decides to defect, turning over secret Russian documents to his new country's government. After realizing the importance of the Russian documents, Gouzenko and his family are swiftly put into protective custody. Gene Tierney plays Anna Gouzenko (his wife) in this spy thriller.

Filmography

That Wonderful Urge. 1948, Twentieth Century–Fox.

Director Robert B. Sinclair. *Producer* Fred Kohlmar. *Writing Credits* Jay Dratler, William Lipman and Frederick Stephani (story). *Running time* 82 mins. *Release Dates* 20 November 1948, U.S.A.

Cast: Tyrone Power (Thomas Jefferson Tyler), **Gene Tierney (Sara Farley)**, Reginald Gardiner (Count André de Guyon), Arleen Whelan (Jessica Woods), Lucile Watson (Anut Cornelia Farley), Gene Lockhart (Judge Parker), Lloyd Gough (Duffy, Chronicle Editor), Porter Hall (Attorney Ketchell), Richard Gaines (Whitson, Farley's Executive), Taylor Holmes (Attorney Rice).

A remake of the 1937 comedy *Love News*, *That Wonderful Urge* again teams Tyrone Power with Gene Tierney. Power reprises his role from the earlier film and plays the handsome reporter, Thomas Jefferson Tyler. He actively pursues a flighty heiress, Sara Farley, played by Gene Tierney (Loretta Young played her role in the 1937 version). Tired of constant suitors, Sara (Gene Tierney) unexpectedly announces that she has married Thomas, and she forces him to go along with her plan. After a string of screwball scenes, the two of them finally concede they're really in love after all.

Interesting Trivia: That Wonderful Urge was the third and last time that Gene and Tyrone Power co-starred. Their other films were *The Razor's Edge* and *Son of Fury*. Tyrone Power's premature death ended any future pairing on the silver screen. If he had lived, there's no doubt they would have worked together on many more occasions. They clicked as an on-screen couple and were genuinely fond of each other off screen.

Whirlpool. 1949, Twentieth Century–Fox.

Director Otto Preminger. *Producer* Otto Preminger. *Writing Credits* Guy Endore (novel), Ben Hecht and Andrew Solt. *Cinematographer* Arthur C. Miller. *Running time* 98 mins. *Release Dates* 28 November 1949, U.S.A.

Cast: **Gene Tierney (Ann Sutton)**, Richard Conte (Dr. William Sutton), José Ferrer (David Korvo), Charles Bickford (Lt. Colton), Barbara O'Neil (Theresa Randolph), Eduard Franz (Martin Avery), Constance Collier (Tina Cosgrove), Fortunio Bonanova (Feruccio di Ravallo).

Based on the novel by Guy Endore. Gene plays the part of Ann Sutton, a kleptomaniac. Richard Conte plays Dr. Bill Sutton, Jose Ferrer plays David Korvo, and Charles Bickford plays Lt. Colton. On one of her many shoplifting experiences, Ann gets caught, but eventually she is saved by hypnotist David Korvo.

She becomes entangled in his life and the lives of his friends, Tina Cosgrove, played by Constance Collier, and Theresa Randolph, played by Barbara O'Neil. The latter character is a focal point in the story after her murder points toward Ann (Gene Tierney) as the major suspect.

Filmography

David had a major operation before the murder took place, so he was immobile. His alibi is airtight. However, Ann's fingerprints are on the glass found in the murdered woman's library, along with Ann.

The mystery deepens when the investigative officer discovers that the dead woman was also a patient of Ann's psychiatrist husband. It really is a whirlpool of intrigue and suspense. A classic on-the-edge-of-your seat whodunit, a genre that today's filmmakers so often mistakenly ignore.

Night and the City. 1950, Twentieth Century–Fox.

Director Jules Dassin. *Producer* Samuel G. Engel. *Writing Credits* Austin Dempster (uncredited), Jo Eisinger, Gerald Kersh (novel). *Cinematographer* Mutz Greenbaum (as Max Greene). *Running time* 96 mins U.S.; 101 mins U.K. *Locations* Piccadilly Circus, London, England, Silver Fox Cafe, St. Martin's Lane, London; Thames Embankment, London; Trafalgar Square, London; Westminster Bridge, London; Hammersmith Bridge, London; St. Paul's Cathedral, London; the Demolished Shot Tower, South Bank, London. *Production Dates* July 1949–October 1949; *London Film Studio*, Shepparton, U.K. *Release Dates* April 1950, U.K.; 9 June, 1950, U.S.A.

Cast: Richard Widmark (Harry Fabian), **Gene Tierney (Mary Bristol)**, Googie Withers (Helen Nosseross), Hugh Marlowe (Adam Dunne), Francis L. Sullivan (Phil Nosseross, Silver Fox Club), Herbert Lom (Kristo), Stanislaus Zbyszko (Gregorius the Great), Mike Mazurki (The Strangler), Charles Farrell (Mickey Beer), Ada Reeve (Molly the Flower Lady), Ken Richmond (Nikolas, as Kenneth Richmond).

Night and the City teams Gene with Richard Widmark. Widmark plays Harry Fabian, a petty hustler and con man who goes after the bigger dollars in the London underworld. Not content with making small amounts of money on two-bit scams, he strikes up the idea of becoming a top London wrestling promoter. Big mistake!

Gene plays his girlfriend, Mary Bristol, the woman he promises a life of ease and comfort after his latest scam takes off. Fabian eventually creates a tangled web of lies, deceit and corruption. We see him on the run throughout most of the movie, proving there is no such thing as "easy money." Filmed mostly on location in London between July and October of 1949 and released in New York City on June 9th, 1950, the film was shot in the classic film noir style of the late '40s and '50s.

Interesting Trivia: An alternate British version of *Night and the City* exists that includes deleted scenes not seen in the American version. There are also different title credits, an opening scene with Widmark and Tierney that isn't anywhere to be seen in the American version, and an alternate score composed by Benjamin

Filmography

Frankel. These changes extend the U.K. version to 101 minutes, instead of the U.S. version of 96 minutes.

Where the Sidewalk Ends. 1950, Twentieth Century–Fox.

Director Otto Preminger. *Producer* Otto Preminger. *Writing Credits* Ben Hecht (screenplay), Robert E. Kent (adaptation), Frank P. Rosenberg (adaptation), William L. Stuart (novel) and Victor Trivias (adaptation). *Cinematographer* Joseph LaShelle. *Running time* 95 mins. *Location* New York City. *Release Dates* 26 June 1950, U.S.A., premiere; 7 July 1950, U.S.A., nationwide.

Cast: Dana Andrews (Det. Sgt. Mark Dixon, 16th Precinct), **Gene Tierney (Morgan Taylor [Paine]**), Gary Merrill (Tommy Scalise), Bert Freed (Det. Sgt. Paul Klein, Dixon's partner), Tom Tully (Jiggs Taylor, Morgan's Father), Karl Malden (Det. Lt. Thomas, 16th Precinct Detectives Commander), Ruth Donnelly (Martha, owner of Martha's Cafe), Craig Stevens (Ken Paine), Don Appell (Willie Bender), Neville Brand (Steve, Scalise Hood), Barry Brooks (Thug), Oleg Cassini (Oleg the Fashion Designer), John Close (Hanson), Anthony George (Thug), Kathleen Hughes (Secretary), Lou Krugman (Mike Williams), Louise Lane (Secretary), Louise Lorimer (Mrs. Jackson), Ian MacDonald (Casey), John McGuire (Gertessen), David McMahon (Harrington), Grayce Mills (Mrs. Tribaum, Paine's Landlady, as Grace Mills), Lou Nova (Ernie, Scalise Hood), Peggy O'Connor (Model), Stephen Roberts (Gilruth, as Steve Roberts), Robert F. Simon (Insp. Nicholas Foley, as Robert Simon), Phil Tully (Det. Ted Benson, 16th Precinct), Harry von Zell (Ted Morrison, Man killed at Scalise's place), David Wolfe (Sid Kramer, Scalise Hood).

Dana Andrews plays tough New York City cop Mark Dickson. He accidentally kills a murder suspect while giving him some roughhouse treatment, and in order to protect himself he covers the murder up. He sets up enough evidence to pin the blame on a well-known racketeer, a criminal who has committed similar crimes in the past. A perfect plan, or is it?

Gene plays the role of Morgan Taylor. She's the girlfriend of Ken Paine, played by Craig Stevens. A model by day and an escort in a sleazy gambling club at night, Gene soon crosses paths with Dickson and becomes emotionally involved with him. As the corrupt cop Dickson somehow gains the audience's sympathy, we slowly watch as his conscience gets the better of him.

With the combination of Otto Preminger, Dana Andrews and Gene Tierney, *Where the Sidewalk Ends* proved to be no *Laura*, but in its own right it had something else to give. Without making comparisons, it was (and still is) a perfect example of classic film noir.

Interesting Trivia: This was the fifth and last time that Gene co-starred with Dana Andrews. Prior to *Where the Sidewalk Ends*, they were both in *Belle Starr*,

Filmography

The Iron Curtain, *Laura* and *Tobacco Road*. They remained good friends long after their last appearance together on screen.

Close to My Heart. 1951, Warner Bros.

Director William Keighley. *Producer* William Jacobs. *Writing Credits* William Keighley (uncredited) and James R. Webb (novel and screenplay). *Cinematographer* Robert Burks. *Running time* 90 mins. *Release Dates* 1 January 1951, U.S.A.

Cast: Ray Milland (Brad Sheridan), **Gene Tierney (Midge Sheridan)**, Fay Bainter (Mrs. Morrow), Howard St. John (I.O. Frost), Mary Beth Hughes (Arlene), Ann Morrison (Mrs. Barker), James Seay (Heilner), Baby John Winslow (Himself), Eddie Marr (Taxi Driver Dunne), John Alvin (Haggard Man), Rodney Bell (Young Parent), Nan Boardman (Woman Patient), Ralph Byrd (Charlie), Elizabeth Flournoy (Receptionist), Fred Graham (Guard), Lois Hall (Young Mother).

Gene plays the role of Midge Sheridan in *Close to My Heart*. Ray Milland plays Brad Sheridan, her husband, in what turns out to be a soppy melodrama about the adoption process. It does, however, have a twist. The happy couple find out their newly adopted baby's biological father is a convicted murderer. The question of whether or not such evil character is a biological or environmental component is brought up. Not bearing to part with their baby, they decide, or rather convince themselves, that it must be environmental, they so keep the child and live happily ever after.

The Mating Season. 1951, Paramount.

Director Mitchell Leisen. *Producer* Charles Brackett. *Writing Credits* Charles Brackett, Richard L. Breen, Caesar Dunn (play) and Walter Reisch. *Cinematographer* Charles Lang. *Running time* 101 mins. *Release Dates* 12 January 1951, U.S.A.

Cast: **Gene Tierney (Maggy Carleton)**, John Lund (Val McNulty), Miriam Hopkins (Fran Carleton), Thelma Ritter (Ellen McNulty), Jan Sterling (Betsy), Larry Keating (Mr. Kalinger), James Lorimer (George C. Kalenger, Jr.), Gladys Hurlbut (Mrs. Conger), Cora Witherspoon (Mrs. Williamson), Malcolm Keen (Mr. Williamson), Ellen Corby (Annie), Billie Bird (Mugsy), Samuel Colt (Colonel Conger).

In *The Mating Season* Gene plays the role of Maggy Carleton/McNulty, the innocent new bride of Val McNulty, played by John Lund. The always lovable character actor Thelma Ritter plays the role of Ellen McNulty, Gene's new mother-in-law. As the story unfolds we see Maggy and Val setting up house after just being married. Ellen decides it would be nice to pay her son and new daughter-in-law a surprise visit, so she sells her New Jersey hamburger stand and makes the trip west.

When Ellen arrives, her daughter-in-law, Maggy, mistakes her for the maid she's just hired to help out at the lavish party she's throwing for her husband's

Filmography

boss. Ellen goes along with the role of maid and persuades her son not to correct his new wife. At least not yet. The confusion makes for a very funny chain of events with Ritter's performance earning her an Academy Award nomination for best supporting actress of 1952.

On the Riviera. 1951, Twentieth Century–Fox.

Director Walter Lang. *Producer* Sol C. Siegel. *Writing Credits* Hans Adler (play), Valentine Davies, Henry Ephron, Phoebe Ephron, Jesse Ernst (adaptation) and Rudolph Lothar (play). *Cinematographer* Leon Shamroy. *Running time* 89 mins. *Release Dates* 20 April, 1951, U.S.A. *Box Office Take* $2,500,000.

Cast: Danny Kaye (Jack Martin, Henri Duran), **Gene Tierney (Lili Duran**), Corinne Calvet (Colette), Marcel Dalio (Philippe Lebrix), Jean Murat (Felix Periton), Henri Letondal (Louis Foral), Clinton Sundberg (Antoine), Sig Ruman (Gapeaux), Joyce Mackenzie (Mimi, as Joyce MacKenzie), Monique Chantal (Minette), Marina Koshetz (Mme. Louise Cornet), Ann Codee (Mme. Periton), Mari Blanchard (Eugenie), Ethel Martin (Trio Dance Team Member), George Martin (Trio Dance Team Member).

On the Riviera was the second remake of the same story. The original film starred Maurice Chevalier and Merle Oberon. It was called *Folies Bergere* in a film released in 1935. In 1941 the second version, called *Night in Rio*, starred Don Ameche, Alice Faye and Carmen Miranda. This Kaye/Tierney version was the third version. Their strong performances made it the best of the three versions.

Kaye plays dual roles, Jack Martin and Henri Duran. His Duran character is married to Gene, who plays of his very confused wife, Lilli. It's the classic tale of two men so identical in appearance (obviously with Kaye playing both characters) that even a wife can't tell them apart. Kaye once again sings three very animated and comical songs written by his real life wife, lyricist Sylvia Fine. His performance was good enough to win him the 1952 Golden Globe Award for Best Actor in a Comedy or Musical. The film grossed a respectable 2.5 million in U.S. ticket sales.

Interesting Trivia: On the Riviera was the tenth and last time that Gene's then husband, fashion designer Oleg Cassini, worked as the costume designer. Their complete list of movies together as actress and designer are: *The Shanghai Gesture* (1941), *The Razor's Edge* (1946), *The Ghost and Mrs. Muir* (1947) (Gene Tierney's costumes), *That Wonderful Urge* (1948), *Whirlpool* (1949) (costume designer: Gene Tierney), *Where the Sidewalk Ends* (1950), *Night and the City* (1950) (Gene Tierney's costumes), *On the Riviera* (1951) (Gene Tierney's costumes), *The Mating Season* (1951) (Gene Tierney's costumes), and *Close to My Heart* (1951) (Gene Tierney's gowns).

The Secret of Convict Lake. 1951, Twentieth Century–Fox.

Director Michael Gordon. *Producer* Frank P. Rosenberg. *Writing Credits* Ben

Hecht (uncredited), Anna Hunger (story), Jack Pollexfen (story), Oscar Saul, Victor Trivas (adaptation). *Cinematographer* Leo Tover. *Running time* 83 mins. *Release Dates* 3 August 1951, New York City, U.S.A.

Cast: Glenn Ford (Jim Canfield), **Gene Tierney** (**Marcia Stoddard**), Ethel Barrymore (Granny), Zachary Scott (Johnny Greer), Ann Dvorak (Rachel Shaeffer), Barbara Bates (Barbara Purcell), Cyril Cusack (Edward "Limey" Cockerell), Richard Hylton (Clyde Maxwell), Helen Westcott (Susan Haggerty), Jeanette Nolan (Harriet Purcell), Ruth Donnelly (Mary), Harry Carter (Rudy Shaeffer).

The story is set in 1870s California. Jim Canfield (Glenn Ford) is convicted of a crime that he didn't commit. He plans an escape from his Nevada prison with several other inmates, and together they set out for the home of the man that framed him and the real man who committed the crime. On their arrival they find that women now mainly occupy the small farming community. The men have formed a posse and left the women behind while they search for the escapees. Jim soon falls for Marcia, played by Gene. The only problem is that Marcia is engaged to the man who framed him.

Way of a Gaucho. 1952, Twentieth Century–Fox.

Director Jacques Tourneur. *Producer* Phillip Dunne. *Writing Credits* Herbert Childs (novel) and Phillip Dunne. *Cinematographer* Harry Jackson. *Running time* 87 mins. *Release Dates* 16 October 1952, U.S.A.

Cast: Rory Calhoun (Martin), **Gene Tierney** (**Teresa**), Richard Boone (Salinas), Hugh Marlowe (Miguel), Everett Sloane (Falcon), Enrique Chaico (Father Fernández), Lidia Campos (Tia María), Mario Abdah (Horse Dealer), Teresa Acosta (Dancer), Raoul Astor (Police Lieutenant), Lia Centeno (Lady Guest), Kim Dillon (Sentry), Ronald Dumas (Julio), John Henchley (Gaucho Tracker), Oscar Lucero (Dancer), Hugo Mancini (Army Lieutenant), John Paris (Foreman), Alex Peters (Driver), Douglas Poole (Pall Bearer), Claudio Torres (Florencio), Anthony Ugrin (Bit Part), Jorge Villoldo (Valverde), Néstor Yoan (Army Lieutenant).

Shooting on *Way of the Gaucho* started in December of 1951. It would be a three-month location shoot in Argentina. The picturesque scenery of the Pampas and the Andes along with the ancient Spanish buildings and churches makes for a very enjoyable backdrop. Rory Calhoun plays Martin, the Gaucho outlaw whom Teresa, played by Gene, falls in love with. In short this is another, good girl, falls for bad boy love story with breathtaking photography to complement the romance.

Plymouth Adventure. 1952, MGM.

Director Clarence Brown. *Producer* Dore Schary. *Writing Credits* Ernest Gebler (novel) and Helen Deutsch. *Cinematographer* William H. Daniels. *Running time*

Filmography

105 mins. *Release Dates* 14 November 1952, New York City, U.S.A; 28 November 1952, nationwide.

Cast: Spencer Tracy (Capt. Christopher Jones), **Gene Tierney (Dorothy Bradford)**, Van Johnson (John Alden), Leo Genn (William Bradford), Dawn Addams (Priscilla Mullins), Lloyd Bridges (Coppin), Barry Jones (William Brewster), John Dehner (Gilbert Winslow), Tommy Ivo (William Button), Lowell Gilmore (Edward Winslow), Noel Drayton (Miles Standish).

The story follows the English settlers of the 17th century who traveled from England to New England on the *Mayflower*. Spencer Tracy plays Captain Christopher Jones, and Gene plays the pioneer woman, Dorothy Bradford, who although married, falls in love with him. The film was released on November 28, 1952. The special effects team of A. Arnold Gillespie, Warren Newcombe and Irving G. Ries all won an Academy Award for Best Special Effects in a Motion Picture of 1953.

Interesting Trivia: After working with Gene in *Plymouth Adventure*, Spencer Tracy said of her, "Although she was beautiful in her films, they couldn't quite capture all of her. Fortunately I did, even if it was late in my life."

Never Let Me Go. 1953, MGM.

Director Delmer Daves. *Producer* Clarence Brown. *Writing Credits* Roger Bax (novel), George Froeschel and Ronald Millar. *Cinematographer* Robert Krasker. *Running time* 69 minutes. *Location* Cornwall, England. *Release Dates* 1 May 1953, U.S.A.

Cast: Clark Gable (Philip Sutherland), **Gene Tierney (Marva Lamarkins)**, Bernard Miles (Joe Brooks), Richard Haydn (Christopher Denny), Belita (Valentina Alexandrovna), Kenneth More (Steve Quillan), Karel Stepanek (Commissar), Theodore Bikel (Russian Patrol Boat Cop), Anna Valentina (Svetlana Mikhailovna), Frederick Valk (Kuragin), Peter Illing (NKVD Man), Robert Henderson (U.S. Ambassador), Stanley Maxted (John Barnes), Meinhart Maur (Lemkov), Alexis Chesnakov (Gen. Zhdanov).

Never Let Me Go tells the story of an American news writer, Phillip Sutherland (Gable), who has been stationed in Moscow since the war. He falls in love with a Russian ballerina, Marva Lamarkins, played by Gene. After he finds out that she learned the English language in order to communicate after falling in love with him, they rush to the American embassy and marry. Life seems perfect for the newlyweds until Sutherland tries to bring his new wife out of Russia and into the United States. Communist Russia holds her captive and he is forced to temporarily leave her behind while he figures out a way of smuggling his bride into his own country of freedom.

Personal Affair. 1953, Twentieth Century–Fox.

Director Anthony Pelissier. *Producer* Antony Darnborough. *Writing Credits*

Filmography

Lesley Storm. *Cinematographer* Reginald Wyer. *Running time* 82 mins. *Release Dates* 15 January 1954, U.S.A.

Cast: **Gene Tierney (Kay Barlow)**, Leo Genn (Mr. Barlow), Glynis Johns (Barbara Vining), Walter Fitzgerald (Henry), Pamela Brown (Evelyn), Megs Jenkins (Vi), Michael Hordern (Headmaster), Thora Hird (Mrs. Usher*)*, Martin Boddey (Police Inspector), Norah Gaussen (Phoebe), Nanette Newman (Sally).

Gene plays Kay Barlow, the wife of a schoolteacher, Stephen Barlow, played by Leo Genn. When one of his students, Barbara Vining, played by Glynis Johns, falls in love with him, Kay confronts her, only to frighten her enough that she runs away. After Stephen (Leo Genn) goes after the young girl to explain the reality of why her infatuation with him has to end, he returns to town without her and the gossipy rumors of what happened to the missing girl begin to circulate.

With Barbara missing for days, and with his marriage and career crumbling around him, Stephen is accused of raping and murdering the girl. Luckily, before he is convicted of any such crime she returns to town and clears him of any wrongdoing. An entertaining, suspenseful drama.

Black Widow. 1954, Twentieth Century–Fox.

Director Nunnally Johnson. *Producer* Nunnally Johnson. *Writing Credits* Nunnally Johnson and Hugh Wheeler (story). *Cinematographer* Charles G. Clarke. *Running time* 95 mins. *Release Dates* 28 October 1954, New York City, U.S.A.

Cast: Ginger Rogers (Carlotta "Lottie" Marin), Van Heflin (Peter Denver), **Gene Tierney (Iris Denver)**, George Raft (Detective Lt. C.A. Bruce), Peggy Ann Garner (Nanny Ordway), Reginald Gardiner (Brian Mullen, Lottie's Husband), Virginia Leith (Claire Amberly, Nanny's Roommate), Otto Kruger (Gordon Ling, Nanny's Uncle), Cathleen Nesbitt (Lucia Colletti, the Maid), Skip Homeier (John Amberly, Claire's Brother), Hilda Simms (Anne, Sylvia's Hatcheck Girl), Harry Carter (Police Sergeant Welch), Geraldine Wall (Miss Mills), Richard H. Cutting (Police Sergeant Owens, as Richard Cutting), Mabel Albertson (Sylvia, Nanny's Employer).

When a young actress, Nanny Ordway, played by Peggy Ann Gardner, is murdered, suspicion shifts to a fellow actress, the bitchy Carlotta "Lottie" Marin, played by Ginger Rogers. Her husband, Peter Denver, played by Van Heflin, is also a suspect, known to have had a liking for Nanny (Peggy Ann Gardner). A love/hate triangle of murder and deception ensues. Gene plays Iris Denver and is merely a pretty prop in this film. Sadly, she isn't even given the honor of being one of the murder suspects. Given her ability to play evil characters masked by beauty, it would have given this film the extra spice it needs.

The Egyptian. 1954, Twentieth Century–Fox.

Director Michael Curtiz. *Producer* Darryl F. Zanuck. *Writing Credits* Phillip

Filmography

Dunne, Casey Robinson and Mika Waltari (novel). *Cinematographer* Leon Shamroy. *Running time* 139 mins. *Location* Death Valley National Park, California; Red Rock Canyon State Park, Kern County, California. *Release Dates* December 1954, U.S.A. *Budget* $5,000,000. *Gross* $4,250,000.

Cast: **Gene Tierney (Baketamon, Pharoah's sister)**, Michael Wilding (Akhnaton, the Pharoah), Bella Darvi (Nefer), Peter Ustinov (Kaptah), Edmund Purdom (Sinuhe, the Egyptian), Judith Evelyn (Taia, Queen Mother), Henry Daniell (Mekere, High Priest), John Carradine (Grave robber), Carl Benton Reid (Senmut, father of Sinuhe), Tommy Rettig (Thoth, son of Merit), Anitra Stevens (Queen Nefertiti).

A poor orphan, Sinuhe, played by Edmund Purdom, becomes a brilliant doctor in Eighteenth Dynasty Egypt. This is his story, told amid a backdrop of fine acting performances, props and costumes. Gene, in her most scantily clad role to date, plays Baketamon, the sister of the Pharoah, played by Michael Wilding.

This is another one of those solid '50s epic productions that is a spectacle to watch.

Awards and nominations, 1955 Academy Awards, Nominated, Best Color Cinematography, Leon Shamroy.

Interesting Trivia: Marlon Brando was signed to play the lead role, but for reasons unknown, he dropped out before filming began. It took two years for wardrobe designers to research and catalog some 5 million items of clothing and props for the epic production.

Bella Darvi, who played Nefer, was discovered in Europe by Darryl Zanuck and his wife, Virginia, three years prior to this film being made. She played the temptress not only on screen but also in real life, and was the main reason behind Zanuck's marriage breakdown. Her lack of acting ability combined with the Zanuck sex scandal destroyed any hopes of her becoming a Hollywood star.

Although her performance is far from bad in *The Egyptian*, the critics of the day slammed her, and she returned to Europe, depressed and defeated because her Hollywood career had come to such an abrupt and heartbreaking end. She did not recover. Sinking into a world of alcohol and gambling and with mounting debts, she decided death was her only way out. After several failed suicide attempts, she finally succeeded in 1971. At age 42, Bella turned on her kitchen stove and gassed herself.

The Left Hand of God. 1955, Twentieth Century–Fox.

Director Edward Dmytryk. *Producer* Buddy Adler. *Writing Credits* William E. Barrett (novel) and Alfred Hayes. *Cinematographer* Franz Planer. *Running time* 87 mins. *Release Dates* 21 September 1955, New York City, U.S.A.

Cast: Humphrey Bogart (Jim Carmody), **Gene Tierney (Anne Scott)**, Lee J.

Filmography

Cobb (Mieh Yang), Agnes Moorehead (Beryl Sigman), E.G. Marshall (Dr. David Sigman), Jean Porter (Mary Yin), Carl Benton Reid (Father Cornelius, bishop's envoy), Victor Sen Yung (John Wong, church sexton), Philip Ahn (Jan Teng, Buddhist priest), Benson Fong (Chun Tien, husband of dying woman).

Gene plays a beautiful missionary nurse, Ann Scott, who falls in love with Jim Carmody, played by Humphrey Bogart. An American soldier of fortune, Jim gets himself into an awkward predicament and disguises himself as a priest. Feeling ashamed at falling in love with a man of the cloth, Anne battles with her emotions until Jim finally confesses his love for her and reveals that he is nothing more than a man disguised as a priest to escape the Chinese warlord, General Yang, played by Lee J. Cobb.

Interesting Trivia: This film was the beginning of the end for both Gene and Humphrey Bogart. Bogart cradled Gene and helped her with her lines throughout the shoot, but her mental decline was at its peak, and upon the film's completion she would not return to work for seven years.

Humphrey Bogart was diagnosed with cancer on completion of this film. He would live for another 18 months, dying of throat cancer on January 14, 1957.

Advise and Consent. 1962, Columbia.

Director Otto Preminger. *Producer* Otto Preminger. *Writing Credits* Allen Drury (novel) and Wendell Mayes. *Cinematographer* Sam Leavitt. *Running time* 142 mins. *Location* Washington, District Columbia. *Release Dates* 6 June, 1962, U.S.A.

Cast: Franchot Tone (The President), Lew Ayres (The Vice President, Harley M. Hudson), Henry Fonda (Robert A. Leffingwell), Walter Pidgeon (Senate Majority Leader Robert D. Munson), Charles Laughton (Sen. Seabright "Seab" Cooley), Don Murray (Sen. Brigham "Brig" Anderson from Utah), Peter Lawford (Sen. Lafe Smith from Rhode Island), **Gene Tierney (Dolly Harrison)**, Burgess Meredith (Herbert Gelman), Eddie Hodges (Johnny Leffingwell), Paul Ford (Sen. Stanley Danta, Majority Whip), George Grizzard (Sen. Fred Van Ackerman from Wyoming), Inga Swenson (Ellen Anderson), Paul McGrath (Hardiman Fletcher), Will Geer (Senate Minority Leader Warren Strickland).

Another speech-laden political film, directed once again by Otto Preminger. With all the star power he could muster, Preminger pulls off a somewhat seedy, probably accurate look at what goes on behind closed doors in the ever so secretive political arena. Unfortunately, its accuracies do not make for edge-of-your seat viewing.

Interesting Trivia: After a seven-year absence from the silver screen, Gene makes her comeback in *Advise and Consent*. She was once again guided by her favorite director, Otto Preminger, and she made it through production without incident. Getting through this film was a major boost to her confidence.

Filmography

Preminger initially offered the role of a Southern senator to Martin Luther King, Jr. He felt casting a black man in a role that didn't exist in real life would have a positive impact on the public. King thought otherwise. He declined the offer after some serious consideration, on the grounds that it might hinder rather than help the impending civil rights movement.

Advise and Consent was the third and final time that Gene co-starred with Henry Fonda. Their other films were *The Return of Frank James* and *Rings on Her Fingers*. Speaking of working together, this was the fourth and last film collaboration between Gene and Otto Preminger. Their films were *Advise and Consent*, *Laura*, *Where the Sidewalk Ends* and *Whirlpool*. Otto Preminger died of cancer and complications related to Alzheimer's disease on April 23, 1986. He was 79 years old.

Toys in the Attic. 1963, United Artists.

Director George Roy Hill. *Producer* Walter Mirisch. *Writing Credits* Lillian Hellman (play) and James Poe. *Cinematographer* Joseph F. Biroc. *Running time* 90 mins. *Location* Louisiana. *Release Dates* 31 July, 1963, U.S.A.

Cast: Dean Martin (Julian Berniers), Geraldine Page (Carrie Berniers), Yvette Mimieux (Lily Prine Berniers), Wendy Hiller (Anna Berniers), **Gene Tierney (Albertine Prine)**, Nan Martin (Charlotte Warkins), Larry Gates (Cyrus Warkins), Frank Silvera (Henry Simpson, Mrs. Prine's chauffeur), Charles Lampkin (Gus, Handyman).

Adapted from the Lillian Hellman play, *Toys in the Attic* is the story of a Southern family with more than a few skeletons in their closet. Gene plays a small part as Albertine Prine, and although she is similar in age to her on screen son-in-law, Julian Berniers (Dean Martin), some gray hair dye enables her to pull it off.

Awards and nominations, 1964 Academy Awards, Nominated, Best Costume Design, Black and White, Bill Thomas; 1964, Golden Globe Awards, Nominated, Best Motion Picture Actress, Drama, Geraldine Page; 1964, Golden Globe Awards, Nominated, Best Supporting Actress, Wendy Hiller.

Las Cuatro Noches de la Luna Llena (*Four Nights of the Full Moon*).

1963, Independent short.

Director Sobey Martin. *Producer* Unknown. *Writing Credits* Unknown. *Cinematographer* Juan Marine. *Running time* Not known, listed as a "short.

Cast: Dan Dailey, Analia Gade, **Gene Tierney.**

Little known Spanish short subject, not available on VHS.

The Pleasure Seekers. 1964, Twentieth Century–Fox.

Director Jean Negulesco. *Producer* David Weisbart. *Writing Credits* John H. Secondari (novel) and Edith R. Sommer. *Cinematographer* Daniel L. Fapp. *Running time* 107 mins. *Release Dates* 25 December 1964, U.S.A.

Filmography

Cast: Ann-Margret (Fran Hobson), Anthony Franciosa (Emilio Lacaye), Carol Lynley (Maggie Williams), Gardner McKay (Pete Stenello), Pamela Tiffin (Susie Higgins), André Lawrence (Dr. Andres Briones), **Gene Tierney (Jane Barton)**, Brian Keith (Paul Barton), Vito Scotti (Neighbor Man), Isobel Elsom (Dona Teresa Lacaya).

A soap opera type melodrama based on the loves and relationships of three women who share a room together in a Spanish hotel. All of them are seeking rich husbands and trying out as many men for the job as possible. Gene takes a back seat to the new stars of the day here, content with a guest role, playing Jane Barton. Similar to the 1950s film *Three Coins in the Fountain*, this film could be best described as the *Sex and the City* of its day.

Awards and Nominations, 1966 Academy Awards, Nominated, Best Music, Scoring of Music, Adaptation or Treatment, Lionel Newman and Alexander Courage.

Daughter of the Mind. 1969, TV.

Director Walter Grauman. *Producer* Walter Grauman. *Writing Credits* Luther Davis, Paul Gallico (novel). *Cinematographer* Jack Woolf. *Running time* 90 mins. *Release Dates* 9 December 1969, U.S.A.

Cast: Don Murray (Dr. Alex Lauder), Ray Milland (Professor Samuel Constable), **Gene Tierney (Lenore Constable)**, Barbara Dana (Tina Cryder), Edward Asner (Saul Wiener), Pamelyn Ferdin (Mary Constable), Ivor Barry (Dr. Paul Cryder), William Beckley (Arnold Bessmer), George Macready (Dr. Frank Ferguson), John Carradine (Mr. Bosch), Virginia Christine (Helga), Cecile Ozorio (Devi Bessmer), Frank Maxwell (Gen. Augstedt), Bill Hickman (Enemy agent), Hal Frederick (Technician).

A horror/thriller film based on a professor of cybernetics who is convinced his dead daughter is communicating with him from beyond the grave. This was Gene's TV movie debut.

Scruples. 1980, TV miniseries.

Director Robert Day and Alan J. Levi. *Producer* Leonard Katzman. *Writing Credits* Judith Krantz (novel), James Lee. *Cinematographer* Joseph F. Biroc. *Running time* 279 mins. *Release Dates* 25 February 1980, U.S.A.

Cast: Lindsay Wagner (Billy Ikehorn), Barry Bostwick (Spider Elliott), Marie-France Pisier (Valentine O'Neill), Efrem Zimbalist, Jr. (Ellis Ikehorn), Connie Stevens (Maggie McGregor), Nick Mancuso (Vito Orsini), Robert Reed (Josh Hillman), **Gene Tierney (Harriet Toppingham)**, Louise Latham (Mary Ann Evans), Genevieve (Lilianne de Vertdulac), Michael Callan (Alan Wilton), Gary Graham (Jake Cassidy), Sarah Marshall (Susan Arvey), Milton Selzer (Sid Amos), Paul Carr (Pat O'Byrnne).

Filmography

Adapted from the best selling Judith Krantz novel of the same name, *Scruples* is the story of L.A. society and the fashion industry. Originally shown on CBS in six two-hour episodes on February 25, 26 and 28, 1980. Gene had a minor part. It turned out to be her last movie role before officially retiring.

TV Guest Appearances: M*A*S*H (1972), playing Ellen Berent in episode "House Arrest" (episode #3.18), 4 February 1975.

The F.B.I. (1965), playing Faye Simpson in episode "Conspiracy of Silence" (episode #4.23), 2 March 1969.

General Electric Theater (1953), in episode "Journey to a Wedding," 27 November 1960; *What's My Line?* (1950), playing mystery guest, 25 August 1957.

Gene Tierney's star on the Hollywood Walk of Fame is at 6125 Hollywood Boulevard, Hollywood, California. The year of its placement is unknown. On February 9, 1960, Joanne Woodward went down in history as being the first celebrity to be honored in that prestigious concrete strip.

Since then, to commemorate their outstanding achievement in the entertainment business, more than 2,000 entertainers have had a star placed on Hollywood Boulevard. Inside each bronze star is the name of the artist and a logo identifying which of the five categories the honoree belongs to: Motion Pictures (MT), Television (TV), Radio, Recording (Rec) or Live Theatre (LT). Next to winning an Oscar or an equally prestigious career award, it is the pinnacle of an entertainer's career.

Bibliography

Various snippets used in the research of this book (the below mentioned untitled clippings) were all taken from vintage Hollywood magazines and newspapers. Some of the articles were trimmed and pasted into a scrapbook before coming into my possession. Unfortunately, these articles had their original headings trimmed by the scrapbook owner/compiler. In an extensive salvage effort for scholarly purposes, the date of these various untitled clippings has been researched and listed below.

Periodical Articles

"Between You and Me." *Picturegoer/Film Weekly*, May 4, 1941, p. 4.
"Design for Delight." *Photoplay*, unknown date, pp. 45, 129–131.
"Determined Debutante." *Motion Picture*, December 1945, pp. 36, 99–105.
"Don't Elope Gene Tierney." *Photoplay*, 1940, pp. 21, 45.
"Fifteen Thousand Dollars Worth of Clothes for Gene Tierney." *Look*, October 17, 1944, pp. 42–43.
"For Sentimental Reasons." *Movie Stars Parade*, July 1948, pp. 50, 90–91.
"Gene's Affair with Aly." *Screenland*, November 1953, pp. 35, 53.
"Gene with a Capital G." *Silver Screen*, February 1941, pp. 39, 82, 87.
"G.E.T Girl." *Screenland*, undated issue, pp. 43, 112–113.
"Gene Tierney." *Screen Guide*, July 1946, pp. 60–63.
"Gene Tierney: An Honest Star." *Stardom*, undated issue, p. 22.
"Gene Tierney—Final Curtain Call." *Maine Antique Digest,* May 1992, pp.11A, 16A.
"Gene Tierney: Honeymoon Home." *Screenland*, March 1942, pp. 32–34, 63–65.
"Gene Tierney: New Home." *Screenland*, undated issue, pp. 33–35.
"Gene Tierney: No Hope for the Future." *Hollywood Stars Annual*, 1958, pp. 8–9.
"Haunted Beauty." *People*, November 25, 1991, p. 124.
"Hi Gene!" *Movie Play*, March 1949, p. 33.
"Hollywood Fanfare." *Good Housekeeping*, February 1942, p. 8.
"If Your Man's in Camp." *Movie Radio Guide*, April 1943, pp. 44–45.
"Is Gene Tierney Sorry She Married?" *Screen Guide*, November 1941, pp. 10–13.
"It Pays to Be Hurt." *Stardom*, February 1942, pp. 26, 48.
"Laugh or Go Mad." *Silver Screen*, November 1948, pp. 28–29, 61–62.

Bibliography

"Leave Heaven to Her." *Modern Screen*, August 1946, pp. 59, 100–101.

"Let's Pretend You're Mrs. Oleg Cassini." *Motion Picture*, March 1945, pp. 30–31, 119–120.

"Made for the Movies." *Look*, March 1943, pp. 36, 38, 39.

"Meet Gene Tierney." *Movies*, October 1940, p. 47.

"Must You Step on People's Toes?" *Silver Screen*, July 1950, pp. 6.

"My Gene Tierney." *Silver Screen*, December 1946, pp. 35, 71, 72, 74.

"My Luckiest Day." *Cosmopolitan*, February 1947, p. 14.

"Real Life Romance." *Screen Life*, September 1941, pp. 30, 89–90.

"Repeat Performance for Gene." *Silver Screen*, November 1949, pp. 30–31, 62.

"She's Terrific." *Motion Picture*, November 1940, pp. 28, 62–63, 88.

"Taking a Second Look at Love." *Screenland*, June 1954, pp. 40–41, 70.

"Temporary Blonde." *Silver Screen*, August 1945, p. 26.

"Ten Sure Fire Rules for Popularity." *Filmland*, August 1950, pp.30–32.

"The Strange Marriage of Gene Tierney." *Motion Picture*, September 1950, pp. 46–47, 73.

"The Truth About Surprise." *Screenland*, September 1941, pp. 54–55, 84–85.

"They Knew What They Wanted." *Modern Screen*, June 1942, pp. 47–49, 87.

"This Is How It Really Happened." *Photoplay/Movie Mirror*, February 1942, pp. 28–29, 70–72.

"Time Out for Tierney." *Motion Picture*, October 1948, pp. 32–33, 68.

[Untitled clipping.] *Movie Classic*, 1947, pp. 10–11.

[Untitled clipping.] *Movie Fan*, July 1946, pp. 23–29, 107–116.

[Untitled clipping.] *Movieland*, May 1945, pp. 43.

[Untitled clipping.] *Movieland*, April 1961, pp. 38–39, 51.

[Untitled clipping.] *Movie Pix*, August 1954, p. 10.

[Untitled clipping.] *Movie Stars Parade*, September 1942, pp. 31–33.

[Untitled clipping.] *Photoplay*, March 1942, pp. 57–59, 60–61.

[Untitled clipping.] *Photoplay*, August 1944, pp. 50–51, 88.

[Untitled clipping.] *Photoplay*, September 1970, pp. 4.

[Untitled clipping.] *Picture Goer/Film Weekly*, August 23, 1941, p. 18.

[Untitled clipping.] *Screen Guide*, March 1942, pp. 48–49.

[Untitled clipping.] *Screen Mirror*, February 1971, pp. 22–23, 62–63.

[Untitled clipping.] *Spinning Wheel*, August 1950, p. 23–24, 36–37.

[Untitled clipping.] *TV Radio Mirror*, July 1971, p. 16.

"Welcome for a Troubled Beauty." *Life Magazine*, September 29, 1958, pp. 88–90.

"What Every Wife Should Know." *Modern Screen*, July 1948, pp. 60, 104.

"Where Are They Now?" *Newsweek*, January 29, 1968, pp. 18.

"Why Do Hollywood Stars Crack Up?" *Parade*, June 9, 1957, pp. 18–20.

Newspaper Articles

"Babies Are Box Office." *Chicago Sunday Tribune*, June 25, 1944, p. 2.

"Gene Tierney Dead at 70." *New York Post*, November 8, 1991, p. 3.

"Gene Tierney Estate Catalog." *Hart Galleries*, Houston, Texas, February, 7–9, 1992, pp. 1–6.

"Gene Tierney Says Days in Mental Hospital Vital." *Houston Chronicle*, November 16, 1958, pp. 7–8.

"Her Final Curtain Call." *Houston Chronicle*, February 11, 1992, pp. 11A, 16A.

"Obituaries." *The New York Times*, November 8, 1991, p. 40.

[Untitled clipping.] *Chicago American*, Wednesday, July 10, 1957, p. 11.

Bibliography

[Untitled clipping.] *Dallas Morning News*, November 8, 1991, p. 26.

[Untitled clipping.] *Daily News*, November 8, 1991, p. 20.

[Untitled clipping.] *Daily Variety*, November 8, 1991, p. 15.

[Untitled clipping.] *Houston Post*, November 8, 1991, p. 35A.

[Untitled clipping.] *Houston Chronicle*, November 8, 1991, p.3.

[Untitled clipping.] *Houston Chronicle*, August 14, 1988, pp. 4J.

Books

Acker, Ally. *Reel Women: Pioneers of the Cinema, 1896 to the Present*. New York: Continuum, 1991.

Cassini, Oleg. *In My Own Fashion*. New York: Simon and Schuster, 1987.

Chierichetti, David. *Hollywood Costume Design*. New York: Harmony Books, 1976.

Custen, George F. *Twentieth Century–Fox's: Darryl F. Zanuck and the Culture of Hollywood*. New York: Basic Books, 1997.

Davis, Ronald L. *The Glamour Factory: Inside Hollywood's Big Studio System*. Dallas: SMU Press, 1993.

Furia, Phillip. *Skylark: The Life and Times of Johnny Mercer*. New York: St. Martin's Press, 2003.

Geist, Kenneth L. *Pictures Will Talk: The Life and Films of Joseph L. Mankiewicz*. New York: Scribner's, 1978.

Gow, Gordon. *Hollywood in the Fifties*. New York: Barnes and Co., 1971.

Gussow, Mel. *Don't Say Yes Until I Finish Talking: A Biography of Darryl F. Zanuck*. New York: Doubleday, 1971.

Higham, Charles, and Joel Greenberg. *Hollywood in the Forties*. London: A. Zwemmer Ltd., 1968.

Katz, Ephraim. *The Film Encyclopedia*, 2nd ed. New York: HarperCollins, 1994.

Monroe, Marilyn. *My Story*. New York: Stein and Day, 1974.

Palmer, Christopher. *The Composer in Hollywood*. London: Marion Boyars, 1990.

Robertson, Patrick. *The Guinness Book of Movie Facts and Feats*. London: Guinness Publishing Ltd., 1988.

Shipman, David. *The Great Movie Stars: The Golden Years*. New York: Crown, 1970.

Solomon, Aubrey, Jr. *Twentieth Century–Fox: A Corporate and Financial History*. Metuchen, N.J.: Scarecrow, 1988.

Staggs, Sam. *All About: All About Eve*. New York: St. Martin's Press, 2000.

Thomas, Nicholas, ed. *International Dictionary of Films and Filmmakers. Vol 1: Films*. Chicago and London: St. James Press, 1990.

Thomas, Tony. *The Films of the Forties*. New York: Citadel Press/Carol Publishing Group, 1975.

Tierney, Gene, with Mickey Herskowitz: *Gene Tierney: Self-Portrait*. New York: Wyden Books, 1978.

VanDerBeets, Richard. *George Sanders: An Exhausted Life*. Lanham, Md: Madison Books, 1990.

Internet Sources

Denny Jackson's Gene Tierney Page.
Gene Tierney Goddess: Yahoo Groups.
Gene Tierney Online.
http://en.wikipedia.org/wiki/Howard_Hughes
http://www.famoustexans.com/howardhughes.htm
Internet Movie Database.
TV Guide Online.

While the author has made every effort to offer attributions for all quoted matter herein, that has not been possible in some few cases. The author would be grateful for any source information that anyone could provide.

Index

Numbers in *italics* indicate photographs.

Abbott, George 17–19, 24–26
Academy Award nominations: acting 89, 92, 107, 207, 209, 211; art direction 202, 207, 209, 211; costume design 224; direction 95, 115, 182–183, 206, 207; music 89, 92, 202; photography 95, 98, 115, 202, 206, 207, 213, 222; sound 209; special effects 148; writing 95, 115, 207
Academy Award winners 95, 98, 107, 148, 207, 211, 220
actors on loan 41–42, 148
Addams, Dawn *147,* 220
Advise and Consent 110, 181, *182,* 223–224
Albert, Eddie 34, 69
All About Eve 115
Ameche, Don *71, 74, 132,* 205, 218
Anatomy of a Murder 182
Anderson, Judith *94,* 206
Andrews, Dana: *Belle Starr* 40, *41,* 201; *Iron Curtain* 118, 213; *Laura* 92, *94, 193,* 206–207; *Where the Sidewalk Ends 124,* 129, *193,* 216–217
Argentina 142–147, 219
Arizona 46, 209
Arnaz, Desi 34
Aspen, Colorado 174, 179
Associated Press 194
Atkinson, Brooks 19
Azadia 93

Ball, Lucille 34
The Bar Bill 62, 67
Barrymore, Ethel 136, 219
Baxter, Anne 105, 106, 211

A Bell for Adano 28, 97, *98,* 208–209
Belle Starr 40–42, 46, *52,* 201, 216
Belle Tier, Inc. 20, 28, 43, 44, 49–50
Bendix, William 97, 208
Bennett, Joan *192*
Best, Edna 114, 212
Bettina 158
Beverly Hills home 52, 56–59, 72, 87
Bickford, Charles 118, 214
Black Widow 154, 157, 221
The Blue Angel 54
Bogart, Humphrey 158, 181, 222–223
Bond, Ward 30, 200
Bong, Richard 204
boycott of Oleg Cassini 48, 56
Brand, Harry 44
Brando, Marlon 222
Brillanmont School 7, 12–13
Broadway plays 18–19, 26–27, 33, 55, 106, 201
Brontë, Charlotte 175
Brown, Clarence *144,* 148, 220
Brown, Judge 43–44
Bruce, Nigel 30, 200
Butch (dog) 47, *57*
Byington, Spring *71,* 205

Cabot, Bruce 46, 54, 201–202
Calhern, Louis *71,* 205
Calhoun, Rory 142, 219
California homes: Beverly Hills 52, 56–59, 72, 87; Cherokee Lane (honeymoon cottage) 45; Franklin Canyon home 52

Cape Cod 99, 106–107, 161–162
The Cardinal 182
Carney, Art 69
Cashin, Bonnie 90
Cassini, Christina (Tina): adulthood 191, 194, 195, 197; birth & infancy *114,* 117, 120, *129, 133,* 145; custody of 179–180; and G. T.'s mental illness 168–169, 176; traveling with G. T. *114,* 120, *129,* 145, 174
Cassini, Daria: birth & infancy 77–80, *81, 86,* 172; disabilities 1, 83–84, 85, 86–87; early development 80–81, 83; Howard Hughes' help 81, 84, 137; institutionalization 85, 86–88, 154, 179
Cassini, Mrs. (Oleg Cassini's mother) 36, 63–64, 75, 78
Cassini, Oleg, life of: citizenship 37, 62, *66;* early life 36–37; *In My Own Fashion* 180; life after G. T. 152, 179–180
Cassini, Oleg, marriage to G. T.: advising G. T. 104, 132, 134–136, 142, 152–153; close call 122–123; conflicts 55, 60, 104–105, 137–140; and Daria 77–80, 85–86, 87, 89, 96, 102; dating and engagement 35–37; divorce from G. T. 104, 105, 115, 147; on G. T. 37, 96, 179, 195; and G. T.'s mental illness 96, 143–145, 180; home life 45, 46, 47, 56–59, 72–75, 81–82,

231

Index

133–134; long-distance marriage 115–117, 119–120, 122, 142–145; moral support for G. T. 40–42; reconciliations 39–40, 115–116, 119–120, 133–134; relationship with G. T.'s parents 37–39, 42, 44–46, 52, 53, 78–79, 157; separations from G. T. 39, 54, 102, 115, 130, 137; social life 37, 46, 47, 73–74, 75, 116, 130

Cassini, Oleg, military service: Coast Guard 62–64, 75; military intelligence 62, 75–76, 78; U.S. Army Cavalry 64, 70, 72, 78

Cassini, Oleg, professional life: acting debut 123, 216; fashion design (Hollywood) 35, 37, 45, 47–48, 54, 56, 105–106; fashion design (New York) 110, 115–116, 142–145; fashion design for G. T. 36, 54–55, 80, 106, 109, 112–113, 115–116, 123, 207, 218

Cassini, Tina see Cassini, Christina

Catalina Island 60–61

Cherokee Lane home (honeymoon cottage) 45

Chevalier, Maurice 132, 218

China Girl 63, 204–205

Christie, Agatha 88

Church of St. John the Divine 195

Clapboard Road, Connecticut home 46

Claudia 33

Close to My Heart 135, 136, 217, 218

Cobb, Lee J. 223

Coburn, Charles 71, 205

Cohn, Harry 24, 48

Collier, Constance 119, 170

Collier's Magazine 26

Colorado 174, 179

Columbia Hospital, Washington, D.C. 77–80

Columbia Studios 19–20, 22–24, 223

columnists 30, 104, 119–120, 158, 161

Connecticut homes: Clapboard Road 46; Farmington 13; Green Farms 3–5, 133–134, 174, 180; Hartford (Institute for Living) 165–168; Westport 46

Conte, Richard 118, 214

Cornwall, England 144, 145, 149, 212, 220

Costumes: "dangerous" red dress 123–124; Dragonwyck 103; The Ghost and Mrs. Muir 112–113, 115, 218; Jezebel dress 14, 16; Laura 90, 207; masquerade ball 116; The Mating Season 130, 218; Never Let Me Go 143, 146; The Razor's Edge 105–106, 108, 109, 218; The Shanghai Gesture 54–55, 218; Son of Fury 52; Sundown 50, 53; Tobacco Road 30–31, 32; wedding dress 106, 109; Where the Sidewalk Ends 123–124, 125, 218; see also Cassini, Oleg, fashion designs for G. T.

Coward, Noel 96, 120–122

Craig, Marguerite 178

Crain, Jeanne 97

Crawford, Joan 99, 100, 209

Cregar, Laird 200

critics 19, 26

Las Cuatro noches de la luna llena 185, 224

Dailey, Dan 185, 224

Dandridge, Dorothy 202

Darvi, Bella 222

Daughter of the Mind 190, 225

Davies, Mary Lou 26

Davis, Bette 14, 16, 19

Davis, Jim 186

De Niro, Robert 123

Dick, R. A. 111, 212

Dietrich, Marlene 13, 54, 120–122

Divorce: G. T.'s parents 39, 50–51; Howard Lee and Hedy Lamarr 174, 176; and Jack Kennedy 104, 107; Oleg Cassini and G. T. 87, 104–105, 115, 140–142; Oleg Cassini's first 33; Tyrone Power and Anabella 104

dogs 47, 57, 58, 149

Dolin, Anton 150

Dragonwyck 100, 101, 103, 209–211

dress shop job 177–178

Duncan, Mary 55

The Egyptian 155, 157, 221–222

Eisenhower, Dwight D. 172

electric shock therapy 162–163, 165–168

Endore, Guy 118, 214

England 8, 114, 129; see also Cornwall; London

Esseray, Peggy 12

estate auction 195–197

European travels 6–13, 122–123, 150, 152, 154–155

Eye Bank 42, 53

Fairbanks, Douglas, Sr. 7, 12

Fairfield Country Club 14

Farmington, Connecticut home 13

Faye, Alice 132

The FBI 190, 226

Fenady, Andrew 197

Ferrer, José 118, 180, 214

film noir 90, 123, 130, 206, 216

film studios: Columbia 19–20, 22–24, 223; MGM 148, 219–220; Paramount 35, 37, 43, 45, 48, 130, 217; RKO 20; United Artists 54, 153, 201–202, 224; Warner Brothers 14, 217; see also 20th Century–Fox

films starring G. T.: Advise and Consent 110, 181, 223–224; A Bell for Adano 28, 97, 98, 208–209; Belle Starr 40–42, 46, 52, 201, 216; Black Widow 154, 157, 221; China Girl 63, 204–205; Close to My Heart 135, 136, 217, 218; Dragonwyck 100, 101, 103, 209–211; The Egyptian 155, 157, 221–222; The Ghost and Mrs. Muir 100, 111–115, 195, 212–213, 218; Heaven Can Wait 70, 71, 74, 205–206; Hudson's Bay 30, 32, 199–200; The Iron Curtain 117, 118, 213, 217; Laura 89–96, 151, 182, 206–208; Leave Her to Heaven 89, 97–100, 122, 182, 209; The Left Hand of God 158, 159, 181, 222–223; The Mating Season 126–127, 130–132, 217–218; Never Let Me Go 140–141, 143, 145–146, 149–151, 220; Night and the City 114, 120–122, 215–216, 218; On the Riviera 132–133,

232

Index

135, 218; *Personal Affair 153*, 220–221; *The Pleasure Seekers* 184, 187, *189*, 224–225; *The Razor's Edge* 104–106, *108, 109*, 211–212, 214, 218; *The Return of Frank James* 29, *30, 33*, 60, 199, 224; *Rings on Her Fingers* 60, 63, 203–204, 224; *The Secret of Convict Lake 134*, 136, 218–219; *The Shanghai Gesture 51*, 54–56, 59, 202–203, 218; *Son of Fury 52*, 56, 203, 213–214; *Sundown* 46, 48, *50*, 52–54, 201–202, 213; *That Wonderful Urge* 116, *117*, 133, 214, 218; *Thunder Birds* 63, *64–65*, 204; *Tobacco Road* 30–32, 200–201, 217; *Toys in the Attic 183*, 185–186, 224; *Way of a Gaucho 138*, 142–147, 219; *Where the Sidewalk Ends* 121–130, 216–217, 218, 224; *Whirlpool* 118–120, 214–215, 218, 224
Fine, Sylvia 133, 218
Flournoy, Elizabeth *147*
Folies Bergere 132, 218
Fonda, Henry 29–30, 60–61, 199, 203–204, 223–224
Fontaine, Joan 175
Ford, Glenn 69, 136, 219
Ford, John 30, 200
Fort Riley, Kansas Army Base 70, 72, 78
Fort Riley, Kansas home 72–75, 89
The Four Nights of the Full Moon 185
France 36, 107, 122, 150, 154, 158, 191, 195, 197
Franken, Rose 33
Franklin Canyon home (California) 52

Gable, Clark 68–69, *140, 145, 149*, 150–151, 220
Gallagher, Bill 104
Garbo, Greta 70
Gardner, Peggy Ann 221
Garland, Judy 68
Gene Tierney paper doll 78
General Electric Theater 226
Genn, Leo *147*, 220, 221
German measles 72, 79, 85–86, 88
Gershwin, George 94
The Ghost and Mrs. Muir 100, 111–115, 195, 212–213, 218

Gillespie, A. Arnold 148, 220
Gillette, Morgan 69
Ginsburg 48
Golden, John 33
Golden Globe Awards 211, 218, 224
Gone with the Wind 68
Goulding, Ivis *147*
Grauman's Chinese Theatre (Walk of Fame) 101
Grayson, Kathryn *192*
Green Farms, Connecticut home 3–5, 133–134, 174, 180
Grotto Restaurant, Houston 194–195
Gunwalloe Cove 149

Hadyn, Richard *145*, 204, 220
Hakim, Raymond 35
Hambro, Sylvia Muir 8, 120
Harkness Pavilion 162–165
Harper's Bazaar 24, 26
Harrison, Rex 112–113, 212
Hart Galleries auction 195–197
Harvard Lampoon 29
Hayworth, Rita 22–24, *147*, 157
Heaven Can Wait 70, *71, 74*, 205–206
Heflin, Van *154*, 157, 221
Hellman, Lillian 224
Hell's Angels 84
Henie, Sonja 102
Henri, Mademoiselle 8–9
The Herald Tribune 26
Hill, George Roy 184–185, *186*, 224
Hitler, Adolf 69
Hodiak, John 97, 208
Hollywood: attitude toward aging 184; columnists 30, 104, 119–120, 158, 161; publicity 22–24, 34, 104; screen tests 14; social scene 27–28, 34, 56; *see also* studio practices
Hollywood Canteen incident 64, 70–71, 79, 85–86, 88, 192–193
Hollywood homes *see* California homes
The Hollywood Reporter 30
Hollywood studios *see* film studios
Hollywood Victory Committee 69
Hollywood Walk of Fame 101, 226

Hollywood war effort 62, 64–71, 73, 88
Holtzman, Dr. 176
Hospitals: Columbia Hospital, Washington, D.C. 77–80; Harkness Pavilion 162–165; Institute for Living 165–168; Menninger Clinic 171–173, 176–179, 187–188
Hougenauts, Madame 9
Houston, Texas homes 180, 184, 191–192, 194–197
Hudson's Bay 30, *32*, 199–200
Hughes, Howard 20–22, 81, 84–85, 137–140, 188–190, 195
Huston, Walter 55, 101, 202, 210

I Wanted Wings 35
Institute for Living 165–168
The Iron Curtain 117, 118, 213, 217
Iturbi, José *142*

Jane Eyre 175
jewelry 43, 157, 195, 197
Jezebel 14
Jezebel dress 14, *16*
jobs 177–178; *see also* G. T., acting career
Johns, Glynis 221
Johnson, Magic 194
Johnson, Van *147*, 220
Jones, Barry *147*, 220
Jones, Jennifer 89, 207
Josephy, Bill 37
Joslyn, Allyn *71*, 205
Journey to a Wedding 226
Junction City, Kansas home 72–75
Juno (dog) 149

Kansas homes 72–75, 171–173, 178
Kaye, Danny 132–133, 218
Kelly, Grace 179–180
Kennedy, Jack (John F.) 101–104, 105, 106–110, 184, 211
Kennedy, Jacqueline Bouvier 107, 109–110
Khan, Aga 152, 157–158
Khan, Prince Aly 145–147, *150*, 152–154, 157–158, 161, 195
Khan, Karim 158
Khan, Yasmin 147, 157
King, Henry 97, 208
King, Martin Luther, Jr. 224

233

Index

knitting 11, 12, 172, 177
Krantz, Judith 190, 225–226

Lamarr, Hedy 174, 176, 207
Lang, Charles 115, 202, 212, 213
Langan, Jeff 101, 210
Lange, Hope 115
Lange, Jessica 123
Langhorn School 87, 89
Las Vegas, Nevada 43–44, 188–190
LaShelle, Joe 95, 206, 207
Laura 89–96, 151, 182, 206–208; theme song 93–94, 151
Lawford, Peter 204, 223
Leave Her to Heaven 89, 97–100, 122, 182, 209
Lee, Gypsy Rose 182
Lee, Howard: devotion to G. T. 175, 177, 179, 185–187, 193; divorce from Hedy Lamarr 174, 176; engagement to G. T. 176, 179; and G. T.'s mental illness 110, 175–176; marriage to G. T. 110, 175, 180, 184, 191–194; meeting G. T. 174–175, 194; reconciling G. T. with her father 185–187
The Left Hand of God 158, 159, 181, 222–223
Leigh, Vivien 153
Leisen, Mitchell 126–127, 130, 131, 217
Leslie, Natalie 150
Life magazine 50, 53
Little Women 7
Litvak, Anatole 14
location shoots: Argentina 142–147, 219; Arizona 46, 209; California 98, 199, 200, 201, 203, 209, 212, 222; Catalina Island 60–61; Cornwall 144, 145, 149, 212, 220; London 120–123, 150–151, 153–154, 215; Louisiana 224; New Mexico 52–53, 69, 98, 201, 209; New York City 216; Spain 185; Washington, D.C. 184, 223; Wyoming 98, 209
Lockhart, Kathleen 147
Loiewski, Count Alexander 36
Loiewski, Oleg Cassini 43; *see also* Cassini, Oleg
Lombard, Carole 68–69, 150
London 120–123, 150–151, 153–154, 215

Los Angeles homes *see* California homes
Louise (nanny) 4
Louisiana 224
Love Is News 116, 214
Lubitsch, Ernst 70, 205, 206, 209–210
Lund, John 132, 217

Madeline (housekeeper) 59
Maheu, Robert 188–190
Main, Marjorie 71, 205
Malden, Karl 124, 216
The Male Animal 26, 27, 28, 33
Mamoulian, Rouben 93, 206
The Man with Bogart's Face 197
Mankiewicz, Joseph 101, 115, 209–210, 212
Manning, Meredith 12
Marshall, Connie 100, 210
Martin, Dean 183, 185, 186, 224
Martin, Sober 185, 224
Marvin, Lee 59
Maschio, Johnny 35
M.A.S.H. 190, 226
Mason, Dr. Vernon 22
Matheson, Murray 147
The Mating Season 126–127, 130–132, 217–218
Mature, Victor 55, 62, 67, 202
Mayer, Louis B. 48
Mazurki, Mike 129, 215
McCarthy, Faustine 194
McCarthy, Glen, Jr. 194
McConnell, Keith 147
McGuire, Dorothy 33
Menninger, Dr. Karl 171, 178
Menninger Clinic 171–173, 176–179, 187–188
Mental illness *see* G. T., mental illness
Mercer, Johnny 93
Merrill, Gary 125, 216
MGM Studios 148, 219–220
Mildred Pierce 99, 100, 209
Miles, Bernard 145, 220
Milland, Ray 135, 136, 190, 217, 225
Miranda, Carmen 132, 218
The Mirror Crack'd 88
The Mirror Crack'd from Side to Side 88
Miss Porter's School 13
Mitchell, Alleyne 94
Mitchell, Johnny 194
Modern Times 94
Monroe, Marilyn 124

Moore, Constance 35
Morley, Robert 34
Mrs. O'Brien Entertains 18–19
Muir (Hambro), Sylvia 8, 120
Muni, Paul 30, 200
Munson, Ona 51, 55, 202–203

Nathan, George Jean 29
Never Let Me Go 140–141, 143, 145, 146, 149–151, 220
New Mexico 52–53, 69, 98, 201, 209
New York City homes 3, 18, 158, 161, 168–171
New York City location shoots 216
New York critics 19, 26
New York Eye Bank 42, 53
New York Journal American 44
New York Times 15, 19
Newcombe, Warren 148, 220
Night and the City 114, 120, 121, 122, 215–216, 218
Night and the City (alternate British version) 215–216
Night in Rio 132, 218
Ninotchka 70
Nixon, Richard 110

Oberon, Merle 132, 218
Oderkirk, Glen 20
On the Riviera 132–133, 135, 218
O'Neil, Barbara 119, 214
Oscars *see* Academy Awards
Our Town 27, 29

Pallette, Eugene 71, 205
Palmer, Dick 20
paper doll 78
Paramount Studios 35, 37, 43, 45, 48, 130
Paris, France 7, 36, 107, 150, 158, 197
Parker, Dorothy 14
Paust, Dagney 8
Payne, John 105, 211
Pearl Harbor 60–62
Personal Affair 153, 220–221
Peters, Elizabeth Knight 69
Pidgeon, Walter 181, 223
plane crashes 69, 84, 122–123, 190, 204
The Pleasure Seekers 184, 187, 224–225
The Plymouth Adventure 139, 147, 148
Polony, Frank 93

234

Index

Porter, Cole 93
portraits of G. T. *86, 91,* 93, 195, 197, 207
Power, Tyrone: death of 116; *The Razor's Edge* 105, *108,* 211–212; romance with Gene Tierney 104–106; *Son of Fury 52,* 56, 203; *That Wonderful Urge* 116, 117, 214; World War II pilot 69, 105
Preminger, Eric Lee 182
Preminger, Otto: Academy Award nominations 206, 207; *Advise and Consent* 181–184, 223–224; *Laura* 89–96, 206; life of 181–182; perfectionism 93, 94–95, *96,* 119; *Where the Sidewalk Ends* 123–125, 129, 216; *Whirlpool* 118–119, 214
Price, Vincent: *Dragonwyck* 100, 101, 210; *Hudson's Bay* 200; *Laura* 93, 94, 206; *Leave Her to Heaven* 97, 209; reunions *192, 193*
Pritchard, Jeffrey *148*
Pritchard, Owen *148*
The Private Lives of Elizabeth and Essex 14, 19
psychiatrists 153, 161–162, 165–168, 176
publicity practices 34, 44, 104

radio broadcasts *53,* 90, 95
Rainer, Louise *192*
Rainier, Prince 180
Raksin, David 93–94, 207
The Razor's Edge 104–106, *108, 109,* 211–212, 214, 218
Reagan, Ronald 69
Reed, Florence 55
The Return of Frank James 29, *30, 33,* 60, 199, 224
Return to Peyton Place 180
reunions *192, 193*
Ries, Irving G. 148, 220
Ring Two 26
Rings on Her Fingers 60, 63, 203–204, 224
Ritter, Thelma 132, 217, 218
River Oaks apartment, Houston 194
RKO Studios 20
Rocky and Bullwinkle 96
Rogers, Ginger 157, 221
Rooney, Mickey 34
Rosenstein, Arthur *147*
Ruby (maid) 153–154

St. Margaret's School 4
Salami (dog) 58
Sanders, George 46, 56, 114, 116, 202, 203, 212, 213
Scott, Randolph 40, 41–42, 201
Scruples 190, 225–226
The Secret of Convict Lake 134, 136, 218–219
Seiber, Maria 13, 122
Self Portrait by G. T. 193
Seton, Anya 101, 210
The Seven Nights of the Full Moon 185, 224
Sex and the City 225
The Shanghai Gesture 51, 54, 55–56, 59, 202–203, 218
Shields, Betty Ann 12
Shumlin, Howard 26
Solomon and Sheba 116
Son of Fury 52, 56, 203, 213, 214
Spain 185
Stalag 17, 182
Stanwyck, Barbara 40
Stark, Fran 152
Stark, Ray 152
Starr, Belle 43
Sterling, Robert 31
Sternberg, Josef von 54, 202
Stevens, Craig *125,* 130, 216
Stewart, James 66–68, 69
The Still Alarm 90
Stork Club 27, *47*
studio practices: boycotts 48, 56; control over actors' lives 43, 44, 45, 48; loaning actors 41–42, 54, 130, 148; publicity 34, 44, 104; shooting schedules 52–53, 56, 58, 59, 92, 94–95; suspensions 40, 42, 160, 182; underemployment of actors 20, 22, 24, 27, 29, 31
studios *see* film studios
Sundown 46, 48, *50,* 52–54, 201–202, 213
Sutton, John 30, 200
Swan, Betty 12
swimsuit photos 27, *149, 164, 189*
Switzerland 7–12

Talmadge, Billie 178
Taylor, Elizabeth 88
Taylor, Gene 3
A Telephone Call 14
tennis 56, *128*
Texas Film Society 192

Texas homes 180, 184, 191–192, 194–197
Three Coins in the Fountain 187, 225
Thunder Birds 63, *64–65,* 204
That Wonderful Urge 116, *117,* 133, 214, 218
Tierney, Belle Taylore and Daria 78, 83; and G. T.'s mental illness 157, 163–165, 168–169, 171; in Hollywood with G. T. 13–14, 21–22, 31, 106; and Jack Kennedy 102; on location with G. T. 13–14, 21, 151, 174; marriage and divorce 3, 39, 50–51, protection of G. T. 13–14, 31, 158–159, 161; relationship with Oleg Cassini 38–39, 42, 44, 45–46, 78–79, 157; traveling with G. T. 13–14, 19, 21, 174
Tierney, Gene, acting career: Academy Award nomination 99–100, 209; advice from Oleg Cassini 132, 134–136, 142; auditions and screen tests 14, 18, 27; comebacks 1, 89, 96, 174, 176, 181–185, *186,* 190, 223; comedy roles 132, 200, 203–204, 214; dancing 150; early years *10,* 11, 14, *22, 25,* 27–31; film studio contracts 20, 27–29, 31–34, 43–44, 49–50, 97, 164, 174, 187; names and nicknames 24, 29, *82,* 181, 197; pressure from studios 132, 164; publicity 34, *78,* 104; stage roles 15–19, 24–27, 29, 33; success as an actress 1, 2, 29–31, 89, 96, 99, 105, 122, 159, 186; television roles 185, 190, 225–226; work ethic 29, 58–60, *82,* 92, 95, 153–154, 157
Tierney, Gene, beauty: descriptions of 1, 2, 19, 37; portraits *86, 91,* 93, 117, 170, 195–197, 207
Tierney, Gene, dating and romance: Aly Khan 145–147, *150,* 152–153, 161, 195; George Abbott 26; Howard Hughes 20–22, 81, 84, 137, 190; Jack Kennedy 101–104, 105, 106–107, 110, 211; Oleg Cassini 35–37; publicity

Index

dates 34, *67*; Robert Sterling 31; Tyrone Power 104–106, *117,* 214

Tierney, Gene, dreams & premonitions 122–123, 157, 191–192

Tierney, Gene, early life: childhood 3–13; names and nicknames 3, 24; school 4, 5–6, 7, 12–13; society debut 13, 14–16, *23*

Tierney, Gene, family: Aunt Leila 120, 122; births of daughters 77, 80, 117; Christina *114, 129, 133,* 145; conflicts with father 14, 19, 33, 38, 44–46, 49–52, 54; conflicts with mother 42, 44–46; Daria's birth 77–80; Daria's disabilities 78, 79, 80–81, 83, 86–88; grandchildren 194; parents' divorce 39; reconciliation with father 186–187; siblings (*see* Tierney, Howard, Jr.; Tierney, Patricia); Uncle Gene 3

Tierney, Gene, health: illnesses 22, 40–42, 52, 71–72, 167, 201; injuries 111, *112,* 119, 150; pregnancies 70–77, 79, 116, 180; weight control 13, 24, 42; *see also* G. T., mental illness

Tierney, Gene, homes: California 45, 52, 56–59, 72, 87; Connecticut 3–5, 13, 46, 133–134, 174, 180, 193; Kansas 72–75, 171–173, 178; New York City 3, 15, 17, 18, 115, 134, 158, 161, 168–171; Switzerland 7–12; Texas 180, 184, 191–192, 194–197

Tierney, Gene, later life: autobiography 193; death 194–195; friendship with Oleg Cassini 152, 179–180; personal possessions 195–197; retirement 2, 180, 184, 187, 190–195; *see also* G. T., marriage to Howard Lee

Tierney, Gene, marriage to Howard Lee: engagement 176, 179; first meeting 174–175, 194; happiness together 110, 175, 179, 180, 191, 193–194; wedding day 179

Tierney, Gene, marriage to Oleg Cassini: conflicts 55, 60, 102, 104–105, 137–140; dating and engagement 35–37; divorce 104–105, 115, 147, 152–153; elopements 37–39, 42–44, 106; home life 45, *46, 47,* 56–59, 72–75, 81–82, 133–134; long-distance marriage 115–117, 119–120, 122, 142–145; reconciliations 39–40, 115–116, 119–120, 133–134; separations 39, 54, 102, 115, 130, 137; social life 37, *46, 47,* 73–74, *75, 116,* 130

Tierney, Gene, mental illness: art therapy 77; "cold pack" therapy 172–173; contributing factors 164, 187, 192; effects of Daria's birth 78, 79–80, 87–88, 96; electric shock therapy 162–163, 165–168, 172; first signs 142–145, 151, 153, 157, 158–162; hospitalizations 1, 77–80, 162–168, 171–173, 176–179, 187–188; loss of memory 153–154, 157, 161, 163, 168, 172; openness about 110, 175–176, 187–188; outpatient treatment 179, 191–193; psychotherapy 155, 166, 172, 177; work as therapy 177–178, 183–184

Tierney, Gene, war years: film work 63–65, 70, 89–99; Fort Riley, Kansas 70, 72, 78, 89; Hollywood Canteen incident 85, 88; move to Washington, D. C. 75–76; Oleg Cassini's military service 70, 72–75

Tierney, Howard, Jr.: early life 3–4, 7, 12, 14, 39; estrangement from his father 52; and G. T.'s mental illness 161–162, 165, 167, 171; support for G. T. *15,* 102, 161–162, 165, 167, 171

Tierney, Howard, Sr.: control of G. T.'s career 14, 17–19, 27–28, 33, 43–45, 53, 164, 187 (*see also* Belle Tier, Inc.); death of 187; divorce and estrangement 39, 46, 50–52, 172, 187; as family provider 3–5, 13, 30; marriages 39, 49–51; relationship with Oleg Cassini 37, 42, 44–46, 52, 53

Tierney, Patricia (Pat): adult relationship with G. T. 80, 101, 106, 165, 167; early life 3–5, 6–7, 8, 12, 13, 14

Titanic 115

Tobacco Road 30, *31, 32,* 200–201, 217

Topeka, Kansas home 171–173, 178

"Tournie" (Greek roommate) 8, 9, 11

Toys in the Attic 183, 185–186, 224

Tracy, Spencer *139,* 148, 220

20th Century–Fox Studios: contracts with G. T. 27–29, 31–34, 43, 44, 49–50, 97, 164, 174, 187; films with G. T. 199–201, 203–216, 218–219, 221–223; *see also* studio practices; Zanuck, Darryl F.

United Artists Studios 54, 153, 201–202, 224

U.S. Army Air Corps 66–68

U.S. Army Cavalry 64, 70, 72

U.S. Coast Guard 62–64, *75*

U.S. Marine Air Corps 105

Vallee, Rudy 34

Vogue magazine 195

Walk of Fame 101, 226

Wanger, Walter 53, 201

war effort *see* World War II

Warner, Jack 48

Warner Brothers Studio 14, 217

Washington, D.C. 45, 63–64, 75–76, 77, 184, 223

Watt, Richard 26

Way of a Gaucho 138, 142–147, 219

Webb, Clifton: Academy Award nominations 206–207; death of 96; emotional instability 95–96, 206–207; friendship with G. T. 106, 120, 122; *Laura* 90–92, *94,* 206–208; *The Razor's Edge* 105–107, 212

Welles, Orson 147, 175

Westport, Connecticut home 46

What a Life 19

What's My Line? 226

Where the Sidewalk Ends 121–130, 216–217, 218, 224

Whirlpool 118–120, 214–215, 218, 224

236

Index

White House 110, 184
Widmark, Richard 120–121, 123, 215
Wilde, Cornel 97, *99*, 209
Wilkens, Dr. Ann 172–173, 177–178
Williams, Ben Ames 97, 209
Williams, Wayne 69
Winkler, Otto 69
The Wizard of Oz 93
Wood, Natalie 111, 212
Woodward, Joanne 226

World War II: films 63, 64–65, 97, 98, 204, 209; Pearl Harbor 60–62; pilots 66–69, 105, 204; war effort 62, 64–71, 73, 88

Yellow Rose Awards 192
Young, Loretta 116, 214

Zanuck, Darryl F. Academy Award nomination 211; battles with G. T. 40–42, 48, 105–106; battles with Otto Preminger 92, 181–182, 206; boycott of Oleg Cassini 48, 105–106; casting G. T. 40, 96, 97; discovery of Gene Tierney 27–28; on G. T.'s beauty 1; producer for 20th Century–Fox 199–201, 203, 204, 209, 211, 221; screenwriter 204; sex scandal 221–222